T0366736

LOEB CLASSICAL LIBRARY

FOUNDED BY JAMES LOEB 1911

EDITED BY

JEFFREY HENDERSON

SOPHOCLES

III

LCL 483

SOPHOCLES

FRAGMENTS

EDITED AND TRANSLATED BY

HUGH LLOYD-JONES

HARVARD UNIVERSITY PRESS
CAMBRIDGE, MASSACHUSETTS
LONDON, ENGLAND

First published 1996
Reprinted with corrections and additions 2003

LOEB CLASSICAL LIBRARY® is a registered trademark
of the President and Fellows of Harvard College

Library of Congress Control Number 92-19295
CIP data available from the Library of Congress

ISBN 978-0-674-99532-1

Composed in ZephGreek and ZephText by
Technologies 'N Typography, Merrimac, Massachusetts.
Printed on acid-free paper and bound by
The Maple-Vail Book Manufacturing Group

CONTENTS

PREFACE   vii

INTRODUCTION   1

FRAGMENTS OF KNOWN PLAYS   10

FRAGMENTS NOT ASSIGNABLE TO ANY PLAY   344

DOUBTFUL FRAGMENT: *OENEUS*?   418

INDEX   423

PREFACE

I am greatly obliged to James Diggle, who allowed me an early view of a most valuable treatment of a number of Sophoclean fragments, particularly those of the *Ichneutae* (*The Searchers*), and generously found time to read my proofs, effecting many improvements. Mary Lefkowitz gave me most valuable assistance; without her expert guidance I could not have managed to commit this work to writing with a word processor.

The reprinting of this volume in 2003 enabled me to make some additions and corrections. I am obliged to Professor Noel Robertson for helpful suggestions.

HUGH LLOYD-JONES

INTRODUCTION

This collection of Sophoclean fragments, like that of the fragments of Aeschylus in the second volume of the Loeb *Aeschylus*, edited by Herbert Weir Smyth, includes those fragments of which at least one entire verse, or two connected half-verses, is preserved.

I have presented fragments preserved on papyri by the same technique which I employed in the appendix containing papyrus fragments which I added to Smyth's Aeschylus. My model was the *Greek Literary Papyri* contributed to this series by the late Sir Denys Page, and explained by him in the preface to that work.

The numbering is that of a book to which this collection is very greatly indebted, the splendid edition of the fragments of Sophocles by Stefan Radt: *Tragicorum Graecorum Fragmenta* (*TrGF*), volume IV, 1977; corr. ed. 1999. Radt had taken over the numbering of the earlier editor A. C. Pearson, who rounded off the memorable edition of the complete plays by Sir Richard Claverhouse Jebb by the addition of the fragments (*The Fragments of Sophocles*, 1917). By that time papyrus discoveries had already made important additions to the Sophoclean fragments contained in the *Tragicorum Graecorum Fragmenta* of August Nauck (1st ed., 1856; 2nd ed.,

1

1889). Pearson supplied a full commentary, as well as detailed discussions of the various plays. Both are still valuable, although he was often too optimistic about the possibility of guessing at their plots, a matter in which it is often very difficult to arrive at certainty or even probability. Radt was able to take advantage of new discoveries and new research of the sixty years between Pearson's edition and his own, including an excellent edition of the papyrus fragments, apart from the *Ichneutae*, by Richard Carden (*The Papyrus Fragments of Sophocles*, 1974), to which W. S. Barrett supplied an edition of the fragments of the *Niobe*. Radt provides an excellent edition of the texts, and though he does not offer a commentary, his Latin prefatory notes and apparatus criticus contain much valuable information; see my review of his book: *Classical Review* 31 (1981) 175–8.

The reader who wishes for a fuller treatment of any of the problems arising from this collection, or for a text in which the fragments known to us from papyri are presented with the highest possible degree of scholarly exactitude, should consult these works, in the first instance that of Radt, who has increased the value of his edition by a valuable general discussion of the fragments ("Sophokles in seinen Fragmenten," in the *Entretiens de la Fondation Hardt* 29 (1982) 185–231). My work contains a certain number of new suggestions, some of which I have explained in *Studi Italiani di Filologia Classica*, Terza Serie, vol. XII, fasc. ii (1994) 129–148.[1]

---

[1] Two books called *The Lost Sophocles*, both published in 1984, one by Akiko Kiso and one by Dana F. Sutton, are to be used with caution, if at all.

The ancient life of Sophocles says that he wrote 130 plays; the Suda says that he wrote 123. Radt in the article cited above admirably discusses the question of the number; but no satisfying answer is possible, for a variety of reasons. First, a tragedy might have two alternative titles. Four pairs of alternative titles are given by ancient authorities. But there may be more; for it may happen that a Greek play is quoted sometimes by one title and sometimes by another. Thus no one knew that Menander's *Samian Woman* (Σαμία) had an alternative title *The Marriage Alliance* ἡδεία), before passages quoted with the latter title, some of them with a corrupt form of it, turned up in a papyrus which obviously contained part of *The Samian Woman*. It may therefore happen that fragments quoted as from two plays with different titles really belong to the same play. There are even a couple of cases in which we have to reckon with the possibility that the same play had *three* alternative titles; see on the *Thyestes* plays. When a tragedian has written two or more plays with the same title, it is not always possible to determine whether these were different plays or different versions of the same play. Also, an ancient writer who quotes a fragment may give a wrong title to the play it comes from. Thus when we find a fragment spoken by Hippodameia attributed to the *Hippodamia*, a play mentioned in no other place, we cannot help concluding that the fragment really comes from the *Oenomaus*, in which Hippodameia was a character. Still, it is not safe to conclude that a play that is mentioned only once did not really exist; in several cases the existence of plays mentioned only once has been confirmed by new discoveries. No ancient authority says that Sophocles wrote a play called *Eurypylus*, and yet it is

INTRODUCTION

generally agreed that the fragments published under that
title come from a play of that name written by Sophocles
(see the prefatory note to that play). Very often ancient
authorities omit to tell us that a particular play was a satyr
play. Only 13 plays of Sophocles are stated by ancient
authorities to have been satyric, but Radt believes that
Sophocles wrote some thirty satyric dramas. It appears
from an inscription (see on *The Sons of Aleus*) that in at
least one instance Sophocles composed a trilogy or indeed
a tetralogy on a continuous theme, and this may not have
been the only such case. For example, the *Palamedes* and
the two Nauplius plays may have belonged to the same
tetralogy.

Here is a list of the plays of Sophocles in whose exis-
tence we seem to me to have some positive reason to
believe. It coincides with the list of plays against whose
titles Radt has not placed a question mark, except that my
list includes the Κασσάνδρα (not listed by Radt) and
does not include the Ἰφικλῆς or the Οἰκλῆς.

	Ἀθάμας Α′ *and* Β′	Athamas 1 *and* 2
	Αἴας Λοκρός	Ajax the Locrian
	Αἴας Μαστιγοφόρος	Ajax with the Whip
5	Αἰγεύς	Aegeus
	Αἰθίοπες	The Ethiopians
	Αἰχμαλωτίδες	The Captive Women
	Ἀκρίσιος	Acrisius
	Ἀλεάδαι	The Sons of Aleus
10	Ἀλέξανδρος	Alexander
	Ἀλκμέων	Alcmeon
	Ἄμυκος	Amycus
	Ἀμφιάρεως	Amphiaraus

4

Ἀμφιτρύων   Amphitryon
15 Ἀνδρομάχη   Andromache
Ἀνδρομέδα   Andromeda
Ἀντηνορίδαι   The Sons of Antenor
Ἀντιγόνη   Antigone
Ἀτρεύς *or* Μυκηναῖαι   Atreus *or* The Women
    of Mycenae
20 Ἀχαιῶν Σύλλογος   The Gathering of the
    Achaeans
Ἀχιλλέως Ἐρασταί   The Lovers of Achilles
Δαίδαλος   Daedalus
Δανάη   Danae
Διονυσίσκος   The Infant Dionysus
25 Δόλοπες   The Dolopians
Ἑλένης Ἀπαίτησις   The Demand for Helen's
    Return
Ἑλένης Ἁρπαγή   The Rape of Helen
Ἑλένης Γάμος   Helen's Wedding
Ἐπίγονοι   The Epigoni
30 Ἐπὶ Ταινάρῳ Σάτυροι   The Satyrs at Taenarum
Ἔρις   Eris
Ἐριφύλη   Eriphyle
Ἑρμιόνη   Hermione
Εὔμηλος   Eumelus
35 Εὐρύαλος   Euryalus
Εὐρύπυλος   Eurypylus
Εὐρυσάκης   Eurysaces
Ἠλέκτρα   Electra
Ἡρακλείσκος   The Infant Heracles
40 Ἡρακλῆς   Heracles
Ἠριγόνη   Erigone
Θαμύρας   Thamyras

5

	Θησεύς	Theseus
45	Θυέστης Α´, Β´ and Γ´	Thyestes 1, 2 and 3
	Ἴναχος	Inachus
	Ἰξίων	Ixion
	Ἰοβάτης	Iobates
50	Ἱππόνους	Hipponous
	Ἰφιγένεια	Iphigeneia
	Ἰχνευταί	The Searchers
	Ἴων	Ion
	Καμίκιοι	The Men of Camicus
55	Κασσάνδρα	Cassandra
	Κέρβερος	Cerberus
	Κηδαλίων	Cedalion
	Κλυταιμήστρα	Clytemnestra
	Κολχίδες	The Women of Colchis
60	Κρέουσα	Creusa
	Κρίσις	The Judgment
	Κωφοί	The Dumb Ones
	Λάκαιναι	The Laconian Women
	Λαοκόων	Laocoon
65	Λαρισαῖοι	The Men of Larissa
	Λήμνιαι Α´ and Β´	The Women of Lemnos 1 and 2
	Μάντεις or Πολύιδος	The Prophets or Polyidus
	Μελέαγρος	Meleager
70	Μέμνων	Memnon
	Μίνως	Minos
	Μοῦσαι	The Muses
	Μυσοί	The Mysians
	Μῶμος	Momus
75	Ναύπλιος Καταπλέων	Nauplius Sails In
	Ναύπλιος Πυρκαεύς	Nauplius Lights a Fire

	Ναυσικάα *or* Πλύντριαι	Nausicaa *or* The Women Washing Clothes
	Νιόβη	Niobe
	Νίπτρα	The Footwashing
80	Ὀδυσσεὺς Ἀκανθοπλήξ	Odysseus Wounded by the Spine
	Ὀδυσσεὺς Μαινόμενος	The Madness of Odysseus
	Οἰδίπους ἐπὶ Κολωνῷ	Oedipus at Colonus
	Οἰδίπους Τύραννος	Oedipus the King
	Οἰνεύς	Oeneus
85	Οἰνόμαος	Oenomaus
	Παλαμήδης	Palamedes
	Πανδώρα *or* Σφυροκόποι	Pandora *or* The Hammerers
	Πηλεύς	Peleus
	Ποιμένες	The Shepherds
90	Πολυξένη	Polyxena
	Πρίαμος	Priam
	Πρόκρις	Procris
	Ῥιζοτόμοι	The Root-Cutters
	Σαλμωνεύς	Salmoneus
95	Σίνων	Sinon
	Σίσυφος	Sisyphus
	Σκύθαι	The Scythians
	Σκύριοι	The Men of Scyros
	Σύνδειπνοι	Those Who Dine Together
100	Τάνταλος	Tantalus
	Τεῦκρος	Teucer
	Τήλεφος, Τηλεφεία	Telephus, Telepheia
	Τηρεύς	Tereus

	Τραχίνιαι	The Women of Trachis
105	Τριπτόλεμος	Triptolemus
	Τρώιλος	Troilus
	Τυμπανισταί	The Drummers
	Τυνδάρεως	Tyndareus
110	Τυρώ Α′ and Β′	β4 Tyro 1 and 2
	Ὕβρις	Hybris
	Ὑδροφόροι	The Water-carriers
	Φαίακες	The Phaeacians
	Φαίδρα	Phaedra
115	Φθιωτίδες	The Women of Phthia
	Φιλοκτήτης	Philoctetes
	Φιλοκτήτης ἐν Τροίᾳ	Philoctetes at Troy
	Φινεύς Α′ and Β′	Phineus 1 and 2
120	Φοῖνιξ	Phoenix
	Φρίξος	Phrixus
	Φρύγες	The Phrygians
	Χρύσης	Chryses

Satyr plays attested:

Ἄμυκος	Κηδαλίων
Ἀμφιάρεως	Κρίσις
Διονυσίσκος	Κωφοί
Ἐπὶ Ταινάρῳ Σάτυροι	Μῶμος
Ἡρακλείσκος	Σαλμωνεύς
Ἡρακλῆς	Ὕβρις
Ἰχνευταί	

Plays plausibly conjectured to be satyric:

Ἀχιλλέως Ἐρασταί	Ἑλένης Γάμος
Ἔρις	Ἴναχος

8

Κέρβερος   Πανδώρα
Οἰνεύς

A case can be made for regarding as satyr plays the
Ναυσικάα and the Σύνδειπνοι. D

M. L. West, ZPE 126 (1999) 43–65, published frag-
ments of literary text accompanied by musical nota-
tion from cartonnage scraps in the Ashmolean Museum.
One of them (fr. A 12) is identified by a subscription as
Ἀχιλλεὺ[σ] Σοφοκλ[έουσ, which West takes to have
been a work of the younger Sophocles (*TGF* 1, No. 62).

FRAGMENTS OF KNOWN PLAYS

ΑΘΑΜΑΣ Α΄ *and* Β΄

Hesychius in quoting frr. 1–3 and the scholion on Aristophanes, Clouds *255 f, quoted below, show that Sophocles wrote two plays with this title; the outlines of the plot of one of them are known to us, but that of the other is a matter of surmise.*

At Clouds *255 Socrates tells Strepsiades to take the wreath which he is handing him, and Strepsiades replies "Ah, Socrates! Take care you don't sacrifice me, like Athamas!" Athamas, son of Aeolus, was king of Orchomenos in Boeotia, then the home of the Minyae. A scholion explains that in one of the Athamas plays of Sophocles Athamas was wearing a wreath and standing by the altar of Zeus to be sacrificed, when Heracles came up and saved him. Certain manuscripts, and also the Suda and Tzetzes, add that Heracles saved him by explaining that Phrixus, on whose account he was to be sacrificed, was still alive. Athamas had been married to Nephele, a supernatural being whose name means 'Cloud,' but had abandoned her for a mortal, Ino, daughter of Cadmus. Nephele had punished him by sending a drought, and when Athamas sent envoys to ask the Delphic oracle how to put an end to this, Ino bribed the envoys to say that the oracle had declared that Athamas' children by Nephele, Phrixus and Helle, must be sacrificed. In another version of the story Ino*

10

FRAGMENTS OF KNOWN PLAYS

ATHAMAS 1 and 2

herself had caused the drought by roasting the seed of the corn, in order to incriminate her rival's children. Nephele saved her children by sending a ram with a golden fleece to carry them away; some writers say that the ram flew, but according to the best authorities it swam. Helle fell off the ram's back and was drowned, giving her name to the Hellespont, but the ram conveyed Phrixus to Colchis, where he married a daughter of the king, Aeetes.

It has been conjectured that the other Athamas play told how Hera punished Athamas and Ino for having protected the infant Dionysus by driving them both mad, so that Athamas while hunting mistook his son Learchus for a deer and killed him, and Ino threw their other son, Melicertes, into a boiling cauldron. Ino with the dead child jumped into the sea, and was metamorphosed into a sea goddess, Leucothea; Melicertes became the sea god Palaemon. A relief on a cup of the second century B.C. which shows Hermes handing the infant Dionysus to Athamas (illustration in LIMC II 2, p. 700) has been thought to support this identification, since the remains of a name might be supplemented as that of Sophocles.

Sophocles also wrote a Phrixus *(see frr. 721–2); Aeschylus wrote an* Athamas *and Euripides two plays called* Phrixus *and one called* Ino.

11

4

ὡς ὢν ἄπαις τε κἀγύναιξ κἀνέστιος

Choeroboscus on Theodosius, *Canones* 1, 289, 24 Hilgard

5

οἴνῳ παρ' ἡμῖν Ἀχελῷος ἆρα νᾷ

Lexicon Messanense 280 v 22 Σοφοκλῆς Ἀθάμαντι (Rabe: ἀθανατ[.(.)] codd.)

παρ' Headlam: γὰρ codd.

ΑΙΑΣ ΛΟΚΡΟΣ

The post-Homeric epic Iliou Persis *(see also Alcaeus fr. 298 and Euripides'* Trojan Women *69 f) described how during the sack of Troy Ajax the son of Oileus violated Cassandra in the temple of Athena, pulling down the image of the goddess as he did so. Ajax took refuge at the altar of the very goddess he had offended, and so escaped immediate danger. Polygnotus in his famous picture of the sack of Troy showed Ajax at the altar swearing an oath. This was presumably an assertatory oath, in which many of his friends joined him. Odysseus wished the Greeks to stone Ajax; he cannot have cared about the fate of Cassandra, but will have been aware of the danger arising from the offence given to Athena. If he had had his way disaster would have been averted, but the Greeks foolishly spared Ajax. While they were sailing home, Poseidon at the request of Athena raised a tremendous storm. According to one account, Ajax perished near the rocks of Caphereus, at the southeastern point of Euboea;*

12

4

As being without child or wife or hearth . . .

5

So Achelous[a] runs with wine in our place.

[a] The name of the Achelous, which is by far the greatest river of Greece, is sometimes used to mean 'water' in general.

AJAX THE LOCRIAN

according to another, in the neighbourhood of Mykonos, where the Gyraean rocks are located. According to the Odyssey (4, 499 f) Poseidon allowed him to make his way to a rock, and would have spared him in spite of Athena. But Ajax then boasted that he had escaped in spite of the gods, so that Poseidon split the rock with his trident and he was drowned. Another story, followed by Virgil, Aen. 1, 39 f, *was that Athena sank his ship with a thunderbolt, and when he defied her from a rock threw a second bolt at him and killed him.*

Neither the crime of Ajax nor his death can have been depicted on the stage. The testimonia and fragments throw little light upon the plot; but it seems likely that the debate as to what the Greeks were to do about the sacrilege played an important part. One imagines a kind of trial, with Odysseus arguing that Ajax should be punished, and Ajax defending himself. Fr. 10b contains the beginnings of the lines of a dialogue between Ajax and another person, who replies to each of the utterances of Ajax with a negation; this may have come from such an episode.

Fr. 10c shows that Athena actually appeared in person to the Greeks and rebuked them with extreme severity; no doubt she went on to warn them that retribution would follow and that Ajax and many others would pay the penalty of their offence. It seems likely that she spoke towards the end of the play as god from the machine; but it might be argued that her appearance may have come earlier, and that a messenger speech near the end of the play may have described the storm and the end of Ajax.

10a–g Ed. pr. Haslam, P. Oxy. 3151 (Part 44, 1976, 1 f); cf. Haslam, ZPE 22 (1976) 34; Lloyd-Jones, ib. 40; Luppe, *Gnomon* 49 (1977) 738

10c

(remains of one line)

Α]ΘΗΝΑ

ποίου Δρύαντος κεῖνος ἐγγό[νοις ξυνὼν
Τροίαν ἐπεστράτευσεν, Ὠργεῖοι; τ[ίς ἦν
ὃς τἄργα ταῦτα πρὸς θεοὺς ἐμή[σατο;
5 μῶν τῶν ἔνερθεν ἐξανέστηκ[εν μυχῶν
ὁ βυρσοφώνης Ζηνὶ Σαλμωνε[ὺς πρόμος;
τίν[ος ποτ᾿ ἀνδρὸ]ς εἰκάσω τάδ᾿ ἔργ[ματα,
ὅστι[ς μ᾿ ὑβρίζων ἐμὸν] ἀκόλλητον βρέ[τας
κρηπῖδος ἐξέσ]τρεψεν, ἐκ δὲ φοι[βάδα
10 ἔσυρε βωμοῦ παρθέ]νον [θεῶν βία;

2 Ll.-J.   5–6 Ll.-J.   7 ἔργ[ματα Ll.-J.   9 κρηπῖδος
Diggle   φοι[βάδα Luppe   10 ἔσυρε Luppe   end Ll.-J.

14

But where and to whom could such a speech have been delivered?

There are 77 fragments of the papyrus, but apart from 10c all are very small. In 10e the names of two speakers are plausibly restored as those of Antenor's son Helicaon and Agamemnon's herald Talthybius, and 10g 43, 12 appears to mention Cassandra's suitor Coroebus (perhaps also 10g 37,2). Helicaon's father is mentioned in fr. 11. But we cannot be sure that all these fragments come from the same play, and since Helicaon may have been a character in the Eurypylus *(q.v.) and Coroebus is said to have been killed by Neoptolemus, who certainly figured in that play, some of the fragments may have come from that work. See* Tragica Adespota *fr. 637.*

10c

ATHENA

Descendants of what Dryas were his companions when he launched his expedition against Troy, Argives?[a] Who was he who performed these actions against the gods? Has Salmoneus, who made himself a voice by means of hides,[b] risen from the caverns of the underworld to challenge Zeus? What sort of man can I guess was author of these deeds, the man who in his insolence wrenched headlong from its base my image, not fastened there, and dragged the prophetic maiden from the altar in defiance of the gods?

[a] Dryas was the father of the Thracian king Lycurgus, who because of his persecution of Dionysus was proverbial for having fought against a god; the subject of the sentence was presumably Agamemnon.

[b] Salmoneus; see prefatory note to the *Salmoneus.*

11

κατεστίκτου κυνὸς
σπολὰς Λίβυσσα, παρδαλήφορον δέρος

Scholia RVEΓ on Aristophanes, *Birds* 933; Suda σ 956 Adler;
Pollux, *Vocabulary* 7, 70

2 παρδαλήφορον Ellendt: -ηφόρον codd.

12

τὸ χρύσεον δὲ τᾶς Δίκας
δέδορκεν ὄμμα, τὸν δ' ἄδικον ἀμείβεται

Stobaeus, *Anthology* 1, 3, 37 (1, 59, 1 Wachsmuth); cf.
Aristoxenus fr. 50 Wehrli in Athenaeus 12, 546B

13

ἄνθρωπός ἐστι πνεῦμα καὶ σκιὰ μόνον

Stobaeus, *Anthology* 4, 43, 52 (5, 840, 14 Hense)

14

σοφοὶ τύραννοι τῶν σοφῶν ξυνουσίᾳ

Quoted by as many as fourteen authorities, some of whom,
including Plato, *Rep.* 8 p. 568AB and *Theages* 125B, attribute it
to Euripides. There seems to have been a similar line of Euripi-
des, something like ἀγαθὸν τυράννοις αἱ σοφῶν ξυνουσίαι;
see Kassel–Austin on Aristophanes fr. 323.

11

The Libyan jerkin of the dappled servant beast, the skin
worn by the leopard[a] . . .

[a] The commentator on Aristophanes who quotes this frag-
ment says that it refers to the leopard-skin that was hung outside
the door of Antenor (see prefatory note to *The Sons of Antenor*)
to warn the Greeks to spare it because of his friendship with
some of them.

12

The golden eye of Justice sees, and requites the unjust
man.

13

A man is nothing but breath and shadow.

14

Kings are wise because of the company of wise men.

ΑΙΓΕΥΣ

*The outlines of the plot are altogether uncertain. Fr.
19 refers to a river in Trozen, where Theseus was born; fr.
20 seems to refer to his battle with one of the formidable
criminals whom he destroyed on his famous journey from
Trozen to Athens; in fr. 22 someone seems to be asking
Theseus how he managed to get past those criminals; in fr.
24 Aegeus is telling someone, perhaps one of his sons, how
his own father Pandion divided his kingdom between his
sons; and fr. 25 must refer to Theseus' battle with the bull
of Marathon.*

*In one version of the story, which Sophocles followed
in his* Aegeus, *it was before Theseus had been recognised*

20

κέστρᾳ σιδηρᾷ πλευρὰ καὶ κατὰ ῥάχιν
ἤλαυνε παίων

Pollux, *Vocabulary* 10, 160 (2, 237, 23 Bethe)

21

κλύω μὲν οὐκ ἔγωγε, χωρίτην δ' ὁρῶ

Stephanus of Byzantium, *Ethnica* 699, 10

κλύω or ἔκλυον Meineke: ἐκλύωμεν or ἐκλύομεν codd. δ'
Meineke: γ' codd.

AEGEUS

*as the son of Aegeus that Medea, who was then living with
Aegeus, got Aegeus to send him against the bull, and after
his return in triumph tried to poison him, only for his
father to recognise him just in time. In another version,
which Euripides followed in his* Aegeus *and which
Callimachus followed in his* Hecale, *Theseus went against
the bull of his own free will, after he had been recognised.
See Carolin Hahnemann,* Hermes *127 (1999), 385–96.*

Some have suggested that the Aegeus *was identical
with the* Theseus *(q.v.), but if fr. 730 a–g really come from
the latter play, this is most improbable. See frr. 795, 905.*

20

. . . with an iron hammer he pounded his sides and his
back.

21

I do not hear, not I, but I see a native of the place . . .

FRAGMENTS OF KNOWN PLAYS

22

πῶς δῆθ' ὁδουρῶν σμῆνος ἐξέβης λαθών;

Schol. EFGQ (CP) on Pindar, *Pyth.* 2, 57 (2, 42, 9 Drachmann)

σμῆνος Nauck: ὅμοιος codd.: ὁδουρὸν οἷος Valckenaer (ὁδουρὸν CP)

23

ὥσπερ γὰρ ἐν φύλλοισιν αἰγείρου μακρᾶς
κἂν ἄλλο μηδέν, ἀλλὰ τοὐκείνης κάρα
κινεῖ τις αὔρα κἀνακουφίζει πτερόν

Schol. MVBEQ on Homer, *Iliad* 7, 106 Σοφοκλῆς ἐν Αἰγεῖ
Heath: ἐν ἄργει BEQ: ἐν Ἀτρεῖ Barnes

24

ΑΙΓΕΥΣ

ἐμοὶ μὲν ἀκτὰς ὥρισεν μολεῖν πατήρ,
πρεσβεῖα νείμας τῆσδε γῆς . . . . Λύκῳ
τὸν ἀντίπλευρον κῆπον Εὐβοίας νέμει,
Νίσῳ δὲ τὴν ὅμαυλον ἐξαιρεῖ χθόνα
5 Σκίρωνος ἀκτῆς· τῆς δὲ γῆς τὸ πρὸς νότον
ὁ σκληρὸς οὗτος καὶ γίγαντας ἐκτρέφων
εἴληχε Πάλλας

Strabo, *Geography* 9, 1, 6 p. 392 C . . . ἀρκεῖ ταῦτα παρὰ
Σοφοκλέους λαβεῖν· φησὶ δ' ὁ Αἰγεύς, ὅτι ὁ πατὴρ ὥρισεν
ἐμοὶ μὲν ἀπελθεῖν εἰς ἀκτάς, τῆσδε γῆς πρεσβεῖα νείμας·
. . . . . . α Λύκῳ τὸν ἀντίπλευρον κτλ.

1–2 Ll.-J. after H. L. Jones and Radt

20

AEGEUS

22

How did you get out without being noticed by the swarm
of guardians of the road?

23

For as among the leaves of a tall poplar, even if nothing
else is moved, a breeze moves its top and lifts a feather . . .

24

AEGEUS

My father decided that I should go to the coast, assigning
to me the chief position in this land. . . . To Lycus he as-
signed the garden on the side opposite Euboea; and for
Nisus he chose out the neighbouring country of Sciron's
shore;[a] and the southern part of this land fell to the hard
man, who brings up giants, Pallas.[b]

[a] Megara.
[b] Theseus defeated and killed Pallas and his fifty sons.

25

κλωστῆρσι χειρῶν ὀργάσας κατήνυσε
σειραῖα δεσμά

Photius 808 Theodoridis . . . Σοφοκλῆς δὲ ἐν Αἰγεῖ (Reitzen-
stein: ἐναργῆ cod.) τὸν Θησέα στρέφοντα καὶ μαλάττοντα
τοὺς λύγους ποιῆσαι δεσμὰ τῷ ταύρῳ· λέγει δὲ οὕτως·
κλωστῆρσι (Reitzenstein: -ρεσι cod.) κτλ.

ΑΙΘΙΟΠΕΣ

The ancient summary of Sophocles' Ajax begins τὸ
δρᾶμα τῆς Τρωικῆς ἐστι πραγματείας, ὥσπερ οἱ
Ἀντηνορίδαι καὶ Αἰχμαλωτίδες καὶ Ἑλένης ἁρπαγὴ
καὶ Μέμνων. *Though we have no evidence as to its con-
tent, Heyne was probably right when in 1783 he conjec-
tured that the* Aethiopes *was identical with the* Memnon.

28

τοιαῦτά τοί σοι πρὸς χάριν τε κοὐ βίᾳ
λέγω· σὺ δ᾽ αὐτός, ὥσπερ οἱ σοφοί, τὰ μὲν
δίκαι᾽ ἐπαίνει, τοῦ δὲ κερδαίνειν ἔχου

Athenaeus, *Deipnosophists* 3, 122B

1 βίᾳ] βίαν Herwerden

29

τετράπτεροι γὰρ νῶτον ἐν δεσμώμασι
σφηκοὶ κελαινόρινες

Photius Galeanus 22, 15 = Et. Gen. AB = Et. Magn. 385, 1

2 σφηκοὶ] σφηκτοὶ or σφικτοὶ Blaydes

22

AEGEUS

25

Using his hands as distaff and spindle he made them [the withes] soft and so contrived to bind it.[a]

[a] This was done to make a rope with which he could tether and drag along the captured Bull of Marathon.

THE ETHIOPIANS

In all probability, it dealt with the participation in the Trojan War of the Ethiopian prince Memnon, the son of Eos, the goddess of the dawn, by the Trojan prince Tithonus, which had been described in the lost post-Homeric epic Aethiopis. *Memnon killed Nestor's son, Antilochus, but was himself killed by Achilles.*

28

This I say to you to persuade you, not to compel; and do you of your own will act like the wise and praise justice, but cling to profit.

29

For they have four wings on their backs, are pinched because they have straps round them, and they have black noses.[a]

[a] This is thought to allude to the giant ants described by Herodotus 3, 102 f, which are larger than foxes and guard the gold-bearing sand; perhaps they were imagined to be in Memnon's kingdom.

ΑΙΧΜΑΛΩΤΙΔΕΣ

The subject of the play is unknown. Some have conjectured that it dealt with the fate of the Trojan female prisoners after the end of the war. But there is rather more to be said for the conjecture that it dealt with the female prisoners taken by the Greeks before the action of the Iliad *begins; fr. 40 mentions Chryse, the home of Chryseis;*

33a

δάκος [γὰρ οὐδὲ]ν τοῖσιν εὐόργοις ἔπος

Unpublished Oxyrhynchus papyrus ap. Lobel, *ZPE* 19 (1975) 209; Hesychius ε 7048 Latte

34

στρατοῦ καθαρτὴς κἀπομαγμάτων ἴδρις

Harpocration, *Glossary to the Ten Orators* 48, 9

35

ἀσπὶς μὲν ἡμὴ λίγδος ὡς πυκνομματεῖ

Pollux, *Vocabulary* 10, 189

ἡμὴ λίγδος Nauck: ἡμίλιγνος codd. FS: ἡ μίλιγδος cett. πυκνομματεῖ Bentley: πύκνωμά τι codd. ABFS: πυκνὸν πατεῖ CL

36

ὑφῃρέθη σου κάλαμος ὡσπερεὶ λύρας

Schol. V on Aristophanes, *Frogs* 230 and E on 231; Pollux, *Vocabulary* 4, 62

THE CAPTIVE WOMEN

fr. 43 mentions Mynes, the husband of Briseis, and his brother Epistrophus, both killed at Lyrnessus by Achilles; and fr. 34 might refer to Calchas, who in the first book of the Iliad *figures in an incident that involves both women. A. Schöll conjectured that this play was identical with the* Chryses, q.v.

33a
For good-tempered people are not stung by a word.

34
The purifier of the army, skilled in the rites of wiping off (pollution) . . .

35
My shield is as full of eyes as a waxen cast about a statue.

36
You are like a lyre which has had its reed removed.

37

ἐν παντὶ γάρ τοι σκορπὶὸς φρουρεῖ λίθῳ

Schol. on Nicander, *Theriaca* 18 Crugnola

39

καὶ νησιώτας καὶ μακρᾶς Εὐρωπίας . . .

Stephanus of Byzantium, *Ethnica* 287, 8 Meineke

Some word like οἰκήτορας (Meineke) or ἐνοίκους (Ellendt) must have followed.

40

ταύτην ἐγὼ Κίλλαν τε καὶ Χρύσην ‹ἔχω›

Stephanus of Byzantium, *Ethnica* 696, 15 Meineke

‹ἔχω› Casaubon: ‹νέμω› Meineke

41

εἰ μικρὸς ὢν τὰ φαῦλα νικήσας ἔχω

Photius Galeanus 643, 7 = Et. Gen. A = Et. Magn. 789, 41 = Suda φ 141

42

ἔσπεισα βαιᾶς κύλικος ὥστε δεύτερα

Schol. on Sophocles, *O.T.* 750; Suda β 210

37

For under every stone a scorpion is on guard.

39

Islanders and ‹denizens› of wide Europe . . .

40

This Cilla and Chryse I ‹possess›.[a]

[a] These are places in the Troad where Apollo had sanctuaries; see *Iliad* 1, 37 f.

41

. . . if I who am small have won a puny victory.

42

I poured from a small cup as a second . . .

FRAGMENTS OF KNOWN PLAYS

ΑΚΡΙΣΙΟΣ

Acrisius, son of Abas, king of Argos, fought even in the womb with his brother Proetus, who left Argos and ruled in Tiryns. Warned by an oracle that he would be killed by his grandson, Acrisius imprisoned his daughter Danae in a brazen tower, which Zeus entered in the form of a shower of gold to seduce Danae and engender Perseus. Acrisius ordered the mother and child to be put to sea in an ark, which was washed up on the small island of Seriphus. Here Danae was persecuted by the king Polydectes, but was protected by his brother Dictys. After his triumphant return to Seriphus with the head of the Gorgon, Perseus made his way to Argos, where Acrisius resigned the throne to him and himself moved to Larisa in Thessaly for fear of the prophecy. Visiting Larisa to take part in an athletic contest, Perseus threw a quoit which accidentally killed his grandfather.

61

ΧΟΡΟΣ

βοᾷ τις, ὤ· ἀκούετε;
ἢ μάτην ὑλακτῶ;
ἄπαντα γάρ τοι τῷ φοβουμένῳ ψοφεῖ

Stobaeus, *Anthology* 3, 8, 2 (3, 340, 13 Hense): Gnomology in Barberini gr. 4

XO. cod. S (om. MA)   2 ὑλακτῶ] ὑλῶ Hermann, who took βοᾷ . . . ὑλῶ to be a trimeter   3 ἄπαντα Gesner: πάντα codd.

ACRISIUS

Three plays of Sophocles dealt with this myth, the Acrisius, *the* Danae *and the* Men of Larissa. *The* Men of Larissa *evidently dealt with the end of Acrisius; the title indicates this, and note frr. 378 and 380, about an athletic contest. The* Danae *probably dealt with the exposure of Danae and her son; note fr. 165, in which Acrisius must be expressing his fear of the prophecy. Although we have sixteen quotations from the* Acrisius, *none of them gives a clue to the nature of its subject-matter. Brunck thought it was identical with the* Men of Larissa, *but Jacobs thought it was identical with the* Danae. *Fr. 64, which seems to have been uttered by the young Danae, and frr. 66 and 67, which might be uttered by Acrisius in explanation of his fear of the prophecy, seem to indicate that the play dealt with the story of the exposure, and since Sophocles is unlikely to have written two plays about this subject, Jacobs' theory seems likelier than not to be correct.*

61

CHORUS

Someone is shouting! Ho! Do you hear? Am I howling in vain? For if one is frightened, everything makes a noise!

62

ἀλλ᾽ οὐδὲν ἕρπει ψεῦδος εἰς γῆρας χρόνου

Stobaeus, *Anthology* 3, 12, 2 (3, 340, 13 Hense)

63

δῆλον γάρ· ἐν δεσμοῖσι δραπέτης ἀνὴρ
κῶλον ποδισθεὶς πᾶν πρὸς ἡδονὴν λέγει

Stobaeus, *Anthology* 4, 19, 29 (4, 427, 10 Hense)

64

ῥῆσις βραχεῖα τοῖς φρονοῦσι σώφρονα
πρὸς τοὺς τεκόντας καὶ φυτεύσαντας πρέπει,
ἄλλως τε καὶ κόρῃ τε κἀργείᾳ γένος,
αἷς κόσμος ἡ σιγή τε καὶ τὰ παῦρ᾽ ἔπη

Stobaeus, *Anthology* 4, 25, 24 (4, 623, 17 Hense); 4, 23, 28 (4, 579, 10 Hense)

65

θάρσει, γύναι· τὰ πολλὰ τῶν δεινῶν, ὄναρ
πνεύσαντα νυκτός, ἡμέρας μαλάσσεται

Stobaeus, *Anthology* 4, 44, 56 (5, 971, 13 Hense)

66

τοῦ ζῆν γὰρ οὐδεὶς ὡς ὁ γηράσκων ἐρᾷ

Stobaeus, *Anthology* 4, 52, 11 (5, 1076, 3 Hense); 4, 50, 72 (5, 1046, 7 Hense); 4, 50, 9 (5, 1022, 8 Hense)

ACRISIUS

62
But no falsehood lasts into old age.

63
It is clear! A runaway whose legs are fettered says anything that will please.

64
Those who think sensibly hold that brief speech to one's parents and begetters is appropriate, especially when one is a maiden and an Argive by birth, since silence and few words are an ornament to such.

65
Do not worry, lady! Most alarming things that have drawn breath in dreams during the night when day comes grow mild.

66
For no one loves life so much as he who is growing old.

67

τὸ ζῆν γάρ, ὦ παῖ, παντὸς ἥδιον γέρας·
θανεῖν γὰρ οὐκ ἔξεστι τοῖς αὐτοῖσι δίς

Stobaeus, *Anthology* 4, 52, 3 (5, 1074, 12 Hense)

1 ἥδιον Meineke: ἥδιστον codd.

ΑΛΕΑΔΑΙ

*Aleus, king of Tegea, was warned by the Delphic oracle
that if his daughter had a son that grandson would kill his
own sons. He therefore made his daughter Auge priestess
of Athena, so that she could not marry. However, while
Heracles was passing through Tegea Aleus entertained
him in the temple, and he got drunk, with the consequence
that Auge became pregnant. According to one story, her
son Telephus was exposed on Mount Parthenion and was
suckled by a hind. He was brought up by another Arca-
dian king, Corythus, or by his herdsmen, and was later
told by the Delphic oracle to go to Mysia in Asia Minor,
where he found his mother. According to another story,
Aleus gave his daughter to Nauplius, the celebrated pilot,
to be drowned, but Nauplius took her to Mysia and sold
her together with her son to Teuthras, king of that coun-
try. Teuthras married her, and Telephus succeeded him as
king.*

77

ἐνταῦθα μέντοι πάντα τἀνθρώπων νοσεῖ,
κακοῖς ὅταν θέλωσιν ἰᾶσθαι κακά

Stobaeus, *Anthology* 3, 4, 36 (3, 228, 17 Hense)

ACRISIUS

67

For life, my child, is a possession more delightful than any other, because the same people cannot die twice.

THE SONS OF ALEUS

This family history figured in four plays of Sophocles: Aleadae, Mysians, Telephus *and* Eurypylus. *An inscription of the fourth century (*DID 5, 8 *in Snell,* TrGF I, *p. 39) records that Sophocles composed a* Telepheia, *which presumably means a tetralogy about Telephus. Since poets younger than Aeschylus did occasionally compose tetralogies on continuous themes, this is not impossible.*

The Aleadae *presumably told how Telephus killed his uncles, but its fragments throw little light upon its plot, nor does any other author tells us how he came to kill them. One authority says that they were called Hippothous and (possibly) Pereus, others that they were called Cepheus, Lycurgus and Amphidamas. Frr. 84, 86 and 87 seem to suggest that they reproached Telephus with the obscurity of his origin, and that may have led to the quarrel in which he killed them.*

77

But it is here that all the concerns of men go wrong, when they wish to cure evil with evil.

78

τοῖς γὰρ δικαίοις ἀντέχειν οὐ ῥᾴδιον

Stobaeus, *Anthology* 3, 9, 1 (3, 346, 14 Hense)

79

κακὸν τὸ κεύθειν κοὐ πρὸς ἀνδρὸς εὐγενοῦς

Stobaeus, *Anthology* 3, 12, 3 (3, 444, 8 Hense)
κοὐ Gesner: καὶ codd.

80

καὶ γὰρ δικαία γλῶσσ᾽ ἔχει κράτος μέγα

Stobaeus, *Anthology* 3, 13, 22 (3, 457, 10 Hense)

81

ὦ παῖ, σιώπα· πόλλ᾽ ἔχει σιγὴ καλά

Stobaeus, *Anthology* 3, 33, 3 (3, 678, 10 Hense); Plutarch, *Talkativeness* 502E; Arsenius, *Violarium*, p. 488 Walz = Apostol. 18, 62a (CPG 2, 737, 9)

82

τί ταῦτα πολλῶν ῥημάτων ἔτ᾽ ἔστι σοι;
τὰ γὰρ περισσὰ πανταχοῦ λυπήρ᾽ ἔπη

Stobaeus, *Anthology* 3, 36, 11 (3, 692, 12 Hense)

83

μὴ πάντ᾽ ἐρεύνα· πολλὰ καὶ λαθεῖν καλόν

Stobaeus, *Anthology* 3, 41, 4 (3, 758, 5 Hense)
λαθεῖν καλόν Blomfield: λαλεῖν κακόν codd.

78

For it is not easy to resist those who are in the right.

79

Concealment is bad and is not the action of a noble man.

80

For righteous speech has great power.

81

My son, be silent! Silence has many beauties.

82

Why should this still need many words from you? In every place excess is painful.

83

Do not investigate everything! It is best that many things should remain hid.

84

κοὐκ οἶδ᾽ ὅτι χρὴ πρὸς ταῦτα λέγειν,
ὅταν οἵ γ᾽ ἀγαθοὶ πρὸς τῶν ἀγενῶν
κατανικῶνται·
ποία πόλις ἂν τάδ᾽ ἐνέγκοι;

Stobaeus, *Anthology* 4, 1, 6 (4, 2, 12 Hense); Corpus Paroe-
miographorum 716 Elter (see Hense, p. X)

2 γ᾽ Valckenaer: τ᾽ codd. (defended by Robert, assuming that
there was a lacuna after κατανικῶνται)

85

δοκῶ μέν, οὐδείς· ἀλλ᾽ ὅρα μὴ κρεῖσσον ᾖ
καὶ δυσσεβοῦντα τῶν ἐναντίων κρατεῖν
ἢ δοῦλον αὐτὸν ὄντα τῶν πέλας κλύειν

Stobaeus, *Anthology* 4, 13, 22 (4, 351, 5 Hense)

86

A.
παῦσαι· καταρκεῖ τοῦδε κεκλῆσθαι πατρός.
⟨ΤΗΛΕΦΟΣ⟩
εἴπερ πέφυκά γ᾽· εἰ δὲ μή, μείζων βλάβη.
A.
τό τοι νομισθὲν τῆς ἀληθείας κρατεῖ.

Stobaeus, *Anthology* 4, 24, 25 (4, 610, 2 Hense)

Süvern observed that this came from a stichomythia.

84

I do not know what I can say in reply to this, when good men are conquered by ignoble men. What city could put up with this?

85

I think, no one; but consider whether it is not better to defeat one's enemies even by impiety than to be a slave and submit to others.

86

A.

Stop! It is enough to be called the son of this father.

⟨TELEPHUS⟩

If I am his son! But if I am not, the harm is greater.

A.

What people believe prevails over the truth.

87

A.

ὁ δ' εἰ νόθος, πῶς γνησίοις ἴσον σθένει;

B.

ἅπαν τὸ χρηστὸν γνησίαν ἔχει φύσιν.

Stobaeus, *Anthology* 4, 24, 42 (4, 614, 11 Hense); Clement of Alexandria, *Miscellanies* 6, 2, 10, 1 (2, 429, 8 Stählin)

1 πῶς Ll.-J.: τοῖς SM: τις τοῖς A: τις Nauck

88

τὰ χρήματ' ἀνθρώποισιν εὑρίσκει φίλους,
αὖθις δὲ τιμάς, εἶτα τῆς ὑπερτάτης
τυραννίδος θεοῖσιν ἀγχίστην ἕδραν.
ἔπειτα δ' οὐδεὶς ἐχθρὸς οὔτε φύεται
5 πρὸς χρήμαθ' οἵ τε φύντες ἀρνοῦνται στυγεῖν.
δεινὸς γὰρ ἕρπειν πλοῦτος ἔς τε τἄβατα
καὶ πρὸς βέβηλα, χὠπόθεν πένης ἀνὴρ
οὐδ' ἐντυχὼν δύναιτ' ἂν ὧν ἐρᾷ τυχεῖν.
καὶ γὰρ δυσειδὲς σῶμα καὶ δύσθρουν στόμα
10 γλώσσῃ σοφὸν τίθησιν εὔμορφόν τ' ἰδεῖν.
μόνῳ δὲ χαίρειν κἂν νόσων ξυνουσίᾳ
πάρεστιν αὐτῷ κἀπικρύπτεσθαι κακά.

Stobaeus, *Anthology* 4, 31, 27 (5, 740, 17 Hense); vv. 6–10 Plutarch, *On Reading the Poets* 4, 21B

3 θεοῖσιν Conington: ἄκουσιν SM: τ' ἄγουσιν A: θακοῦσιν Salmasius   4–5 del. Hense   6 ἔς τε Gesner: ἔσται Stobaeus: πρός τε Plutarch   7 βέβηλα Vater: τὰ βατὰ Stobaeus, Plutarch   9 δύσθρουν στόμα Jebb: δυσώνυμον codd.   11 κἂν νόσων ξυνουσίᾳ Meineke: καὶ νοσεῖν ἐξουσίᾳ codd.   12 κἀπικρύπτεσθαι Blaydes: -ψασθαι or -ψεσθαι codd.

87

A.

But if he is a bastard, how can he be as strong as those who are legitimate?

B.

Nobility is always legitimate by nature.

88

It is money that finds friends for men, and also honours, and finally the throne sublime of royalty, nearest to the gods. And no one is an enemy to money, or if they are, men deny their hatred of it. For wealth has a strange power to get to places sacred and profane, and to places from which a poor man, even if he effects an entry, could not get what he desires. For wealth makes an ugly person beautiful to look on and an incoherent speech eloquent; and wealth alone can enjoy pleasure even in sickness and can conceal its miseries.

89

νομάς τέ τις κεροῦσσ᾽ ἀπ᾽ ὀρθίων πάγων
καθεῖρπεν ἔλαφος . . .
ἄρασα μύξας . . . καὶ κερασφόρους
στόρθυγγας εἶρφ᾽ ἔκηλος

Aelian, On the Nature of Animals 7, 39 (i, 192, 27 Hercher); νόμος [sic] . . . κεροῦσσα Herodian, On Grammatical Pathology ap. Et. Gen.; καὶ Σοφοκλῆς κεροῦσσαν τὴν Τηλέφου τροφόν Pollux, Vocabulary 5, 76 (1, 282, 12 Bethe); παρὰ δὲ Σοφοκλεῖ καὶ μύξαι οἱ μυκτῆρες ibid. 2, 72 (1, 105, 10 Bethe)

ΑΛΕΞΑΝΔΡΟΣ

This play evidently dealt with the same legend as a work of which we know much more, the Alexandros *of Euripides, on which see Stinton, "Euripides and the Judgment of Paris,"* JHS Suppl. xi (1965) (=Collected Papers on Greek Tragedy (1990) 16 f) *and Coles,* BICS Suppl. no. 32 (1974). *Paris was exposed at birth because of the prophecy that he would cause the ruin of Troy, and was brought up by a herdsman. When his pet bull was taken to be the prize in funeral games held by Priam in honour of the child who had been exposed long before, Paris made his way to the city, entered for the contest, and won all the prizes. Another son of Priam, Deiphobus, quarrelled with*

91a

ἀλλ᾽ οὐκ ἄτλας γὰρ βάσανος ἡ Λυδὴ λίθος

Herodian, On Prosody in General, cod. Vindob. Hist. gr. 10 fol. 25, 19; Harpocration, epitome p. 71 = Suda β 139

89

And a grazing horned deer came down from the high hills
. . . lifting its nostrils . . . and the tines of its horns it went
safely . . .

ALEXANDER

him, and Paris took refuge at the altar of Zeus. He was re-
cognised by Cassandra, who prophesied the city's destruc-
tion, but this did not prevent Priam and Hecuba from tak-
ing back their son.

   Fr. 93 indicates that Sophocles used the same legend as
Euripides, but we have no notion of how he treated it.
Stinton, op. cit. 55 = 58 remarks that "the piquant situa-
tion of the child grown to manhood taking part, unaware,
in his own funeral games, and the ingenious motive, the
recovery of his beloved steer, might well have been Sopho-
cles' own invention."

91a

But since the Lydian stone is no feeble test . . .[a]

   [a] The touchstone used to test gold or silver.

92

οὐ γάρ τι θεσμὰ τοῖσιν ἀστίταις πρέπει

Stephanus of Byzantium, *Ethnica* 139, 18 Meineke

93

βοτῆρα νικᾶν ἄνδρας ἀστίτας. τί γάρ;

Stephanus of Byzantium, *Ethnica* 139, 20 Meineke

ΑΛΚΜΕΩΝ

For the earlier history of Alcmeon (Alcmaeon), see the prefatory note on the Epigoni. *After killing his mother Eriphyle, he came, pursued by her Erinyes, to Psophis in Arcadia, where the king Phegeus purified him of the murder and gave him his daughter, Alphesiboea or in one version Arsinoe, in marriage. As a wedding present he gave to his wife the necklace made by Hephaestus and given to Harmonia, daughter of Aphrodite and wife of Cadmus, for whose sake his mother had betrayed his father, Amphiaraus. But the Erinyes still pursued him, and the Delphic oracle told him to settle in land which had not existed when he killed his mother. He therefore left Psophis and his wife and settled on the alluvial land in the delta of the Achelous, where he married Callirhoe, the daughter of the river god. He was now released from the madness inflicted by the Erinyes; but Callirhoe begged him to give her the necklace. He therefore made his way*

92

For the rules are not suited to the city-dwellers.

93

. . . that a shepherd should defeat city-dwellers! Of course!

ALCMEON

back to Psophis and told Phegeus that he had promised to dedicate it at Delphi as a condition of his release from madness. But Phegeus discovered the real reason why he wanted it, and on the way back the sons of Phegeus lay in wait for him and killed him.

Since fr. 108 contains words addressed to Alcmeon while he was mad, it is conjectured that this play dealt with the later part of his history; cf. fr. 880, where there is mention of Alphesiboea. We know more of Euripides' play on this subject, 'Αλκμέων διὰ Ψωφῖδος *(Alcmeon in Psophis); for a papyrus fragment of this, see Austin, Nova Fragmenta Euripidea, p. 83 = fr. 86 Kannicht. A less likely subject for the Sophoclean play is the story of how Alcmeon had two children, Amphilochus and Tisiphone, by Tiresias' daughter Manto, and left them with Creon, king of Corinth, dealt with by Euripides in his* 'Αλκμέων διὰ Κορίνθου *(Alcmeon in Corinth). See fr. 958.*

108

εἶθ᾽ εὖ φρονήσαντ᾽ εἰσίδοιμί πως φρενῶν
ἐπήβολον καλῶν σε

Porphyry, *Homeric Questions*, *Il.* 283, 7 Schrader = 5, 4
Sodano; Eustathius, *Od.* 1448, 5

ΑΜΥΚΟΣ

*This satyr play was evidently concerned with the box-
ing match between Polydeuces, in Bithynia with the Argo-
nauts, and Amycus, the barbarous king of the Bebryces
in Bithynia, who used to challenge all strangers to box
with him. Apollonius of Rhodes 2, 1–97 says that Amycus
was killed; Theocritus 22, 27–134 says that Polydeuces*

111

γέρανοι, χελῶναι, γλαῦκες, ἰκτῖνοι, λαγοί

Athenaeus, *Deipnosophists* 9, 400B (παρὰ Σοφοκλεῖ ἐν
᾽Αμύκῳ σατυρικῷ); id., 9, 400C; γλαῦκες . . . λαγοί Eustathius,
Od. 1534, 14 and unknown grammarian ap. Hermann, *De emen-
danda ratione Graecae grammaticae* I (1801) 320, 9 = Cramer,
Anecdota Parisina 4, 245, 23

112

σιαγόνας τε δὴ μαλθακὰς τίθησι

Athenaeus, *Deipnosophists* 3, 94E

ALCMEON

108

I wish that I could see you sane, in control of your mind!

AMYCUS

spared his life. The play seems to have influenced several
works of art; see LIMC I 1, 738 f. Several of these show sa-
tyrs in conjunction with the main characters; perhaps the
satyrs had been enslaved to Amycus and were liberated
after his defeat.

111

Cranes, tortoises, owls, martens, hares . . .

112

. . . and makes his jaws soft.

FRAGMENTS OF KNOWN PLAYS

ΑΜΦΙΑΡΕΩΣ

Several of those who quote fragments specify that this play was satyric; but it is not easy to guess which incident in the life of Amphiaraus lent itself to satyric treatment. Some have suggested that the play dealt with the time when Amphiaraus, knowing that the expedition of his brother-in-law Adrastus against Thebes would end in disaster, went into hiding to avoid having to accompany him. Others have thought of the part taken by Amphiaraus in

113

ὁ πινοτήρης τοῦδε μάντεως χοροῦ

Schol. VΓ Ald. on Aristophanes, *Wasps* 1510

πινοτήρης Dindorf: πινοτὴρ VΓ: πιννοτήρης Ald.

121

καὶ Σοφοκλῆς δὲ τούτῳ παραπλήσιον ἐποίησεν ἐν
Ἀμφιαράῳ σατυρικῷ τὰ γράμματα παράγων ὀρχού-
μενον

Athenaeus, *Deipnosophists* 10, 454F

AMPHIARAUS

the foundation of the Nemean Games, featured in the
Hypsipyle *of Euripides. Comedies with this title were*
written by Aristophanes, Apollodorus of Carystus, and
Philippides, and tragedies by Cleophon ŏphon?) *and*
perhaps Carcinus II; the comedy of Aristophanes dealt
with happenings at the oracular and healing shrine of
Amphiaraus at Oropus on the Boeotian border of Attica
which was established after his death. See fr. 958.

113
The sentinel crab of this prophetic chorus[a] . . .

[a] The Pinna is a bivalve shellfish, and the metaphor is taken
from "the so-called Pinna-guard, a little crab which makes its
home within the Pinna's shell, and acts as sentinel" (D'Arcy
Thompson, *A Glossary of Greek Fishes*, 1957, 202).

121
In a similar way Sophocles in the satyr play *Amphiaraus*
brings on a man who dances the letters.[a]

[a] Athenaeus has just quoted a number of passages from plays
in which an illiterate person describes the letters of a particular
word.

ΑΜΦΙΤΡΥΩΝ

Amphitryon, son of Alcaeus, king of Tiryns, married Alcmene, daughter of his uncle Electryon, but was not allowed to consummate the marriage until he had avenged the death of her brothers on the Taphii and their king Pterelaus. While he was absent on this campaign Zeus came to his house in the form of its owner. Alcmene gave birth to twins, Iphicles who was the son of Amphitryon and Heracles who was the son of Zeus. In the Alcmena *of Euripides Amphitryon was about to burn his*

122

ἐπεὶ δὲ βλάστοι, τῶν τριῶν μίαν λαβεῖν
εὔσοιαν ἀρκεῖ

Schol. LR on Sophocles, *OC* 390 (26, 5 de Marco)

1 μίαν] μιᾶς Meineke

ΑΝΔΡΟΜΑΧΗ

If there was really such a play, it must have been about Hector's wife, who after his death became the concubine of Neoptolemus, and later the wife of Helenus (see Euripides, Andromache*). But there is only one quotation, and "Andromache" may be a mistake for "Andromeda."*

AMPHITRYON

AMPHITRYON

wife alive for her supposed infidelity, but Zeus saved her, extinguishing the fire with a heavy shower of rain. Having accidentally killed his father-in-law, Amphitryon was obliged to leave Tiryns for Thebes. As an old man he figures in the Heracles *of Euripides, where he is present when Heracles in a fit of madness kills his wife and children.*

Which of these episodes furnished the plot of Sophocles' play we have no means of knowing.

122

And when it has come into being, it is enough for one of the three to attain safety.[a]

[a] There is no way of knowing to what this refers.

ANDROMACHE

ΑΝΔΡΟΜΕΔΑ

The *Catasterisms attributed to Eratosthenes and the commentaries on Aratus tell us that in this play Cassiepeia, wife of Cepheus and mother of Andromeda, boasted that she (and not her daughter, as in some versions) was more beautiful than the Nereids, with the result that Poseidon sent a sea monster which began to devastate their country, and could only be stopped from doing so if Andromeda was exposed to it. This monster was killed by Perseus, on his way back to Seriphus with the head of the Gorgon Medusa. Phineus, to whom*

126

†ἡμιουτον† κούρειον ἡρέθη πόλει·
ἀρχῆθέν ἐστι τῷ Κρόνῳ θυηπολεῖν
γένος βρότειον τοῖσι βαρβάροις νόμος.

Hesychius, *Lexicon* κ 3859 Latte

1 ἡμιουτον] δημιόθυτον Tucker: alii alia   2–3 Ll.-J.:
νόμος γάρ ἐστι τοῖς βαρβάροις θυηπολεῖν βρότειον ἀρχῆθεν
γένος τῷ Κρόνῳ cod.: alii alia

127

ἵπποισιν ἢ κύμβαισι ναυστολεῖς χθόνα;

Athenaeus, *Deipnosophists* 11, 482D; Eustathius, *Il.* 1205, 49

ANDROMEDA

Andromeda had been affianced, tried to assert his claim to her, but Perseus disposed of him and his followers by showing them the head.

How Sophocles treated this story, which was also the subject of a celebrated play of Euripides, we have no means of knowing. Casaubon conjectured that it was a satyr play, on the dubious ground that it mentioned Pans (fr. 136). If fr. 133 really belongs to it, this possibility is somewhat strengthened, since the manuscript which preserves it, together with frr. 389a and 1083, may have contained a collection of satyr plays by Sophocles.

126

. . . was chosen as a . . . sacrifice for the city. For from ancient times the barbarians have had a custom of sacrificing human beings to Kronos.[a]

[a] Baal (wrongly called Moloch), to whom the Carthaginians offered human sacrifices, was identified by the Greeks with Kronos.

127

Are you voyaging to the land on horses or in boats?

FRAGMENTS OF KNOWN PLAYS

128

μηδὲν φοβεῖσθε προσφάτους ἐπιστολάς

Phrynichus, *Ecl.* 351 Fischer

φοβεῖσθε V: -αι Xbc

128a

ἡ δυστυχὴς ἀθῷος ἐκκρεμωμένη

Herodian, *On Prosody in General*, cod. Vindob. Hist. gr. 10 fol. 3, 27

ἐκκρεμωμένη West: ενκρεμανομενη cod.

129

ἰδοὺ δαφοινὸν μάσθλητα δίγονον

Et. Gen. AB = Et. Magn. 272, 3; Photius Lex. δ 509; cf. Hesychius, *Lexicon* μ 333

δαφοινὸν Photius: δὲ φοινὸν Et. Gen., Et. Magn.: δὲ φοίνιον Brunck

133

P. Oxy. 2453 fr. 49, which contains small fragments of eight verses, has as the beginnings of successive lines (6 and 7) ζευξίλεως[and τῷ Λιβυκῷ[. ζευξίλεως ('yoking the people', i.e., ruling them) is attested by Hesychius, *Lexicon* ζ 127 Latte as occurring in this play.

128
Do not be afraid of new letters!

128a
. . . the unfortunate one hanging here, intact . . .

129
See the bloody double goad!

133

ΑΝΤΗΝΟΡΙΔΑΙ

Antenor, a noble Trojan whose wife, Theano, was priestess of Athena, and who had entertained Menelaus and Odysseus in his house when they came as ambassadors to demand the return of Helen, not only urged the other Trojans to hand her over, but saved his guests from being put to death. In this way he established friendly relations with the Greeks. Strabo, Geography 13, 1, 53 p. 608 says that "according to Sophocles during the capture of Troy a leopard-skin was placed in front of Antenor's door to indicate that his house was to be left unplundered [see fr. 11]. So Antenor and his sons with the surviving Eneti got safely to Thrace and from there crossed over to the place called Enetica on the Adriatic. And Aeneas with his father Anchises and his son Ascanius

137

ὄρνιθα καὶ κήρυκα καὶ διάκονον

Athenaeus, *Deipnosophists* 9, 373C

ΑΤΡΕΥΣ *or* ΜΥΚΗΝΑΙΑΙ

See on Θυέστης *and see fr. 738*

140

μὰ τὴν ἐκείνου δειλίαν, ᾗ βόσκεται,
θῆλυς μὲν αὐτός, ἄρσενας δ' ἐχθροὺς ἔχων

Schol. on Euripides, *Hippolytus* 307

THE SONS OF ANTENOR

assembled his people and sailed off." In Homer the Eneti
are a Paphlagonian tribe who fight for Troy under their
king Pylaemenes; with them Antenor was traditionally
supposed to have founded the settlement of the Veneti in
Italy, and in particular the city of Patavium (Padua). Ac-
cording to Bacchylides 15 he had fifty sons, and eleven of
his sons are named in Homer; on Helicaon, see Ajax the
Locrian *(fr. 10e) and the* Eurypylus. *Some of the sons were*
thought to have settled in Cyrene.

Carl Robert suggested that this play was identical with
the Laocoon, *and Blass and Wilamowitz that it was iden-*
tical with the Ἑλένης Ἀπαίτησις (The Demand for
Helen's Return): *in both cases there is insufficient evi-*
dence. For recent speculations about this play, see M.
Leigh, JHS 118 (1998), 82–100.

137

. . . bird both herald and minister[a] . . .

[a] This probably refers to the eagle.

ATREUS *or* THE WOMEN OF MYCENAE

140

By his cowardice, which he feeds on, he that is female
himself but has enemies who are male!

ΑΧΑΙΩΝ ΣΥΛΛΟΓΟΣ

See on Σύνδειπνοι

143

ὡς ναοφύλακες νυκτέρου ναυκληρίας
πλήκτροις ἀπευθύνουσιν οὐρίαν τρόπιν

Pollux, *Vocabulary* 10, 133 (2, 229, 25 Bethe)

1 ναυαγίας codd. FS

144

σὺ δ᾽ ἐν θρόνοισι γραμμάτων πτυχὰς ἔχων
νέμ᾽ εἴ τις οὐ πάρεστιν ὃς ξυνώμοσεν

Schol. BD on Pindar, *Isthm.* 2, 68 (3, 222, 11 Drachmann)

1 πτυχὰς Meursius: πτύχας codd.

144a

φάλανθον Νέστορος κάρα

Lexicon of Cyril, Madrid manuscript, ed. Naoumides, *GRBS* 9 (1968) 269

THE GATHERING OF THE ACHAEANS

See on Those Who Dine Together

143
Since the pilots of the nighttime voyage are guiding with their rudders the wind-sped keel.

144
But do you on your chair who hold the tablets with the writing mark off any who has sworn the oath but is not present!

144a
. . . the white[a] head of Nestor . . .

[a] See Chantraine, *Dictionnaire Etymologique de la langue grecque* s.v. φάλανθος.

ΑΧΙΛΛΕΩΣ ΕΡΑΣΤΑΙ

Casaubon's deduction from fr. 153 that this was a satyr play is surely right; clearly the satyrs aspired to be the lovers of Achilles. Achilles' father Peleus and his tutor Phoenix were both characters; but we know nothing of the plot. Mount Pelion is a likely haunt of satyrs, and Chiron's cave there, where Achilles was educated, may have been the scene.

Were there other lovers? Heracles was one in the Her-

149

τὸ γὰρ νόσημα τοῦτ᾽ ἐφίμερον κακόν·
ἔχοιμ᾽ ἂν αὐτὸ μὴ κακῶς ἀπεικάσαι.
ὅταν πάγου φανέντος αἰθρίου χεροῖν
κρύσταλλον ἁρπάσωσι παῖδες εὐπαγῆ,
5 τὰ πρῶτ᾽ ἔχουσιν ἡδονὰς ποταινίους·
τέλος δ᾽ ὁ θυμὸς οὔθ᾽ ὅπως ἀφῇ θέλει,
οὔτ᾽ ἐν χεροῖν τὸ κτῆμα σύμφορον μένειν.
οὕτω δὲ τοὺς ἐρῶντας αὐτὸς ἵμερος
δρᾶν καὶ τὸ μὴ δρᾶν πολλάκις προσίεται.

Stobaeus, *Anthology* 4, 20, 46 (4, 460, 7 Hense)

1 ἐφίμερον Arsenius: ἐφήμερον codd.   3 φανέντος]
χυθέντος Blaydes   4 παῖδες εὐπαγῆ Campbell, Nauck: παι-
διαισαγῆ cod. S: παιδιαῖς ἄγη MA   6 θυμὸς Dobree:
χυμὸς codd.: κρυμὸς Meineke: 'lac. after χυμὸς?' Campbell
7 κτῆμα] πῆγμα Gomperz   8 οὕτω δὲ Schneidewin: οὔτε
codd.   9 προσίεται Meineke: προ- codd.

THE LOVERS OF ACHILLES

acles *of the proto-Cynic Antisthenes, and since Heracles
figures in many satyr plays some people have suggested
that he was a character in this play. But Antisthenes' alle-
gorical motive is patent, and he is not a reliable witness.
In Aeschylus' Achillean trilogy Achilles is the* ἐραστής *of
Patroclus; Plato in the* Symposium *(180A) complains that
in Homer Patroclus is the older of the two. Perhaps he fig-
ured in the play of Sophocles.*

149

For this disease is an attractive evil; I could make quite a
good comparison. When ice appears out of doors, and
boys seize it up while it is solid, at first they experience
new pleasures. But in the end their pride will not agree to
let it go, but their acquisition is not good for them if it
stays in their hands. In the same way an identical desire
drives lovers to act and not to act.

150

⟨ΠΗΛΕΤΣ⟩

τίς γάρ με μόχθος οὐκ ἐπεστάτει ⟨τότε⟩;
λέων δράκων τε, πῦρ, ὕδωρ

Schol. on Pindar, *Nem.* 3, 60 (3, 51, 17 Drachmann)

1 ⟨τότε⟩ Blaydes

151

The scholia on Apollonius Rhodius 4, 816 say that according to Sophocles in *The Lovers of Achilles* Thetis left Peleus because he reviled her. They attribute to the author of the early epic *Aegimius* ([Hesiod] fr. 300) the story that Thetis used to throw the children she bore to Peleus into a cauldron to see if they were mortal. According to others, they say, she threw them into a fire. The story that she dipped her son in the Styx to make him invulnerable, gripping him by the heel, which therefore did not become invulnerable, is shown by works of art to be as early as the Hellenistic age; see *LIMC* I 1 54.

It would appear from the hypothesis to Aeschylus' *Women of Etna* (my Appendix to the LCL *Aeschylus*, pp. 595–6, *TrGF* iii pp. 126–7) that this play contained at least one change of scene.

152

ἢ δορὸς διχόστομον πλῆκτρον.
[δίπτυχοι γὰρ ὀδύναι μιν ἤρικον
Ἀχιλληίου δόρατος]

150

⟨PELEUS⟩

What kind of trouble did not afflict me ⟨then⟩? Lion, dragon, fire, water . . .[a]

[a] Thetis changed shape repeatedly before Peleus managed to capture her.

151

152

. . . or the two-mouthed point of the spear. [For the double pain of the spear of Achilles shattered him.]

Schol. on Pindar, *Nem.* 6, 85b (3, 112, 5 Drachmann)

Casaubon saw that only the first line was from Sophocles; Page, *PMG* 1015 rightly prints the rest as a lyric fragment of unknown authorship.

153

ΦΟΙΝΙΞ

παπαῖ, τὰ παιδίχ᾽, ὡς ὁρᾷς, ἀπώλεσας

Synagoge B 1, 324, 11, etc.

154

σὺ δ᾽, ὦ Σύαγρε, Πηλιωτικὸν τρέφος

Athenaeus, *Deipnosophists* 9, 401C, etc.

155

γλώσσης μελίσσῃ τῷ κατερρυηκότι

Schol. on S., *O.C.* 481

μελίσσῃ Ellendt: μελίσσης cod. L: καὶ μελίσσης RM

156

ὁ δ᾽ ἔν θ᾽ ὅπλοις ἀρρῶξιν Ἡφαίστου τέχνῃ

Choeroboscus on Theodosius, *Canones* 1, 415, 4 Hilgard

δ᾽ ἔν θ᾽ Schneider: δ(έ) ἔνθ᾽ codd.   τέχνῃ Dindorf:
τεχνίτου codd.: Ἡ. ‹σοφοῦ θεῶν› τεχνίτου Mekler

157

ὀμμάτων ἄπο

λόγχας ἵησιν

Hesychius, *Lexicon* o 736 Latte

ὀμμάτων ἄπο λόγχας Casaubon: ὀμματοπάλογχα cod.

153

PHOENIX

Ah, you have lost your beloved, as you see![a]

[a] The grammarians quote this fragment as an example of the term παιδικά being used of a male person; this is the commonest usage, but they explain that it can also be applied to females.

154

... and you, Syagrus,[a] you who were reared on Pelion ...

[a] The name of a hound, as those who quote the fragment explain.

155

... to him who flowed with the honey of his tongue ...

156

But he, with arms unbreakable through the art of Hephaestus ...

157

He darts spears from his eyes.

FRAGMENTS OF KNOWN PLAYS

ΔΑΙΔΑΛΟΣ

We know nothing about the plot. Daedalus may well have been another title for the Men of Camicus, q.v., *or for the* Minos, q.v.; *but the many stories about Daedalus, after whom three comedies were named, could have furnished material for several plays. Frr. 160 and 161 testify that the play contained something about Talos, who according to Simonides fr. 568 in PMG and Apollonius Rhodius 4, 1638 f was a giant made of bronze who*

158

εἵλλει μὲν εἴσω τόνδ᾽ ἀχαλκεύτῳ πέδῃ

Geneva scholia on Homer, Φ 282 (5, 190, 32 Erbse)

εἵλλει Mette: ἐλληημενήσω cod.   τόνδ᾽ Diels: τὸν δ᾽ cod.: τῇδ᾽ Nicole   ἀχαλκεύτῳ Diels: ἔα χαλκευτῷ cod.

162

ἀλλ᾽ οὐδὲ μὲν δὴ κάνθαρος
τῶν Αἰτναίων ⟨γε⟩ πάντως

Schol. LP on Aristophanes, *Peace* 73

2 ⟨γε⟩ πάντως Pearson: πάντων codd.

ΔΑΝΑΗ

This play may have been the same as the Acrisius, q.v. *Welcker and Meineke guessed that it was a satyr play, and indeed Aeschylus wrote a satyr play, the* Δικτυουλκοί *(Hauling in the Net), about the arrival of Danae and Perseus on Seriphus.*

64

DAEDALUS

guarded the island of Crete by walking all round it three times daily. Simonides said that he was made by Hephaestus and was given to Minos, but Apollonius said that he was given by Zeus to Minos' mother Europa. In this play it appears from fr. 160 that he destroyed intruders by consuming them with fiery heat, and from fr. 161 that he was stated to be mortal. Daedalus came to Crete as a refugee from Athens; one wonders how he got past Talos.

158
He confines him inside with a fetter not of bronze.

162
But it is not a beetle, one of those from Etna, either.[a]

[a] Very large beetles were thought to be found on Mount Etna. Attempts to identify newly discovered objects are common in satyr plays; cf. *Ichn.* fr. 314, 308, in its context.

DANAE

165

οὐκ οἶδα τὴν σὴν πεῖραν, ἓν δ᾽ ἐπίσταμαι·
τοῦ παιδὸς ὄντος τοῦδ᾽ ἐγὼ διόλλυμαι

Schol. LGMR on S., *Ajax* 1

ΔΙΟΝΥΣΙΣΚΟΣ

*This was certainly a satyr play; in fr. 171 Silenus or the
Chorus is talking of the infant Dionysus, just as in Aeschy-
lus' Dictyulci fr. 275 (in the LCL Aeschylus = 47a Radt),*

171

ὅταν γὰρ αὐτῷ προσφέρω βρῶσιν διδούς,
τὴν ῥῖνά μ᾽ εὐθὺς ψηλαφᾷ κἄνω φέρει
τὴν χεῖρα πρὸς ⟨τὸ⟩ φαλακρὸν ἡδὺ διαγελῶν

Lexicon Messanense fol. 283r, 18

2 ῥῖνά μ᾽ Nauck: ῥῖναν cod.

172

⟨ΧΟΡΟΣ⟩

πόθεν ποτ᾽ ἄλυπον ὧδε
ηὗρον ἄλθος ἀνίας;

Synagoge 385, 18 Bekker = Photius 1058 Theodoridis

2 ἄλθος Tucker: ἄνθος cod. See M.W. Haslam, *Glotta* 70,
1992, 35–8.

DANAE

165

I do not know what you mean by an 'attempt'; but one
thing I do know, that if this child is alive I am dead.

THE INFANT DIONYSUS

*785 f the Chorus talks of the infant Perseus. Fr. 172 indi-
cates that in this play the lately born Dionysus discovers
wine, as in the* Ichneutae *the lately born Hermes discovers
the lyre.*

171

For when I offer him the drink I'm giving him, at once he
tickles my nose, and brings up his hand to the smooth sur-
face, smiling sweetly.

172

‹CHORUS›

Wherever did I find the flower that cures pain like this?

FRAGMENTS OF KNOWN PLAYS

ΔΟΛΟΠΕΣ

The Dolopes were a Thessalian tribe, over whom Peleus made Phoenix king (Iliad 10, 484). This play may well have been identical with the Phoenix. *The name of Phoenix occurs at fr. 1132, 4, 6. If this is the play parts of which are preserved in frr. 1130–33, it was a satyr play, but it is hard to see how Phoenix could have been related*

174

εὐναῖος ἄν που δραπέτιν στέγην ἔχων

Herodian, *On Prosody in General*, cod. Vindob. Hist. gr. fol. 3v; Photius Galeanus 36, 12 = Et. Gen. B = Et. Magn. 393, 43

ἄν που Herodian: εἴη Photius, etc.

ΕΛΕΝΗΣ ΑΠΑΙΤΗΣΙΣ

This play was thought by Blass and Wilamowitz to have been identical with the Antenoridae, *q.v.; they may well be right. According to the lost epic* Cypria, *the embassy of Odysseus and Menelaus took place after the Greeks had landed near Troy and Protesilaus and Cycnus had been killed. Others made it happen before the Greeks left Tenedos on their way to Troy. It was the subject of a dithyramb of Bacchylides (15) and a not uncommon*

THE DOLOPIANS

to the situation to which fr. 1130 belongs. The play of that name by Euripides told of the blinding of Phoenix by his father Amyntor, whose concubine had falsely accused him; in Homer, he had seduced the concubine to gratify his mother. But Peleus took him to Chiron to have his sight restored, and then set him up as king of the Dolopes; Sophocles may have told a similar story.

174

in my lair, where I would have the home of a runaway[a] . . .

[a] The expression translated "in my lair" is one used of hares, so that the speaker seems to be comparing himself with a hare that continually changes its form. Perhaps Phoenix is speaking of the time between his expulsion by his father and his coming to Peleus.

THE DEMAND FOR HELEN'S RETURN

theme in art; see Beazley, Proceedings of the British Academy 43 (1957) 233 f. *Strabo tells us (frr. 180, 180a) that according to this play the prophet Calchas died in Pamphylia; presumably this event was prophesied. Fr. 177 lends some colour to the view of Hermann and Boeckh that it was a satyr play; they took the passage of Aristides quoted under* Ἑλένης Γάμος (Helen's Wedding) *to come from the* Ἑλένης Ἀπαίτησις. *See fr. 872.*

FRAGMENTS OF KNOWN PLAYS

176

καὶ γὰρ χαρακτὴρ αὐτός· ἐν γλώσσῃ τί με
παρηγορεῖ Λάκωνος ὀσμᾶσθαι λόγου

Schol. MTAB on Euripides, *Phoenissae* 301 (1, 288, 2
Schwartz)

1 αὐτός· Ll.-J. (αὐτὸς Hermann): αὐτὸς codd.

177

γυναῖκα δ᾽ ἐξελόντες ‹ἐξ ἐδωλίων
τὴν› τοῦ Μεν‹ελέω τλήμον᾽,› ἢ θράσσει γένυν
τέως ἔωλον γραφι‹δίοις› ἐνημμένοις

Erotian, θ 5 Nachmanson

1–2 suppl. Ll.-J., who transposed τοῦ μὲν from its place after
τέως in line 3   3 γραφι‹δίοις› suppl. Hermann

178

ἐμοὶ δὲ λῷστον αἷμα ταύρειον πιεῖν
καὶ μὴ 'πὶ πλεῖον τῶνδ᾽ ἔχειν δυσφημίας

Schol. VEΓΘ on Aristophanes, *Knights* 84b; Suda ν 539

2 μὴ 'πὶ Wecklein: μή γε VE: μήτε ΓΘ

ΕΛΕΝΗΣ ΑΡΠΑΓΗ

See on Ἑλένης Γάμος

176

Yes, the accent is the same! Something about his speech coaxes me into scenting a Laconian way of talking.

177

. . . and taking from the palace the wretched wife of Menelaus, who tortures her cheek, till lately faded, with pencils that she digs in.

178

But for me it is best to drink bull's blood,[a] and not to endure any longer these people's slanders.

[a] Themistocles was popularly believed to have committed suicide by drinking bull's blood, which was supposed to be poisonous.

THE RAPE OF HELEN

See on Helen's Wedding

ΕΛΕΝΗΣ ΓΑΜΟΣ

We know nothing of the plot; but the play is usually conjectured to have dealt with Helen's wedding to Paris. If that is correct, it was probably identical with the Ἑλένης Ἁρπαγή (The Rape of Helen) mentioned in the hypothesis (i.e., ancient summary) of the Ajax. *According to Homer (Il. 3, 443 f) they first made love on the island of*

181

πέπων ἐρινὸς ‹παντελῶς› ἀχρεῖος ὢν
ἐς βρῶσιν ἄλλους ἐξερινάζεις λόγῳ

Athenaeus, *Deipnosophists* 3, 76C

1 suppl. Scaliger

ΕΠΙΓΟΝΟΙ

This play is quoted three times, the Eriphyle *(q.v.) seven times; most scholars have believed that the two plays were identical. The prophet Amphiaraus knew that the expedition of the Seven against Thebes would end in disaster, and was unwilling to take part in it. But Polynices bribed his wife Eriphyle with the golden necklace given as a wedding present to Harmonia, wife of Cadmus the founder of Thebes and daughter of Aphrodite, in*

185

ὀλόμενε παίδων, ποῖον εἴρηκας λόγον;

Lynceus in Athenaeus, *Deipnosophists* 13, 584D

HELEN'S WEDDING

Cranae, on the Laconian Gulf; others say it was on Cythera, or on the island of Helene off the southeast coast of Attica. Aristides 46, 307, 14 tells how in a play of Sophocles satyrs were overcome with lust at the sight of Helen, which has been held to indicate that this play was a satyr play.

181

You are a ripe wild fig that though itself quite useless makes others good to eat by your talk.

THE EPIGONI

order to persuade her husband to accompany them. Amphiaraus charged his son Alcmeon with the duty of taking vengeance upon his mother, and this he did, in one version before and in another after the expedition of the Epigoni, the sons of the Seven, including Alcmeon himself, who took the city. See on Alcmeon *and on* Amphiaraus; *one cannot rule out the possibility of a trilogy* Epigonoi, Eriphyle, Alcmeon, *with the* Amphiaraus *as its satyr play. See frr. 846, 958, 890.*

185

Most calamitous of sons, what a word have you uttered![a]

[a] Eriphyle must have said this to Alcmeon, perhaps just before he killed her.

186

audisne haec, Amphiarae, sub terram abdite?

Cicero, *Tusculan Disputations* 2, 60 says that this verse "from the *Epigoni*" was quoted by the Stoic philosopher Cleanthes; Nauck guessed that the original was κλύεις τάδ᾽, Ἀμφιάραε, γῆς κεύθων κάτω; Since the *Epigoni* of Sophocles was more celebrated than that of Aeschylus, it is probably from this play.

187

ΑΛΚΜΕΩΝ

ἀνδροκτόνου γυναικὸς ὁμογενὴς ἔφυς.

ΑΔΡΑΣΤΟΣ

σὺ δ᾽ αὐτόχειρ γε μητρὸς ἥ σ᾽ ἐγείνατο.

Plutarch, *On Reading the Poets* 13, 35C; id., *How to Profit from Your Enemies* 5, 88F quotes line 1 only. Again it is conjectured that the fragment comes from this play.

188

φιλεῖ γὰρ ἡ δύσκλεια τοῖς φθονουμένοις
νικᾶν ἐπ᾽ αἰσχροῖς ἢ ᾽πὶ τοῖς καλοῖς πλέον

Stobaeus, *Anthology* 3, 38, 27 (3, 713, 11 Hense)

189

ὦ πᾶν σὺ τολμήσασα καὶ πέρα γυνή,
κάκιον ἀλλ᾽ οὐκ ἔστιν οὐδ᾽ ἔσται ποτὲ
γυναικὸς ἣ ᾽πὶ πῆμα γίγνεται βροτοῖς

Stobaeus, *Anthology* 4, 22, 173 (4, 557, 7 Hense)

1 γυνὴ MA: γύναι S   3 ἣ ᾽πὶ Bothe: ἢ εἴ τι codd.

186

Do you hear this, Amphiaraus, where you are hidden underground?

187

ALCMEON

You are the brother of a woman who killed her husband!

ADRASTUS

And you are the murderer of the mother who gave you birth![a]

[a] Adrastus, king of Argos and leader of the expedition of the Seven against Thebes, was brother of Eriphyle and uncle of Alcmeon. A fragmentary passage of Philodemus' book on music seems to imply that in this play a dispute between Alcmeon and Adrastus was put an end to by the power of music.

188

For victims of envy find that ill repute wins out over shameful rather than over honourable actions.

189

O woman whose shamelessness has stopped at nothing and has gone yet further, no other evil is or ever will be worse than a woman who was born to give pain to mortals!

190

τὸ κοῖλον Ἄργος οὐ κατοικίσοντ᾽ ἔτι

Schol. LRMT on S., *O.C.* 378

κατοικήσοντ᾽ Casaubon: -σαντ(α) codd.

ΕΠΙ ΤΑΙΝΑΡΩΙ
(*or* ΕΠΙΤΑΙΝΑΡΙΟΙ) ΣΑΤΥΡΟΙ

See on Ἡρακλῆς

ΕΡΙΣ

We know nothing of the plot; but the guess that this play dealt with the appearance of Eris, goddess of strife, at the wedding of Peleus and Thetis, when she threw down the golden apple which was the cause of the Judg-

199

ἐγὼ δὲ πεινῶσ᾽ αὖ πρὸς ἴτρια βλέπω

Athenaeus, *Deipnosophists* 14, 646D

πεινῶσ᾽ αὖ Musurus: πεινωσαγαυ cod.

ΕΡΙΦΥΛΗ

See on Ἐπίγονοι *and fr.* 958

THE EPIGONI

190
. . . he will not reside any longer in hollow Argos.

THE SATYRS AT TAENARUM

See on Heracles

ERIS

ment of Paris, seems not unlikely, and if it is right the play may well have been identical with the Κρίσις. *The* Κρίσις *was a satyr play, and fr. 199 looks as if it came from one.*

199
And I [fem.], being hungry, look again at the cakes.

ERIPHYLE

See on The Epigoni *and fr. 958*

201a

⟨ὦ⟩ γλῶσσ᾽, ἐν οἴοις ἀνδράσιν τιμὴν ἔχεις,
ὅπου λόγοι σθένουσι τῶν ἔργων πλέον

Stobaeus, *Anthology* 2, 15, 27 (2, 189, 22 Wachsmuth)

1 οἴοις Dindorf: οἶσιν codd.: γλῶσσ᾽ ἐν κενοῖσιν . . . ἔχει
Jacobs

201b

ὅπου δὲ μὴ τἄριστ᾽ ἐλευθέρως λέγειν
ἔξεστι, νικᾷ δ᾽ ἐν πόλει τὰ χείρονα,
ἁμαρτίαι σφάλλουσι τὴν σωτηρίαν

Stobaeus, *Anthology* 4, 1, 7 (4, 2, 17 Hense)

1 τἄριστ᾽ Dobree: τὰ ῥᾶ(ι)στ(α) codd.

201c

γήρᾳ προσῆκον σῷζε τὴν εὐφημίαν

Stobaeus, *Anthology* 4, 50, III 89 (5, 1055, 4 Hense)

προσῆκον Gaisford: προσηκόντως A, προσόντως M: alii
alia

201d

ἀρετῆς βέβαιαι δ᾽ εἰσὶν αἱ κτήσεις μόναι

Stobaeus, *Anthology* 3, 1, 1 (3, 3, 3 Hense)

μόναι] μόνης Naber

ERIPHYLE

201a

O tongue, among what sort of men do you enjoy honour,
in a place where words have more strength than deeds!

201b

But where it is not possible to say with freedom what is
best, and the worse prevails in the city, mistakes upset
safety.

201c

Maintain restraint in speech, as is proper to old age!

201d

The only possessions that are permanent are those of
excellence.

201e

ἀνδρῶν γὰρ ἐσθλῶν στέρνον οὐ μαλάσσεται

Stobaeus, *Anthology* 3, 7, 6 (3, 309, 13 Hense)

201f

πῶς οὖν μάχωμαι θνητὸς ὢν θείᾳ τύχῃ;
ὅπου τὸ δεινόν, ἐλπὶς οὐδὲν ὠφελεῖ

Stobaeus, *Anthology* 4, 35, 30 (5, 863, 7 Hense)

201g

ἄπελθε· κινεῖς ὕπνον ἰατρὸν νόσου

Clement of Alexandria, *Miscellanies* 6, 2, 10, 3 (2, 429, 12 Stählin)

ἄπελθε· κινεῖς Nauck: ἄπελθ᾽ ἐκείνης codd.

ΕΡΜΙΟΝΗ

This play dealt with much the same events as the Andromache *of Euripides, as we know from a summary given by Eustathius, Od. 1479, 10. While Menelaus was away at Troy his daughter Hermione had been promised to Orestes by her grandfather Tyndareus, but since Menelaus at Troy had promised her to Neoptolemus, she*

202

ἀλλ᾽ ὦ πατρῴας γῆς ἀγυιαίου πέδον

Stephanus of Byzantium, *Ethnica* 23, 3 Meineke

ἀγυιαίου] -αῖον? Bothe

ERIPHYLE

201e

For the hearts of noble men do not go soft.

201f

Then how shall I who am mortal fight against events ordained by the gods? Where there is formidable power, hope is of no use.

201g

Go away! You are disturbing sleep, the healer of sickness.

HERMIONE

was transferred to him. But after Neoptolemus had gone to Delphi to avenge his father's death upon Apollo and had been killed there by Machaereus, she went back to Orestes, and became the mother of Tisamenus. There is no evidence that Orestes helped to plot the death of Neoptolemus in this play, as he does in that of Euripides. See on the Φθιωτίδες (The Women of Phthia).

202

But, O plain of my native country with its city roads . . . !

ΕΥΜΗΛΟΣ

Eumelus was the son of Admetus and Alcestis; he fought in the Trojan War, and was the owner of famous horses, with which he competed in the funeral games of

ΕΥΡΥΑΛΟΣ

Parthenius, Love Romances 3 summarizes the plot. Odysseus on the way back from Troy, visiting Epirus "because of certain oracles," was entertained by the king Tyrimmas and left his daughter Euippe with child. When he was old enough her son Euryalus made his way to Ithaca to find his father, bearing tokens of recognition. but Odysseus was away, and Penelope, knowing the truth,

ΕΥΡΥΠΥΛΟΣ

Ed. pr.: P. Oxy. 1175, ed. Hunt, part ix, 1912, p. 86, Plates iii and iv; P. Oxy. 2081 (b), part xvii, 1927, 74 f. See Wilamowitz, *NJKB* 29 (1912) 449–453 = *Kl. Schr.* i 347–53; Pearson i 146–165; Page, *GLP* no. 4; Carden 1–51 (with bibliography); Radt 195–229; Lloyd-Jones, *ZPE* 92 (1992) 55–58.

No ancient author says that Sophocles wrote a play with this name, but Tyrwhitt in 1794 remarked that the duel between Eurypylus and Neoptolemus, mentioned by Plutarch, On the Restraint of Anger 10, 458D as having been described by Sophocles, indicated that Sophocles was the author of the play Eurypylus mentioned by Aristotle. The papyrus reveals a coincidence with words of

EUMELUS

EUMELUS

Patroclus and later, according to Apollodorus, won first prize in the chariot race at those of Achilles. Two one-word quotations tell us nothing; but note frr. 851 and 911.

EURYALUS

told him when he returned that the new arrival was plotting to murder him, so that he himself killed his son, in ignorance of his identity. Soon after this, the summary continues, Odysseus was killed by the spear made of the spine of a roach. Although Parthenius does not mention the name, we recognise the allusion to the story of his death at the hands of his son by Circe, Telegonus. We have no fragments.

EURYPYLUS

this play quoted by Plutarch (fr. 210, 9), and since it was written by the same hand as P. Oxy. 1175, containing the Ichneutae, *it is likely to be by the same author.*

Telephus, the son of Heracles by the Tegean princess Auge, was king of Mysia in Asia Minor (see on the Aleadae), *and married Priam's sister Astyoche. The Greeks on their way to Troy at first landed by mistake in Mysia, and were opposed by Telephus, at first successfully. But he was wounded by Achilles, and after the Greeks had departed he was told by a prophet that his wound could be cured only by the spear that had inflicted it. Accordingly he travelled to Aulis, where the Greek army was encamped, and persuaded Achilles to use his spear to heal the wound, promising in return that he would guide the Greeks to Troy. At the same he gave an undertaking that neither he nor any of his family would assist the Trojans.*

After the deaths of Hector and Achilles, the Trojans were in dire straits. Telephus was now dead, but his son Eurypylus was a hero of the kind they needed. At first he refused to help them, owing to the undertaking given by his father. But Priam induced his sister, Eurypylus' mother, to persuade her son to help him, bribing her with the gift of the golden vine which Zeus had given to an earlier king of Troy in return for his beautiful son Ganymedes, carried off to become Zeus' cupbearer.

This story supplied the background to the action of the play, of which we know nothing except what the papyrus tells us. According to the stories told in the lost epics of the

208

[A.]

αμε[..]..[
φήμη γὰρ α[

[B.]

ἐδεξάμην τ[ὸ ῥηθέν, αἴσιος δέ μοι
κόραξ ἐπᾴδ[ει τῆσδ᾽ ἀπ᾽ ἀρχαίας δρυός.

[A.]

5   ἄριστος, ὦ δύσ[τηνε, μάντις ὢν ὅδε
κράζει θυηλῆ[ς Ἄρεος ὡς ἤδη πέλας.
                    (*remains of 5 lines*)

    3 τ[ὸ ῥηθέν Murray   end Ll.-J.
    4–5 Ll.-J.   6 Ll.-J. (Ἄρεος Murray)

84

Trojan cycle and in the Posthomerica, *the extant epic of
the Roman Imperial period by Quintus of Smyrna,
Eurypylus performed great deeds, killing among many
others Nireus, the handsomest of the Greeks, and
Machaon, the famous doctor. But in the end he was killed
in a duel with the son of Achilles, Neoptolemus.*

*The only fragment known from quotation is that
quoted by Plutarch; but we have 121 fragments of the
play, all from the papyrus. Only about ten of these are of
any substance. By far the largest is fr. 210, which shows
that the report of the Messenger who came to Astyoche,
apparently in Troy, to describe her son's death, was di-
vided into two halves by a kommos, or scene of lamenta-
tion, performed by Astyoche and the Chorus, which evi-
dently consisted of women.*

*The Messenger describes how the body of Eurypylus
lay close to the body of another warrior, with whom he
had fought a common fight (fr. 210, 50). The evidence of
vase paintings (see* LIMC 4, 2, p. 55) *seems to indicate
that this was Helicaon, the son of the Trojan Antenor who
survived the siege and founded a colony in the West; see
Hugh Lloyd-Jones in* ZPE 92 (1992), 55–8.

208
[A.]

. . . For an omen . . .

[B.]

I welcome the presage; and a crow is singing to me with
favourable voice from this ancient oak tree here.

[A.]

He is the best of prophets, unhappy one, and crows be-
cause he is already near to a sacrifice to the war god.

210

⟨ΑΓΓΕΛΟΣ⟩

                ]σα[

                ]ην μεταιχ[μι

[ἄκομπ᾽ ἀλοιδόρητα δ]ιαβεβλημ[ένοι

[ἠραξάτην ἐς κύκλα χ]αλκέων ὅπλων

10   ]σ.[..].τέρου·

                ] ἄνευ δορὸς

                πα]λαίσμασιν

                ]ματι·

                ]ν πρὸς οὐραν[ὸν

15   ]δ᾽ ἐστενάζετο

                ὀ]ργάνων στένει

                π]άλλει χερὸς

                ]γματος φυγὼν

                ]ς δορὸς

20 ἔγχος   ]μέσον

                ].ιται πρόσω

                ]υρησας κάτω

                ].των φάος

                Ἀ]χιλλέως

25   ]ουσδ᾽ ἰωμένη

8 Pearson, from Plutarch, *The Control of Anger* 10, 458E καὶ
τὸν Νεοπτόλεμον ὁ Σοφοκλῆς καὶ τὸν Εὐρύπυλον ὁπλίσας
'ἐκόμπασεν (ἄκομπ᾽ Badham) ἀλοιδόρητα᾽ φησί, 'ἐρρηξάτην
. . . ὅπλων᾽   9 Wilamowitz, from Plutarch (ἠραξάτην
Diggle: ἐρρηξάτην Plutarch)   20 ἔγχος (from a note in
the margin) Hunt

210

⟨MESSENGER⟩

. . . the space between the armies . . . Standing opposite
each other without boasts, without abuse, they struck at
the orbs of one another's brazen shields . . . the other (10)
. . . without the spear . . . wrestling . . . to the sky . . . was la-
mented (15) . . . for the lack of instruments . . . brandishes
. . . arm . . . escaping . . . the spear . . . the middle . . . the
lance (20) . . . far off . . . (guarding) below . . . of Achilles[a]
. . . healing (25) . . .

[a] There is evidently an allusion to the spear of Achilles, which
healed Telephus but which has now in the hands of Neoptolemus
killed his son.

T]ήλεφον λέγω·
ἰ]άσατο·
]κ̣ νους ταχὺς
col. ii   καθεῖλ' ἔσω τα [πλ]ευρά[

ΑΣΤΤΟΧΗ

30   οἰοῖ, οἰ[οῖ].
διπλοῦς ἀνεστέναξ[α c. 11 letters]φα[. . .]

⟨ΧΟΡΟΣ⟩

πατρο[c. 15 letters   ]
ραν· ἐπ[c. 14 ll.]μος ἴδε τέκνων.

⟨ΑΣΤ.⟩

τρίτην δ' ἐπ' ἐμ[ὲ c. 11 ll.] ⟨ΧΟ.⟩ καὶ γὰρ οὖν
35   προσάγαγ' ωδι[.] ιγ[. . .]ν διαίνεις·
ἐπεὶ κτησίων φρενῶν ἐξέδυς.

⟨ΑΣΤ.⟩

ὦ δαῖμον ὦ δύσδαιμον, ὦ κείρας ἐμέ.

⟨ΧΟ.⟩

ἀγχοῦ προσεῖπας· οὐ γὰρ ἐκτὸς ἑστὼς
σύρει δὴ φύρδαν.

⟨ΑΣΤ.⟩

40   ἐπισπάσει δίκᾳ με.

⟨ΧΟ.⟩

    δίκᾳ ναί.

⟨ΑΣΤ.⟩

ἀλλ' ὡς τάχιστ' ἄριστα.

    40 δίκᾳ Winnington-Ingram: δίκα Π

88

... I mean Telephus ... healed ... swiftly brought down
...

<ASTYOCHE>

Woe, woe! I lament ... double ...

<CHORUS>

... of his father ... saw ... of the children.

<AST.>

And ... a third ... upon me.

<CH.>

Yes, indeed, he has brought ... you are drenching ..., for
you have departed from the sense that you possess.

<AST.>

O spirit that are an evil spirit, O my destroyer!

<CH.>

Close at hand is he whom you address; he stands not far
off, and drags you in all confusion!

<AST.>

He will draw me in with justice!

<CH.>

With justice, yes!

<AST.>

Soonest is best!

⟨ΧΟ.⟩

ἐέ·

τί φήσομεν, τί λέξομεν;

⟨ΑΣΤ.⟩

45 τίς οὐχὶ τοὐμὸν ἐν δίκᾳ βαλεῖ κάρα;

⟨ΧΟ.⟩

δαίμων ἔκειρεν — οὐ δίκᾳ; — σε, δαίμων.

⟨ΑΣΤ.⟩

ἦ κἀμβεβᾶσι το⟨ῖ⟩ν νεκρο⟨ῖ⟩ν πρὸς τῷ κακῷ

γέλωτ᾽ ἔχοντες α[ἰν]ὸν Ἀργεῖοι βίᾳ;

⟨ΑΓ.⟩

οὐκ ἐς τοσοῦτον ἦλθον ὥστ᾽ ἐπεγχανεῖν,

50 ἐπεὶ πάλαισμα κοινὸν ἠγωνισμένοι

ἔκειντο νεκροὶ τυτθὸν ἀλλήλων ἄπο,

ὁ μὲν λ[α]κητός, ὁ δὲ τὸ πᾶν [.].[....]ο.

ο]ὖ μὴν Ἀχαι[ῶν σπάνι]ος ἦ[ν αὐτοῦ φό]νος.

(remains of ten lines)

] κυρῶν ἔτι

65 ἔ]ρρηξεν νότος.᾽

τοιαῦτα πολλῶ[ν....]ν ἐρρόθει στόμα·

πολλὴ δὲ σινδών, πολλὰ δ᾽ Ἰστριανίδων

ὕφη γυναικῶν ἀνδ[ρὸ]ς ἐρριπτάζετο

νεκρῷ διδόντος οὐδὲν ὠφελουμένῳ.

47 κἀμβεβᾶσι Pearson: και βεβασι Π   suppl. Diggle
48 α[ἰν]ὸν Ll.-J.   52 λ[α]κητός Ll.-J.: δ[.]κητος Π
53 ο]ὖ μὴν Koerte   end Ll.-J.: ὀλίγ]ος ἦ[ν μάχη φό]νος
Kamerbeek   69 διδόντος Pearson (who later changed his
mind): διδοντες Π

⟨CH.⟩

Alas! What shall we say, what words shall we utter?

⟨AST.⟩

Who shall not do justice and strike off my head?

⟨CH.⟩

The spirit has destroyed you; did he not do justice?

⟨AST.⟩

Did the Argives trample on the corpses with violence,
laughing with a dire laughter, to crown this evil?

⟨ME.⟩

They did not get so far as to insult them. For they who
had endured the ordeal together lay dead near to one
another, the one lacerated, and the other[a] altogether . . .
But there was no little carnage among the Achaeans in
that place . . .

(remains of ten lines)

. . . the south wind shattered" . . . Such was the mournful
clamour from many mouths. And many a linen garment,
and many robes that Istrian women[b] had woven were
thrown upon him, as a man bestowed their work upon a
corpse it could not benefit. And Priam, lying upon his

---

[a] The other body may have been that of Helicaon; see prefatory note.

[b] Istros is the Greek name for the Danube; Herodotus 4, 74 says that the Thracians make garments that look like linen out of hemp (κάνναβις).

70 ὁ δ' ἀμφὶ πλευραῖς καὶ σφαγαῖσι κείμενος,
    πατὴρ μὲν οὔ, πατρῷα δ' ἐξαυδῶν ἔπη,
    Πρίαμος ἔκλαιε τὸν τέκνων ὁμαίμονα,
    τὸν παῖδα καὶ γέροντα καὶ νεανίαν,
    τὸν οὔτε Μυσὸν οὔτε Τηλέφου καλῶν,
75 ἀλλ' ὡς φυτεύσας αὐτὸς ἐκκαλούμενος·
    'οἴμοι, τέκνον, προὔδωκά σ' ἐσχάτην ἔχων
    Φρυξὶν μεγίστην ⟨τ'⟩ ἐλπίδων σωτηρίαν.
    χρόνον ξενωθεὶς οὐ μακρὸν πολλῶν κακῶν
    μνήμην παρέξεις τοῖς.[.......]οις ἀεί,
80 ὅσ' οὔτε Μέμνων οὔτε Σα[ρπηδών ποτε
    π[έν]θη π[οήσ]α[ς κ]αίπερ αἰχ[μητῶν ἄκροι
                (remains of four lines)

    77 ⟨τ'⟩ Pearson

211
⟨ΑΣΤ.⟩

    μίδας καὶ τὸ[ν ἀδελφὸν
    Ἰδαῖον βασιλ[ῆα
    Πρίαμον, ὅς μ[ε τάλαιναν
    πάσᾳ κατάρ[ατον
5   ἔπεισεν ἀβου[λίᾳ
    ἔ[ργο]ν ἔρξαι.
        μναμοσ[
        προλι[π
        οὔποτ[

    1,3 Ll.-J. (ὅς μ[ε Brizi)   4 Diehl

mangled body, though not his father spoke as though he
were, weeping for the kinsman of his sons, at once boy
and elder and young man, calling on him not as a Mysian
nor as son of Telephus, but invoking him as though begot-
ten by himself. "Ah, my son, I betrayed you, though I
had in you the last and greatest hope of salvation for the
Phrygians. Though you were not our guest for long, you
will leave the memory of many sorrows for ever to . . . ;
neither Memnon nor Sarpedon caused so many sorrows,
though they were foremost among spearmen . . ."

(*remains of four lines*)

211

⟨AST.⟩

. . . the lord of Ida, my brother Priam, who in all foolish-
ness persuaded me, the wretch, to do an accursed act.

(*remains of three lines*)

10 ἰὼ δόρυ Τηλ[εφείῳ
παιδὶ συγκύ[ρσαν πικρόν.
ὦ λόγχα, σῶτ[ειρα πατρός,
δ]όμου σ᾿ ἀμ[ετέρου πάλαι

10 Ll.-J.   11 πικρόν Ll.-J.   12 σῶτ[ειρα Wilamo-
witz: πατρός Ll.-J.   13 Ll.-J. (δ]όμους ἀμε[τέρους
Bucherer)

212

]χι τευχ[
]σαι Διὸς
]..[.]ς εὐτυχεῖ θανών·   .
πα]γκάλως δ᾿ ἀπώλετο
5   ]σι θε[σ]μὸν ἱδρῦσθαι τὸ νῦν
] κοινόθακα λάξοα
Τη]λέφου ξυνουσίαν
δ]εῖπνα πλησιαίτατος
]ι τῶδε, μηδ᾿ ἄνευ
10   ]·ι τικτούσῃ τε[.]·[
]θ[·]σιν· ο[··]αρος
] ὀρφανὴ προσηδ[
νεό]δροπον πλόκον
΄]πε[...]ναλ-
15   ]ειν[....]αν
] ναν·[

13 Pearson

94

Ah, spear that proved bitter for the son of Telephus! O spearpoint, saviour (of his father) . . . you . . . long ago . . . of our house . . . !

212

. . . died . . . fortunate . . . he made a glorious end . . . ordinance . . . there be established now (5) . . . statues that may sit together . . . the company of Telephus . . . close at hand . . . feasts . . . for him, and not without . . . giving birth to (10) . . . bereft of . . . newly cut coil of hair . . .
(remains of three lines)

FRAGMENTS OF KNOWN PLAYS

ΕΥΡΥΣΑΚΗΣ

Eurysaces, the son of Ajax by Tecmessa, appears as a child in the Ajax, *where his uncle Teucer is to take him to his grandfather Telamon in Salamis. According to Attic legend he and his brother Philaeus made over Salamis to Athens and settled on the Athenian mainland, Philaeus at Brauron and Eurysaces at Melite; distinguished Athenian*

ΗΡΑΚΛΕΙΣΚΟΣ

There are only three quotations, and in one of these (fr. 225) Ἡρακλείσκῳ *is a variant for* Ἡρακλεῖ σατυρικῷ, *so that Schneidewin and others have thought the two plays to be the same. The citation in fr. 223a shows that it*

223a

κρεῖσσον θεοῖς γὰρ ἢ βροτοῖς χάριν φέρειν

Orion, *Florilegium* 5, 9; *Leiden Florilegium* 98; *Munich Florilegium* 102

θεοῖς Orion: θεῷ cett.

223b

τὸν δρῶντα γάρ τι καὶ παθεῖν ὀφείλεται

Orion, *Florilegium* 6, 6; and (without the poet's name) Schol. on Pindar, *Nem.* 4, 50b and Arrian, *Anabasis* 6, 13, 5; cf. Aeschylus, fr. 456

τῶι δρῶντι Arrian.

EURYSACES

families claimed descent from them. Justin 44, 3 says that Teucer after founding Salamis in Cyprus returned to the old Salamis, but was driven away by Eurysaces and founded Galicia in Spain; but it seems unlikely that Sophocles told this story. There is only one quotation. See on the Τεῦκρος, which may have been the same play.

THE INFANT HERACLES

was a satyr play. We have no knowledge of the plot, but a play about the infant Heracles might be expected to deal with the story of his killing the two snakes sent by Hera against him and his brother Iphicles, told by Pindar, Nem. 1 and Paean 20 and Theocritus 24.

223a

For it is better to oblige gods than to oblige mortals.

223b

For the doer is bound to suffer somewhat.

ΗΡΑΚΛΗΣ

The plot is unknown. Some have suggested that it was identical with the Ἐπὶ Ταινάρῳ Σάτυροι (The Satyrs at Taenarum), *others with the* Ἡρακλεΐσκος (The Infant Heracles), *and others with the* Κέρβερος (Cerberus). *Taenarum was situated at the southern point of the promontory west of the Gulf of Laconia, and a cavern there was famous as a descent to the underworld. Although some authors say that he came by way of*

225

. . . συνέλεγον τὰ ξύλ᾽, ὡς ἐκκαυμάτων
μή μοι μεταξὺ προσδεήσειεν

Pollux, *Vocabulary* 7, 109 (2, 82, 20 Bethe); 10, 110 (2, 223, 8 Bethe)

226

τρέφουσι κρήνης φύλακα χωρίτην ὄφιν

Stephanus of Byzantium, *Ethnica* 699, 12 Meineke

τρέφουσι Jacobs: στρέφουσι codd.   φύλακα Tyrwhitt:
φύλλα καὶ codd.

HERACLES

*Trozen, Heracles is also said to have brought up Cerberus
by this route as the last of his labours for Eurystheus,
which favours the suggestion that the play may have been
identical with the* Cerberus. *The curious statement of
Eustathius,* Il. *297, 37 that according to Herodian the sa-
tyrs at Taenarum were called Helots seems to mean that in
this play they were slaves in Laconia, just as in several sa-
tyr plays they endured other kinds of temporary servi-
tude, and could therefore be called Helots.*

225

I was collecting the wood, so that I should not need fuel in
the meantime.

226

They feed the guardian of the spring, the local snake.

ΗΡΙΓΟΝΗ

Erigone was the daughter of Clytemnestra by Aegisthus, who according to one account accused Orestes when he was tried before the Areopagus for the murder of his mother. After his acquittal she was said to have hanged herself, a story that served as one of the alternative explanations of the origin of the Athenian festival of swings, the Aiora. Another story is that after killing her brother Aletes Orestes was about to kill Erigone when Artemis saved her and made her a priestess in Attica. Another legend has it that Orestes married her; she was said to have been mother of Penthilus, that son of Orestes from whom one of the noblest families of the Lesbos of Sappho and Alcaeus, at one time dominant in the island, traced their descent. See on the Thyestes *plays.*

235

ἃ δὲ
δόξῃ τοπάζω, ταῦτ᾽ ἰδεῖν σαφῶς θέλω

Photius Galeanus 595, 7 = Et. Magn. 762, 12 = Suda τ 773

236

νῦν δ᾽ †εἰρὴ ὕποφρος ἐξ αὐτῶν† ἕως
ἀπώλεσέν τε καὐτὸς ἐξαπώλετο

Erotian, *Medical Lexicon* υ 10 Nachmanson

The passage is cited as an example of the use of ὕπαφρος—of which ὕποφρος is evidently a corruption—to mean κρυφαῖος.

ERIGONE

*Another Erigone was the daughter of Icarius, a peas-
ant who received the gift of wine from Dionysus, and
when some of the peasants to whom he gave it became
drunk and were thought by their friends to have been poi-
soned, was murdered by these people. Conducted to her
father's body by their faithful dog Maera, Erigone hanged
herself; this story also served to account for the festival of
the Aiora. Ribbeck tried to show that this story provided
the plot of Sophocles' play; but there is little indication
that it was at all well known before the Alexandrian poet
Eratosthenes wrote his* Erigone, *so that it is likelier that
the play was about the daughter of Aegisthus. Accius'*
Erigona, *which may well have been based on Sophocles'
play, contained mention of Aegisthus and of Orestes.*

235

What I guess at I should like to see clearly.

236

But now . . . secret . . . from them, until he killed and was
killed himself.

ΘΑΜΥΡΑΣ

*This play is sometimes quoted as "Thamyris"; that is
how the name appears in Homer, but "Thamyras" is the
Attic form. Homer, Il. 2, 594 f tells how the Thracian
Thamyris boasted that he could surpass even the Muses
with his song, and they in anger maimed him (πηρὸν
θέσαν), and took away his power to sing and his skill in
playing the lyre. The pseudo-Euripidean Rhesus 916 f
speaks of an actual contest between Thamyras, son of
Philammon, and the Muses, after which they blinded him.
The story that he had one blue and one black eye was*

237

Θρῆσσαν σκοπιὰν Ζηνὸς Ἀθῴου

Herodian, *On Prosody in General*, cod. Vindob. Hist. gr. 100
fol. 3r; Eustathius, *Il.* 358, 39

238

πηκταὶ δὲ λύραι καὶ μαγαδίδες
τά τ᾽ ἐν Ἕλλησι ξόαν᾽ ἡδυμελῆ

Athenaeus, *Deipnosophists* 14, 636F

240

πρόποδα μέλεα τάδε σε κλέομεν
τρόχιμα βάσιμα χέρεσι πόδεσι

Choeroboscus on Hephaestion, *Enchiridion* 217, 5 Cons-
bruch; Anonymus Ambrosianus, *De re metrica* 2, 12 Studemund

1 κλέομεν Herwerden: κλαίομεν Choerob.: κλαίομαι Anon.

THAMYRAS

*explained by Lessing as deriving from the mask worn by
the actor who played the part, which had one blue eye,
which he presented to the audience before the blinding,
and one black eye, which he presented after it. The story
that if he had won Thamyras was to have enjoyed the fa-
vours of one, or in another version of all, of the Muses may
derive from comedy; Antiphanes wrote a comedy called*
Thamyras. *Another anecdote that may derive from com-
edy is the story that Sophocles himself played the harp in
the performance of this play. See the* Μοῦσαι (The
Muses), *which may have been the same play.*

237

. . . the Thracian watchtower of Zeus of Athos[a] . . .

[a] "Athos is not particularly high," wrote Wilamowitz, "1000 m.
lower than Olympus, but is particularly impressive to seafarers
because of its position and the shadow which near sunset it casts
as far as Lemnos"; see fr. 776.

238

Joiner-made lyres and harps that give octave concords,
and the instruments carved from wood to give sweet mu-
sic that exist among the Greeks[a] . . .

[a] The two kinds of harp specified both came from Lydia; see
M. L. West, *Ancient Greek Music* 70 f.

240

These melodies in which we celebrate you get the feet
forward, arms and legs moving swiftly!

241

ᾤχωκε γὰρ κροτητὰ πηκτίδων μέλη
λύρᾳ μόναυλοι † τε χειμωντεως
ναος στέρημα κωμασάσης †

Athenaeus, *Deipnosophists* 4, 175F

2 μόναυλοι Epitome of Athenaeus: μοναύλοις A

242

ἐκ μὲν Ἐριχθονίου ποτιμάστιον ἔσχεθε κοῦρον
Αὐτόλυκον, πολέων κτεάνων σίνιν Ἄργεϊ κοίλῳ

Schol. LRM on S., *O.C.* 378

244

ῥηγνὺς χρυσόδετον κέρας,
ῥηγνὺς ⟨δ'⟩ ἁρμονίαν χορδοτόνου λύρας

Plutarch, *The Control of Anger* 5, 455C

2 suppl. Herwerden

245

μουσομανεῖ δ' ἐλήφθην
ἀνάγκᾳ, ποτὶ δ' εἵραν
ἔρχομαι, ἔκ τε λύρας
ἔκ τε νόμων, οὓς Θαμύρας
περίαλλα μουσοποιεῖ.

Plutarch, *Not Even a Pleasant Life is Possible on Epicurean Principles* 11, 1093D

1 δ' ἐλήφθην Ll.-J.: δ' ἐλάμφθην a AEB Mon.: δὲ λάφθην X gcd   2 ἀνάγκᾳ Ll.-J.: δαν καὶ τὸ codd.   δ' εἵραν Campbell: ποτὶ δειράν, ποτίδειραν codd.   3 δ' after ἔρχομαι deleted by Campbell

THAMYRAS

241

For gone are the songs resounding from the striking of the harp; the lyres and . . . single pipes . . .

242

She had at the breast a son by the mighty one who goes underground, a son, Autolycus, one that would plunder many treasures in hollow Argos.[a]

[a] See Hesiod fr. 64, 14 f for Philonis, who having been impregnated by two gods on the same night bore Autolycus to Hermes and Philammon, father of Thamyras, to Apollo.

244

Breaking the horn bound with gold, breaking the harmony of the strung lyre . . .

245

And I was seized by an urge to be mad for music, and went to the place of assembly, an urge inspired by the lyre and by the measures with which Thamyras makes music supremely.

ΘΗΣΕΥΣ

This play, which is quoted only once, may have been identical with the Aegeus, *q.v., or with the* Phaedra, *q.v.; but see frr. 730a–g and 905.*

ΘΥΕΣΤΗΣ Α΄, Β΄ *and* Γ΄

Sophocles apparently wrote three plays about Thyestes. P. London Inv. 2110 (see Radt, p. 239) appears to mention a 'third Thyestes' of Sophocles. Fr. 140 is quoted as from the Women of Mycenae, *fr. 141 as from* Atreus *or the* Women of Mycenae, *and fr. 260a as from the* Thyestes *or the* Atreus, *so that all these plays may be identical. For another possible case of three alternative titles for the same play, see on the* Ὀδυσσεὺς Ἀκανθοπλήξ *(Odysseus Wounded by the Spine). See also on the* Ἠριγόνη *(Erigone), which may have been an alternative title of one of the Thyestes plays.*

The Thyestes *or* Atreus *probably dealt with the story of the golden lamb (see fr. 738) and the Thyestean feast. One of the three was called* Thyestes in Sicyon; *this must have dealt with the story that after his brother Atreus had given him his own children's flesh to eat Thyestes was told by an oracle that the crime could be avenged only by a son*

THESEUS

THESEUS

THYESTES 1, 2 and 3

begotten by him on his own daughter. He accordingly made his way to Sicyon, where his daughter Pelopia had been sent for the sake of safety, and with his head covered raped her. The same authority who tells us this, the mythographer Hyginus, also tells us that Atreus, not knowing that Pelopia was the daughter of Thyestes, married her, and brought up her son Aegisthus as his own. Later Thyestes fell into the hands of his brother, who handed him over to Aegisthus to be killed. But the two somehow discovered the secret of Aegisthus' real parentage. On learning this Pelopia killed herself. But Aegisthus took the bloody sword with which she had done so to Atreus, telling him that the blood was that of Thyestes, and later when Atreus was sacrificing by the sea murdered him and restored his father to power. Some believe that this narrative furnished the material for two plays of Sophocles. But there is room for doubt; Euripides too wrote a Thyestes, *as did at least six other tragedians.*

Emily Vermeule, PCPS 213 (1987), 122–152, *has argued that a vase by the Darius Painter may illustrate a scene from this play.*

247

σοφὸς γὰρ οὐδεὶς πλὴν ὃς ἂν τιμᾷ θεούς.
ἀλλ᾿ εἰς θεοὺς ὁρῶντα, κἂν ἔξω δίκης
χωρεῖν κελεύῃ, κεῖσ᾿ ὁδοιπορεῖν χρεών·
αἰσχρὸν γὰρ οὐδὲν ὧν ὑφηγοῦνται θεοί

Orion, *Florilegium* 5, 10; *Leiden Florilegium* 99; *Munich Florilegium* 103 (line 1)

1 ὃς Seyffert: ὃν codd.   θεούς Beynen: θεός codd.: θεόν Seyffert   Meineke thought, probably rightly, that vv. 2–4 had been wrongly attached to v. 1; if so, vv. 2–4 probably come from a different play   2 θεοὺς] θεόν σ᾿ Meineke: θεούς σ᾿ Nauck

255

ἔστι γάρ τις ἐναλία
Εὐβοιὶς αἶα· τῇδε βακχεῖος βότρυς
ἐπ᾿ ἦμαρ ἕρπει. πρῶτα μὲν λαμπρᾶς ἕω
κεκλημάτωται χλωρὸν οἰνάνθης δέμας·
5 εἶτ᾿ ἦμαρ αὔξει μέσσον ὄμφακος τύπον,
γλυκαίνεταί τε κἀποπερκοῦται βότρυς·
δείλῃ δὲ πᾶσα τέμνεται βλαστουμένη
καλῶς ὀπώρα κἀνακίρναται ποτόν

Schol. MTAB on Euripides, *Phoenissae* 227 (1, 281, 15 Schwartz)

2 Εὐβοιὶς αἶα L. Dindorf: εὐβοίσασα B: -ησασα MTA   4 χλωρὸν Bergk: χῶρον MTA: χῶρος B   οἰνάνθης Barnes: εὐανθὴς B: -ὲς MTA   6 γλυκαίνεται Meineke: καὶ κλίνεται codd.   8 καλῶς ὀπώρα Barnes: ὀπώρα καλῶς codd.

247

For no one is wise but he who honours the gods; but you must look to the gods, and even if you are ordered to go outside justice, you must go that way; for no guidance that the gods give is shameful.

255

For there is a seagirt land, Euboea; there a bacchic vine grows for a day. Firstwhile dawn shines brightly the green vine-shoot puts forth its tendril; then the middle of the day makes the unripe grape grow large, and the fruit gains sweetness and takes on dark colour; and in the evening the crop comes to a fine growth and is harvested, and the drink is mixed.

256

πρὸς τήν‹δ᾽› ἀνάγκην οὐδ᾽ Ἄρης ἀνθίσταται

Stobaeus, *Anthology* 1, 4, 5 (1, 71, 19 Wachsmuth)

τήν‹δ᾽› (sc. τὸν ἔρωτα) suppl. M. L. West (cf. Plato, *Symp.* 196C 8 καὶ μὴν εἴς γε ἀνδρείαν Ἔρωτι οὐδ᾽ Ἄρης ἀνθίσταται)

257

ὡς νῦν τάχος στείχωμεν· οὐ γὰρ ἔσθ᾽ ὅπως
σπουδῆς δικαίας μῶμος ἅψεταί ποτε

Stobaeus, *Anthology* 3, 29, 1 (3, 626, 6 Hense)

1 ὡς νῦν Dindorf: ὡς νῦν codd.
2 ἅψεταί Valckenaer: ἅπτεται codd.

258

ἔχει μὲν ἀλγείν᾽, οἶδα· πειρᾶσθαι δὲ χρὴ
ὡς ῥᾷστα τἀναγκαῖα τοῦ βίου φέρειν.
ἐκ τῶν τοιούτων χρή τιν᾽ ἴασιν λαβεῖν

Stobaeus, *Anthology* 4, 44, 20 (5, 963, 8 Hense)

Cf. Euripides, *Helen* 253–4 ἔχεις μὲν ἀλγείν᾽, οἶδα· σύμφορον δέ τοι | ὡς ῥᾷστα τἀναγκαῖα τοῦ βίου φέρειν. Two quotations may have been confused; Badham deleted line 2, at the same time emending χρή in line 3 to δή, and Hense thought it possible that only line 3 was by Sophocles.

256

Against this constraint not even the war-god resists.[a]

[a] Probably the constraint of love.

257

Then let us go quickly! For blame can never attach to hurry that is justified.

258

His lot is painful, I know; but one must try to bear as easily as possible the constraints of life. From such things one must find a way of healing.

259

ἔνεστι γάρ τις καὶ λόγοισιν ἡδονή,
λήθην ὅταν ποιῶσι τῶν ὄντων κακῶν

Stobaeus, *Anthology* 4, 48, 27 (5, 1015, 5 Hense)

1 καὶ] κἂν Wagner

260

. . .

καίπερ γέρων ὤν· ἀλλὰ τῷ γήρᾳ φιλεῖ
χὠ νοῦς ὁμαρτεῖν καὶ τὸ βουλεύειν ἃ δεῖ

Stobaeus, *Anthology* 4, 50, 16 (5, 1023, 11 Hense)

260a

†μούνῳ†
καὶ Ζεὺς τροπαῖος εἰσεκώμασεν τόποις

Herodian, *On Prosody in General,* cod. Vindob. Hist. gr. 10,
fol. 3, 19 (Σοφοκλῆς Θυέστῃ ἢ Ατρεῖ)

2 εἰσεκώμασεν Ll.-J.: ἐσκεκόμισται cod.

ΙΝΑΧΟΣ

Ed. pr. of P. Oxy. 2369: Lobel, *P. Oxy.* xxiii, with Plate III; Ed.
pr. of P. Tebtunis 692: Hunt and Smyly, *Tebtunis Papyri* III
(1933), with Plate I; Pfeiffer, *S. B. Bay. Akad.* (1938) 23–62 (on
269cde); id., ibid. 1958, 3–41 (on 269ab); Page, *GLP* no. 6;
Lloyd-Jones, *C.R.* 15 (1965) 241–3 = AP i 397–400); Carden, *PFS*
(1974) 52–93 (with bibliography); Sutton, *Sophocles'* Inachus
(1979); Seaford, *C.Q.* 30 (1980) 23–9; S. R. West, *C.Q.* 34 (1984)
92–102.

259

For there is a certain pleasure in words, if they cause one
to forget the troubles that one has.

260

. . . although I am an old man. but age is often accompa-
nied by good sense and the ability to make the plans one
needs to make.

260a

And Zeus the god of trophies has stormed into the place.

INACHUS

*Despite the numerous quotations and two fairly large
papyrus fragments, many details of the plot remain uncer-
tain, and although it is highly probable that this was a sa-
tyr play, we cannot be absolutely sure even of this. The re-
mains supply no direct indication of its satyric character;
but the nature of the lyrics, the behaviour of the Chorus
when afraid, and certain features of the plot seem to show
that this is likely.*

Frr. 270 and 271 seem to come from an address by the Chorus on its entry to Inachus, the river god who was the first legendary ruler of Argos. There is a story that Inachus was punished by Poseidon with a drought for choosing Hera and not him to be the patron of the country, and fr. 286, together with the obscure fragments 284 and 285, have been thought to indicate that this drought existed at the beginning of the play. In fr. 269a a speaker who is almost certainly Inachus is telling the Chorus about a mysterious stranger, who at first was praised for doing great good, but has now been detected in doing great evil (22 f). In his next speech (32 f), Inachus describes how the stranger has changed his daughter into a cow. The stranger is presumably Zeus, who has transformed Io because his wife Hera, the patroness of Argos, has learned of his love for that person. The coming of Zeus has brought great fertility to the land (frr. 273, 275, 277). The "sooty barbarian" of fr. 269a, 54 seems therefore to have been none other than Zeus. Epaphus, the son Io later bore to him, was black, and it appears that Zeus was black when he engendered him. Chthonic deities were often imagined as being black, the colour of earth, and in frr. 273 and 283 there is mention of Pluto (Plouton). That name denotes the ruler of the underworld, otherwise called Hades, or else the Zeus of the underworld, in his capacity as god of wealth. Seaford's conjecture, that it was this Zeus, rather than the Zeus who reigns on Olympus, who figured in the play, may well be right.

Argos, the herdsman with many eyes, was a character in the play (see frr. 281 and 281a, and note fr. 269a, 56). Hera presumably set him to guard the cow. Fr. 272 indicates that Iris, the messenger of Hera, put in an appear-

ance; perhaps Io was handed over to Argos at her in-
stance. Various accounts of the parentage of Argos are
given, but he is said by some to have been a giant, born of
earth, so that fr. 269d, 19 may well refer to him.

   If the Chorus really consisted of satyrs, what are they
doing in Argos? I suspect that in the scene beginning with
fr. 270 they offered their services to Inachus, perhaps as
herdsmen. This would account for their behaviour in fr.
269c. The Chorus is terrified by the presence of an invisi-
ble person, whom they first imagine to be Hades, but who
turns out to be the messenger of Zeus, Hermes, who has
been there before and who has now returned. Have the sa-
tyrs been engaged by Inachus to watch over the cow? If
so, they may have found themselves uncomfortably situ-
ated between Hera's agent, Argos, and Zeus' agent, Her-
mes. At 40 f there is a dialogue between adversaries, of
whom one is probably Hermes. His first words refer to the
terror of his adversaries, who are presumably the Chorus.
The person he is talking with may be the leader of the
Chorus; but at 46 there is mention of a club, which both
literature and vase painting indicate to have been Argos'
weapon (cf. fr. 281). In fr. 269d there is another dialogue
between adversaries. One of these must be Hermes; the
other has been taken to be Inachus, on account of line 23.
But this could be supplemented in such a way that
Inachus need not be the person addressed, and the allu-
sion to Earth in line 18 may well be to Earth as the mother
of Argos, so that it is not unlikely that the person convers-
ing with Hermes is not Inachus, but Argos.

   In all versions of the story, Hermes kills Argos, and he
must have done so in this play. But in all versions he man-
ages to kill one who was clearly a most formidable

adversary not by means of superior strength, but by so playing his pipe that all the many eyes of Argos close in sleep, leaving him at his opponent's mercy. We know that Argos came on "singing" (fr. 281a). I suspect that Hermes challenged him to a musical competition. One can imagine this as being punctuated by the ludicrous comments of the satyrs, whose assistance would have been of little use

269a

(minimal remains of 14 lines, 7–20)

⟨ΙΝΑΧΟΣ⟩

].[...]. ος ἦ 'νθάδε·
]τε τὸν θεοστυγῆ
τὸν] ξένον νοῶ τίς ἦν
διὰ] θυρῶν τὸ πᾶν μύσος.

25 πρόσθεν γὰρ ἔρξας πόλ]λ' ἐπηνέθη καλά,
τὰ νῦν δὲ δρῶν με πάντ' ἐ]φηυρέθη κακά.
καὶ νῦν πέφευγε· φροῦδο]ς ἐξ ἐνωπίων
φύλακας λαθὼν βέβηκε], φηλώσας ἐμέ.

⟨ΧΟΡΟΣ⟩

ἀλλ' οἴχεται μὴν κἄστ' [ἐλεύθερος πάλιν
30 τὰ σὰ σκοτώσας ὄμμ[αθ'· ἃ δέ σε δείν' ἕδρα
ταῦτ' οὐκέτ' ἴδρις εἰμί, δείν[' εἰ χρὴ καλεῖν.

⟨ΙΝ.⟩

εἰ δεινά; πῶς γὰρ οὐχ; ὃς αἰσ[χύνειν ἔτλη
σεμνὰς τραπέζας ἐν δόμοι[ς φιλοξένοις.
ὁ δ' ἀμφὶ χεῖρα παρθέν[ῳ βαλὼν μόνον

25 Pfeiffer, Ll.-J.　　26 Pfeiffer　　27–30 Ll.-J.
31–3 Diggle　　34–5 Ll.-J.

116

to Argos. Did they form the jury, as the allusions to voting
in frr. 288 and 295 might suggest?

In the best-known version of the story, the cow is then
pursued by a gadfly, sometimes identified with or accom-
panied by the ghost of Argos, and starts on a long journey
that will end in Egypt. Whether this journey featured in
this play it is impossible to tell.

If Pfeiffer (op. cit., p. 34) was right in seeing an allu-
sion to this play in Aristophanes, Acharnians 390 (see fr.
269c, 19), then it was produced before 425 B.C.; but one
cannot be quite certain.

269a
⟨INACHUS⟩

. . . than here . . . I know who the . . . god-detested . . .
stranger was . . . through the doors . . . the whole pollu-
tion. For earlier he was praised for having done much
good, but now he has been detected in doing me every
kind of evil. And now he has fled; he is gone from the
front of the palace, unnoticed by the guards, having de-
luded me.

⟨CHORUS⟩

Indeed he is gone, and is free again, having cast darkness
on your eyes. But as to the terrible things he was doing to
you, I still do not know if we must call them terrible.

⟨IN.⟩

If they are terrible? Surely they are, since he dared to pol-
lute the sacrosanct table in the hospitable house! But he
simply laid his hand on the girl Io and was gone, moving

35 Ἰοῖ δι᾽ οἴκων οἴχεται σ[πεύσας δρόμῳ
κόρης δὲ μυκτὴρ κρατ.[
ἐκβουτυποῦται κα..[
φύει κάρα ταυρῶ[.]..[
αὐχὴν ἐπ᾽ ὤμοι[ς
40 ποδῶν δὲ χηλ[αὶ
κροτοῦσι θράν[
γυνὴ λέαινα π.[
ἧσται λινεργ[
τοιαῦτα..[
45 ὁ ξεῖνος α..[

<XO.>

ἄφθογγός εἰμ[ι
ἔ.[....].ε.[.].[
.κ.[
ὁ ξεῖνος ουθυ...[
50 ἄπιστα το.....[
        ἰώ, Γᾶ, θεῶν [μᾶτερ
        ἀξυνετ.[
        ὁ πολυφάρμ[ακος
κάρβανος αἰθὸς..[
55 ὁ μὲν ε.[
ὁ δ᾽ αἰολωπὸν α.[

269b

...
]...[   ]..ν.[
].ς ἔχ᾽ αὐτόν, ὦ ἰοῦ ἰοῦ[
                ]..[

rapidly through the rooms. The girl's nostril . . . took on cow shape . . . the neck . . . upon her shoulders . . . grew a head like a bull's . . . cloven feet . . . strike the floorboards . . . a woman-lioness sitting, worked in linen . . . Such is . . . the stranger . . .

⟨CH.⟩

I am speechless . . . the stranger . . . incredible . . . Ah, Earth, mother of the gods! . . . unknowing . . . the wizard . . . the sooty barbarian . . . the one . . . the other . . . the man with flashing eyes . . .

269b

Hold him! Ah, ah!

119

269c

(*fragments of fifteen lines, including* 7] σύριγγος δὲ
κλύω,   8 σ]ταθμου[,   9 τὴν [βά]σιν βοῶ[ν,
13]ποδίζεται)

⟨ΧΟ.⟩

πολὺ πολυιδρίδας
ὅτις ὅδε προτέρων
ὄνομ' εὖ σ' ἐθρόει,
τὸν Ἀιδοκυνέας
20   σκότον ἄ⟨β⟩ροτον ὑπαί.

⟨?⟩

τὸν Διὸς μὲν οὖν ἐρώτων ἄγγελον, μέγαν τρόχιν,
εἰκάσαι πάρεστιν Ἑρμῆν πρὸς τὰ σὰ ψοφήματα.

⟨?⟩

αὐτὸν εἶπας, αὐτόν, ὅς μοι δεῦρ' ἀνέστρεψεν πόδα.

⟨?⟩

δευτέρους πόνους ἔοικας πρὶν μύσαι κενοὺς ἐλᾶν.

⟨ΧΟ.⟩

25   ὠή· ἐσορᾷς;
λῷστον ἀπὸ πόδ' ἔχειν·
μανία τάδε κλύειν.
σὺ γὰρ οὖν, Ζεῦ, λόγων
κακὸς εἶ πίστεως
30   ....θεοβ[λαβ
.......].ουβ.[..........]η πορπαφόρος

* * *

26 Ll.-J.

INACHUS

269c

⟨ CH. ⟩

Very, very knowing was whoever it was among those of the
past who rightly called you by your name, beneath the un-
canny darkness of the cap of Hades![a]

⟨ ? ⟩

No, from the noises you are making we can guess that it is
the messenger of Zeus' amours, the great errand-runner,
Hermes!

⟨ ? ⟩

Hermes himself, yes, himself, who has turned back to-
wards me.

⟨ ? ⟩

You are likely to have a second effort go for nothing be-
fore you can wink!

⟨ CH. ⟩

Ho! Do you see? It's best to keep away! It drives you mad
to hear it! In truth, Zeus, your word cannot be trusted! . . .
accursed . . . with a clasp . . .

* * *

[a] The cap of Hades made its wearer invisible; it was so called
because the name Hades was etymologised as meaning "the in-
visible one."

ψιθυρᾶν μάλ' αἰολᾶ[ν.
πάντα μηχανᾷ τὸ Δῖον ὡς[τὸ Σισύφου γένος.
⟨ΧΟ.⟩
ἦ ῥα τάχα Διὸς αὖ,
35   Διὸς ἄρα λάτρις ὅδε;
ἐπί με πόδα νέμει.
[ἔχε με· πόδα νέμει]
ἐμὲ †χερακονιει†
μέγα δέος ἀραβεῖ.

⟨?⟩
40   τῶν ἐναντίων τὸ τάρβ[ος
⟨?⟩
τοῦ κάτω Διὸς φαλαγγ[
⟨?⟩
δωμάτων γ' εἰ μὴ 'πελᾷ[
⟨?⟩
ποῦ δὲ χρὴ πόδα στατίζε[ιν
⟨?⟩
πρὸς τί...ς φόνον βλεπ[
⟨?⟩
45   μη.......ωκ' ἀγῶνο[ς
⟨?⟩
μὴ λέγ' α...ἐκ κορύνης [
⟨?⟩
οἴζομαι λα......ριμ[
........[.........]..[

33 Pfeiffer   37 at first omitted, added later in small let-
ters; del. Maas   38 μάχαιραν ἀκονᾷ?

122

. . .very subtle whispers. The sons of Zeus[, like those of Sisyphus,] are up to every trick!

⟨CH.⟩

Is it Zeus, is it Zeus indeed whose lackey he is? He's coming at me! . . . There's terror in the sound of him!

(*remains of 9 lines*)

269d

(fragments of eleven lines)

]αριστε[

].....

]ἄριστα δ' οὐ

15   ] ἐξηῦρον ὠμότητά τ[ε

]πησομ.....κ...τ.[

]ον δοντ' ἀλεύσομεν θο[

].αι χρησε..ζεσ...κ.[

]αρευν.. ἡ φύσασα γῆ

20   ]οντι πείθεσθαι καλῶς

] ταῦτα· μὴ λέξῃς πλέω.

⟨IN.⟩

ἀλλ' αὖθις εἶ]πον Ζηνὸς αἰάξαι λάτριν.

⟨ΕΡΜΗΣ⟩

τρὶς αὐτὸς οὐ] πάρεστιν Ἰνάχῳ λόγ[ος.

⟨IN.⟩

Διὸς πεφυκὼς] ὀλίγον ἰσχύεις ὅμ[ως.

25   ]...δυντοστ[

].εσανδρ[

]το..[

22–4 Page (23 τρὶς αὐτὸς Ll.-J.: δὶς οὗτος Page)

269e

]..[..]...τας

].....λάτριν

]....ς καλῶς

]...[.].

124

269d

... best ... found ... and cruelty (15) ... we shall avoid
... Earth who bore him ... to render honourable obedi-
ence to ... (20)

⟨HERMES⟩

... Say no more!

⟨IN.⟩

[Once more] I have told the lackey of Zeus that he may go
and howl!

⟨HE.⟩

Inachus shall not say [the same] words [thrice]!

⟨IN.⟩

[Though you are son of Zeus,] you have little strength.

269e

270

XO.

Ἴναχε νᾶτορ, παῖ τοῦ κρηνῶν
πατρὸς Ὠκεανοῦ, μέγα πρεσβεύων
Ἄργους τε γύαις Ἥρας τε πάγοις
κἂν Τυρσηνοῖσι Πελασγοῖς

Dionysius of Halicarnassus, *Antiquities of Rome* 1, 25, 2

4 κἂν Ll.-J.: καὶ codd.

271

XO.

ῥεῖ γὰρ ἀπ᾽ ἄκρας
Πίνδου Λάκμου τ᾽ ἀπὸ Περραιβῶν
εἰς Ἀμφιλόχους καὶ Ἀκαρνᾶνας,
μίσγει δ᾽ ὕδασιν τοῖς Ἀχελῴου

* * *

5   ἔνθεν ἐς Ἄργος διὰ κῦμα τεμὼν
ἥκει δῆμον τὸν Λύρκειον

Strabo, *Geography* 6, 2, 4 (p. 271); Hesychius λ 1432

5 ἔνθεν Erfurdt: ἐνθένδε codd.
6 Λύρκειον Jebb: Λυρκίου codd.: Λυρκείου Tyrwhitt

272

EP.

γυνὴ τίς ἥδε, συλὰς Ἀρκάδος κυνῆς;

Schol. on Aristophanes, *Birds* 1203

συλὰς Pfeiffer: συληνάς, κυλῆνας codd.

270

CH.

Flowing Inachus, son of the father of fountains, Oceanus,
you who have mighty power in the fields of Argos and the
mountains of Hera and among the Pelasgians who are
Etruscans . . .

271

CH.

For he flows from the summit of Pindus and from Lacmus
of the Perrhaebians to the Amphilochians and Acarnan-
ians, and mingles with the waters of Achelous . . . From
there he crosses the sea to Argos and comes to the com-
munity of Lyrcus.[a]

[a] The river Inachus in Epirus was believed to flow under the
sea and emerge as the river of the same name in Argos.

272

HE.

Who is this woman, who has stolen the Arcadian cap?[a]

[a] It seems that Hermes, who was born in Arcadia, has sighted
Iris, messenger of Hera, wearing a cap like his own, and jocularly
accuses her of stealing it.

FRAGMENTS OF KNOWN PLAYS

273

Πλούτωνος δ' ἐπείσοδος

Schol. on Aristophanes, *Wealth* 727

δ'] ἤδ' Porson

274

πάνδοκος ξενόστασις

Pollux, *Vocabulary* 9, 50 (2, 160, 14 Bethe)

275

[τοῦ Διὸς εἰσελθόντος πάντα μεστὰ ἀγαθῶν ἐγένετο.]

Schol. on Aristophanes, *Wealth* 807

276

σιροὶ κριθῶν

Schol. on Demosthenes 8, 45

277

ξανθὰ δ' Ἀφροδισία λάταξ
πᾶσιν ἐπεκτύπει δόμοις

Athenaeus, *Deipnosophists* 15, 668B

1 ξανθὰ Radt: -ὴ codd.   2 πᾶσιν Meineke: παισὶν
cod.   ἐπεκτύπει Nauck: ἐπεκύπτει cod.

273

... and the entry of the god of Wealth ...

274

... the guesthouse that receives all[a] ...

[a] This must mean Hades.

275

[When Zeus entered every place became full of good things.]

276

... silos full of barley ...

277

And the drops of red wine sacred to Aphrodite splashed all over the palace.[a]

[a] An allusion to the game of kottabos; see note on fr. 537.

278

εὐδαίμονες οἱ τότε γέννας
ἀφθίτου λαχόντες
[θείας]

Schol. on Aristophanes, *Peace* 531

1 γέννας Bergk: γενεᾶς codd.   3 del. Herwerden

279

τραχὺς ᾧ χελώνης κέρχνος ἐξανίσταται

Erotian, *Medical Lexicon* κ 8 Nachmanson
ᾧ del. Elmsley: ὡς cod. D

281

Aristophanes, *The Women in Assembly* 76–81:

ΓΥΝΗ
ἔγωγέ τοι τὸ σκύταλον ἐξηνεγκάμην
τὸ τοῦ Λαμίου τουτὶ καθεύδοντος λάθρᾳ.
. . .

ΠΡΑΞΑΓΟΡΑ
νὴ τὸν Δία τὸν σωτῆρ' ἐπιτήδειός γ' ἂν ἦν
τὴν τοῦ πανόπτου διφθέραν ἐνημμένος
εἴπερ τις ἄλλος βουκολεῖν τὸ δήμιον.

Schol. Γ on v. 80 ἀναφέρει δὲ τοῦτον ἐπὶ τὸν παρὰ Σοφο-
κλεῖ ἐν Ἰνάχῳ Ἄργον   Schol. R on v. 81 ὡς τὴν Ἰὼ ὁ
Ἄργος ἐν Ἰνάχῳ Σοφοκλέους

INACHUS

278

Fortunate were they who in those days were granted an immortal birth!

279

. . . on which a hard excrescence like the shell of a tortoise comes up.

281

Aristophanes, *The Women in Assembly* 76–81:

SECOND WOMAN
I have carried off the stick of Lamias while he was asleep!
. . .

PRAXAGORA
By Zeus the Preserver, he'd be just the man to wear the leather jerkin of the All-Seeing One and play the herdsman with the public as his cow!

Schol. in MS. Γ on line 80: "He is referring to Argos in Sophocles' *Inachus*."
Schol. in MS. R on 81: "As Argos does with Io in the *Inachus* of Sophocles."[a]

[a] Clearly the thing that has made Praxagora think of Argos is the club which Argos carried; see the prefatory note above.

281a

Schol. on Aeschylus, *Prometheus Bound* 574a Σοφοκλῆς
ἐν Ἰνάχῳ καὶ ᾄδοντα αὐτὸν (sc. Ἄργον) εἰσάγει.

282

ἐπήνεσ᾽· ἴσθι δ᾽, ὥσπερ ἡ παροιμία,
ἐκ κάρτα βαιῶν γνωτὸς ἂν γένοιτ᾽ ἀνήρ.

Stobaeus, *Anthology* 4, 5, 9 (4, 199, 6 Hense)

283

τοιόνδ᾽ ἐμοὶ Πλούτων᾽ ἀμεμφείας χάριν

Schol. on Aristophanes, *Wealth* 727 (cf. fr. 273)

284

πατὴρ δὲ ποταμὸς Ἴναχος
τὸν ἀντίπλαστον νομὸν ἔχει κεκμηκότων

Hesychius, *Lexicon* α 5460 Latte

2 νομὸν ἔχει Ellendt: ἔχει νόμον cod.

286

πάντα δ᾽ ἐρίθων ἀραχνᾶν βρίθει

Suda α 3750 Adler

287

ἐπίκρουμα χθονὸς Ἀργείας

Hesychius, *Lexicon* ε 4904 Latte

INACHUS

281a

Sophocles in the *Inachus* actually brings him on singing.

282

Well done! But know that, as the proverb has it, a man can get a reputation from very small things.

283

Such is the god of Wealth whom . . . for me, so as to avoid blame . . .

284

And her father, the river Inachus, occupies the region that is like that of the dead.

286

And everything is loaded with cobwebs.

287

. . . feet beating on the ground of Argos . . .

288

κναμοβόλον δικαστήν

Hesychius, *Lexicon* κ 4343 Latte

κναμόβολον Brunck

289

χειμῶνι σὺν παλινσκίῳ

Harpocration, *Glossary to the Ten Orators* 232, 7 Dindorf

291

ἀναιδείας φάρος †πίων

Hesychius, *Lexicon* α 4321 Latte

ΙΞΙΩΝ

A single quotation (fr. 296) and an inscription (DID A 4b 6 f) credit Sophocles with an Ixion. We know nothing of its plot, but if there was such a play it presumably dealt with some part of the story dramatised in Aeschylus' trilogy in which the Ixion *followed the* Perrhaebides. *Having*

ΙΟΒΑΤΗΣ

Iobates was the king of Lycia who was father of Stheneboea, wife of Proetus, king of Tiryns. It was he to whom Proetus sent Bellerophon when Stheneboea accused him of having tried to rape her (Il. 6, 155 f). Obeying the instructions given in the σήματα λυγρά ("deadly signs") in the folded tablet which Proetus had given Bellerophon to present to him, the king sent him against formidable antagonists, the Chimaera, the Solymi and the Amazons, and also sent men to ambush him. But

INACHUS

288

... a juror who throws in his voting bean[a] ...

[a] The one-word fragment 295 consists of the word κημός, which denotes a funnel-shaped box into which jurors put the pebbles with which they voted; see the prefatory note above.

289

... with a storm that brings back darkness ...

291

... a coat ... of shamelessness ...

IXION

been purified by Zeus himself for the treacherous murder of his father-in-law, Ixion attempted an approach to Hera. Zeus made a replica of Hera out of a cloud, and on it Ixion begat the race of Centaurs. He was then punished by being bound to a revolving wheel in Hades.

IOBATES

the gods lent Bellerophon the winged horse Pegasus, and he survived all these ordeals, so that when the king realised that he was the noble child of a god, he gave him his daughter's hand and half his kingdom. Later Bellerophon showed hybris and lost the favour of the gods, so that he fell from Pegasus; one version of the story, that of Hyginus, makes his marriage with the king's daughter come after that event. We have no knowledge of the plot of Sophocles' play. Euripides wrote both a Stheneboea *and a* Bellerophon.

297

καὶ σχῆμα νῷν τι λαμπρὸν ἐνδεῖξαι βίου

Lexicon Messanense fol. 281r 25 (Σοφοκλῆς Ἰοβάτῃ Nauck: Ἰοκ΄στῃ codd.)

σχῆμα νῷν τι Diggle (σχῆμα Blaydes): νῶιν τι σῆμα cod.

298

τὸν Ἀΐδαν γὰρ οὐδὲ
γῆρας οἶδε φιλεῖν

Stobaeus, *Anthology* 4, 52, 10 (5, 1076, 1 Hense)

ΙΠΠΟΝΟΥΣ

Tydeus was the son of Oeneus, king of Calydon, not by his wife Althaea, the mother of Meleager and Deianeira, but by Periboea, daughter of Hipponous, king of Olenus. There is one Olenus in Aetolia, not far from Calydon, and one in Achaea; it seems that the original version of the story featured the Aetolian Olenus, but in Hesiod and later the Achaean Olenus is the one mentioned. According to the early epic Thebais, *Oeneus sacked Olenus and*

300

ἐξ Ὠλένου γῆς φορβάδος κομίζομαι

Stephanus of Byzantium, *Ethnica* 707, 12 Meineke

IOBATES

297

. . . and to display to us two a brilliant pattern of life.

298

For not even old age knows how to love Hades.

HIPPONOUS

carried off Periboea; but according to the Hesiodic Cata-
logue *of* Women *Hipponous found his daughter to be
pregnant and sent her to Oeneus to be killed. There was a
story that the infant Tydeus was reared by swineherds.
We know nothing of the plot of this play. Pollux,* Vocabu-
lary *4, 111 says that it contained a passage in which the
Chorus spoke in the poet's own person; but this statement
may well be due to a misunderstanding.*

300

For I am being brought from the rich land of Olenus.[a]

[a] Presumably an utterance of Periboea; this sounds like the
Achaean rather than the Arcadian Olenus.

301

πρὸς ταῦτα κρύπτε μηδέν· ὡς ὁ πάνθ᾽ ὁρῶν
καὶ πάντ᾽ ἀκούων πάντ᾽ ἀναπτύσσει χρόνος

Clement of Alexandria, *Miscellanies* 6, 2, 10, 9 (2, 430, 6 Stählin)

302

σωτηρίας γὰρ φάρμακ᾽ οὐχὶ πανταχοῦ
βλέψαι πάρεστιν, ἐν δὲ τῇ προμηθίᾳ . . .

Orion, *Florilegium* 4, 2

2 προμηθίᾳ Schneidewin: -εία cod.

ΙΦΙΓΕΝΕΙΑ

We do not know the plot of this play; but there are indications that it dealt with the same events as the Iphigeneia in Aulis *of Euripides. We know from Proclus' summary that in the post-Homeric epic* Cypria, *as in Euripides, Agamemnon sent for his daughter on the pretext that she was to be married to Achilles, and that at the moment when she was about to be sacrificed to still the winds Artemis substituted a hind and carried her off to Tauris in the Crimea. Envoys were sent to Clytemnestra to ask her to convey her daughter to Aulis; in one version of the story*

305

ΟΔΥΣΣΕΥΣ

σὺ δ᾽ ὦ μεγίστων τυγχάνουσα πενθερῶν

Photius Galeanus 410, 4 = Suda π 963 Ὀδυσσεύς φησι
πρὸς Κλυταιμνήστραν περὶ Ἀχιλλέως

138

HIPPONOUS

301

In view of that, conceal nothing! For all things are un-
folded by all-seeing and all-hearing time.

302

For one cannot see recipes for safety everywhere, but in
foresight . . .

IPHIGENEIA

*these envoys were Odysseus and the herald Talthybius, in
another Odysseus and Diomedes. Bergk inferred from the
mention of leisure in fr. 308 that the soldiers' chorus in
Ennius'* Iphigeneia *(fr. xcix Jocelyn) was based on Sopho-
cles, but this can hardly be substantiated. Zielinski's sug-
gestion that the play was set in Argos and centred on the
embassy cannot be verified, but neither can it be ruled
out.*

*Welcker suggested that this play might have been iden-
tical with the* Κλυταιμήστρα *(Clytemnestra), q.v.*

305

ODYSSEUS
(to Clytemnestra)
But you, who are getting for your daughter a husband
with great parents . . .

306

ὀξηρὸν ἄγγος οὐ μελισσοῦσθαι πρέπει

Appendix proverbiorum 4, 27

307

νόει πρὸς ἀνδρὶ χρῶμα πουλύπους ὅπως
πέτρᾳ τραπέσθαι γνησίου φρονήματος

Athenaeus, *Deipnosophists* 12, 513B

1 νόει] νοῦν δεῖ Porson   πρὸς ἀνδρὶ] παρ' ἀνδρὶ Reiske:
πρὸς ἄνδρα Gomperz   χρῶμα Reiske: σῶμα cod.

308

τίκτει γὰρ οὐδὲν ἐσθλὸν εἰκαία σχολή

Stobaeus, *Anthology* 3, 30, 6 (3, 664, 12 Hense)

IXNEΥΤΑΙ

Ed. pr. Grenfell and Hunt, *P.Oxy.* ix (1912) no. 1174, p. 30;
Hunt, *P.Oxy.* xvii (1927) p. 72. See Wilamowitz, *Neue Jahrbücher
für das kl. Altertum* 29 (1912) 453–76 = *Kl. Schr.* 353–383;
Pearson, *Fragments of Sophocles* i, p. 244; Maas, *DLZ* (1912)
2783 f = *Kl. Schr.* 43 f; *BKW* 32 (1912) 1075 f = *Kl. Schr.* 44 f;
Page, *GLP* iii (1941) 26–53, whose prefatory note and translation
I have adapted; Siegmann, *Untersuchungen zu Sophokles'
Ichneutai* (1941); Radt, *Tragicorum Graecorum Fragmenta*, vol.
4 (1977) 274–308; Maltese: *Sofocle, Ichneutae: Introduzione,
testo critico, interpretazione e commento* (1982), with photo-
graphs of the whole papyrus; see Maltese for a full bibliography.
See Diggle, *ZPE* 112 (1996), 3–17.

140

IPHIGENEIA

306

It is not proper to put honey in a vessel that has held vinegar.

307

In dealing with your husband, know how to change the colour of your true thoughts, like a polyp on a rock.[a]

[a] Perhaps advice given by Clytemnestra to her daughter.

308

For nothing good results from casual leisure.

THE SEARCHERS

The characters are Apollo, Silenus, a Chorus of Satyrs, the mountain nymph Cyllene, and Hermes. The scene of the action is Mount Cyllene in Arcadia. Apollo has lost his cattle; he has sought them vainly in Northern Greece, and has now come to the Peloponnese. He promises a reward to their discoverer. Silenus enters and offers the aid of himself and his sons the satyrs, in return for a prize of gold and release from slavery. Slavery to whom? In other satyr plays the satyrs sometimes get lost and are temporarily enslaved to a master other than their usual master, Dionysus, and in this play Apollo himself and Pan, an important god in Arcadia, have both been suggested. However, I believe that Apollo is promising emancipation from their regular servitude to his brother Dionysus. It is true that they usually enjoy being slaves to Dionysus, but it may well have been imagined that they would prefer not to be slaves at all.

After a short ode, the Chorus and its leader advance on the track of the cattle. Confused prints are discovered, leading to the entrance to a cave. The Chorus is suddenly alarmed by a strange sound, which appears to issue from underground. Silenus reproaches the satyrs for their cowardice, and contrasts therewith the courage which he himself frequently displayed when he was young. The chase is resumed; the matter has been disputed, but I believe that Wilamowitz was right to interpret line 174 as indicating that three paths met at the mouth of the cave, and that a section of the satyrs moved along each of them in order to arrive there. Silenus joins the satyrs at what seems to be the point of danger, but as soon as he has heard the strange sound shows himself to be an even greater coward than his sons. At last they beat loudly on the roof of the underground cave, and Cyllene, the nymph of the mountain, emerges and asks what is the meaning of their uproar. She informs them that she is nursing a son of Zeus and of Maia, the daughter of Atlas. This child—Hermes, grown marvellously in a few days—has fashioned an instrument of music from the shell of a tortoise. This is not easy to explain to the satyrs, who are not only ignorant of tortoises, but do not yet know what music is. From this comes the noise which has alarmed them. Now it appears that Hermes has used a cowhide to stretch over the tortoise shell, and the satyrs at once presume that the possession of this cowhide proves that Hermes is the thief of Apollo's cattle. The fragment ends with an altercation between Cyllene and the Chorus, she denying and they insisting that Hermes must be the thief.

The same story is told in the Homeric Hymn to Hermes; but Sophocles diverges from the Hymn's version at several points. Scholars have argued that he must have had some authority for his departures from the Hymn's version, but all of these may easily have been made by the poet in order to adapt the story to his own purposes. Hermes must have propitiated Apollo, as in the Hymn, by the gift of the newly discovered lyre, something which took on special importance in the hands of its new owner. Did the satyrs receive the promised reward? If I am right in believing that it was from their customary servitude to Dionysus that Apollo promised to release them, they did not. Satyrs do not commonly cut an heroic figure in satyric dramas, and these satyrs have shown the same cowardice and boastfulness as other satyrs, so that I suspect that Apollo had a good reason for withholding the reward. In forming a judgment as to the play's quality, we should remember that the discovery of the thief and the confrontation between the two gods, which are missing, must have formed the climax to which the whole action was designed to lead up. We have no means of knowing how long the play was; it may not have been longer than eight hundred lines. Wilamowitz argued for an early date in Sophocles' career, but our knowledge of satyric drama in general and that of Sophocles in particular is so limited that we cannot date the play with any confidence.

314

⟨ΑΠΟΛΛΩΝ⟩

(*remains of six lines*)

κήρυγμ' Ἀπόλλων πᾶσι]ν ἀγγέλλω [β]ροτο[ῖς
θεοῖς τε πᾶσι· δῶρ' ὑπισ]χνοῦμαι τελεῖ[ν,
βοῦς εἴ τις ἐγγὺς εἶδεν εἴτ' ἀ]πόπροθεν·

10   δειν]ὸν [γὰρ οὖν ἄλγημα δύσ]λοφον φρενί
ἔπεσ]τ' ἀ[φαιρεθέντι βο]ῦς ἀμολγάδας
μόσ]χους [τε πάσας καὶ νόμευμ]α πορτίδων.
ἄπα]ντα φρ[οῦδα, καὶ μάτη]ν ἰχνοσκοπῶ
λαθ]ραῖ' ἰόν[των τῆλε βου]στάθμου κάπης

15   θεῶ]ν ὡς τέχνη[σιν· ἀλλ' ἐ]γὼ οὐκ ἂν ᾠόμην
οὔτ' ἂ]ν θεῶν τιν' [οὔτ' ἐφημ]έρων βροτῶν
δρᾶσ]αι τόδ' ἔργ[ον οὐδὲ] πρὸς τόλμαν πεσεῖν.
δεῦρ]' οὖν ἐπείπερ [ἦλ]θον, ἐκπλαγεὶς ὄκνῳ
σκοπ]ῶ, ματεύω, παντελὲς κήρυγμ' ἔχων

20   θεοῖ]ς βροτοῖς τε μηδέν' ἀγνοεῖν τάδε·
ἀκολο]υθίᾳ γὰρ ἐμμανὴς κυνηγετῶ·
.....]ων δ' ἐπῆλθ[ο]ν φ[ῦ]λα, τ[οῦ] παντὸς στρατ[οῦ
ζητῶν] τίς [

(*about six lines missing*)

30   ]α Θεσσαλῶν
       ] Βοιωτίας τε γῆς
       ]ταδ[. .].

(*one line missing*)

7–10 Page, after Hunt and Rossbach   11, 14 Pearson
15 θεῶ]ν Ll.-J.   τέχνηι[σιν Siegmann   ἀλλ' ἐ]γὼ Pearson
17 οὐδὲ Vollgraff   18 Siegmann   19 Walker   21 Wilamowitz
23 Murray

314

⟨APOLLO⟩

(remains of six lines)

To every man and every god Apollo makes a proclamation! If anyone has seen my cattle, near or far, to him I promise a reward. Grievous and heavy pain is in my heart; someone has robbed me of my milch-cows, and all my calves and herds of heifers. Not one is left; all are gone unseen, far from the stables, as though by gods' contrivance; vainly I try to trace them. I never should have thought that any god or mortal man would even dare to attempt this deed. So since I have come to this point, distracted with alarm I gaze and search and make full proclamation to gods and men, that none may be unaware. . . . I follow frantic in pursuit. I visited the tribes . . . seeking, which . . . of all the host . . .

(about six lines missing)

. . . of the Thessalians . . . the land of Boeotia . . . this . . .

(one line missing)

```
          ]ς Δωρικο[
35  ........]τον‘ ἐνθ[
    ........]ἥκω ξυμ[μ]αχ[
    .......Κυλ]λήνης τε δυ[σ
    ........].ε χῶρον, ἐς δ’ ὕλ[
    ἀλλ’ εἴτε ποι]μὴν εἴτ’ ἀγρωστή[ρων τις ἢ
40  μαριλοκαυ]τῶν ἐν λόγῳ παρ[ίσταται
    εἴτ’ οὖν ὀρ]είων νυμφογεννή[του γένους
    Σατύρω]ν τίς ἐστι, πᾶσιν ἀγγέλ[λω τάδε,
    τὰ ἔλωρα τοῦ Παιῶνος ὅστις ἂ[ν λάβῃ,
    τῷδ’ α]ὐτόχρημα μισθός ἐσθ’ ὁ κε[ίμενος.
                    ⟨ΣΙΛΗΝΟΣ⟩
45  ἐπεὶ θ]εοῦ φώνημα τὼς ἐπέκλυον
    βοῶ]ντος ὀρθίοισι σὺν κηρύγμασι,
    σ]πουδῇ τάδ’ ἦ πάρεστι πρεσβύτῃ [τελῶν,
    σ]οί, Φοῖβ’ Ἄπολλον, προσφιλὴς εὐε[ργέτης
    θέλων γενέσθαι τῷδ’ ἐπεσσύθην δρ[ό]μω[ι,
50  ἤν πως τὸ χρῆμα τοῦτό σοι κυνηγέσω.
    τ[ὸ] γὰρ γέ[ρα]ς μοι κείμενον χρ[υ]σο[σ]τεφὲ[ς
    μά[λι]στ’ ἐμ[αῖς κόμ]αισ[ι π]ροσθέσθ[αι χρεώ]ν.
    παῖδας δ’ ἐμ[οὺ]ς ὅσσοισι [...]...ε[.]β.[.].[
    π[έμποιμ’ ἂ]ν, εἴπερ ἐκτελεῖς ἅπερ λέγεις.
                    ⟨ΑΠ.⟩
55  σάφ’ ἴσθι, δ]ώσω· μοῦνον ἐμπ[έδου τ]άδε.
```

39 ἀλλ’ εἴτε Diggle (ὡς εἴτε Hunt)
41 εἴτ’ οὖν Diggle   42 Σατύρω]ν Diggle
43 Pearson   45 Diggle
47 τελῶν Diggle   50 ἤν Diggle: ἄν Π   51 Pearson

. . . the Dorian . . . I have come . . . allies . . . of Cyllene
. . . and to a place, . . ., but if any shepherd, farmer, or
charcoal-burner is at hand to hear me, or any nymph-born
wild man of the mountains, I proclaim this to all: whoever
catches the prey taken from Apollo earns forthwith the
reward that lies ready here.

⟨SILENUS⟩

When I heard a god's voice thus raised in loud proclama-
tion, I hurried, fast as an aged person may, when the news
came, to accomplish this, eager to be your friend and
benefactor, Phoebus Apollo, running as you see, hoping to
hunt this treasure down for you. For I am very eager to
place upon my locks the prize of a golden wreath awaiting
me. And my sons . . . eyes . . . I will send out, if you are go-
ing to keep your promise.

⟨AP.⟩

Be assured, I will give the reward; only make good your
word!

---

52 κόμ]αισ[ι Ll.-J.   end Pearson   54 Diehl
55 σάφ᾽ ἴσθι Ll.-J.   δ]ώσω Siegmann

⟨ΣΙ.⟩

τὰ[ς βοῦς ἀπάξω σ]οι· σὺ δ' ἐμπέδου [δόσι]ν.

⟨ΑΠ.⟩

ἕξει σφ' ὅ γ' εὑ]ρών, ὅστις ἔσθ'· ἑτ[οῖμ]α δ[έ.

(*fragments of four lines*)

⟨ΣΙ.⟩

τί τοῦτο; πῶ[ς *about* 16 *letters*]εις.

⟨ΑΠ.⟩

63   ἐλεύθερος σὺ [πᾶν τε γένος ἔσται τέκν]ων.

ΧΟ(ΡΟΣ) ΣΑΤΤ(ΡΩΝ)

(*fragments of twelve lines*)

76   ξὺν ἅμα θεὸς ὁ φίλος ἀνέτω
πόνους προφήνας
ἀρίζηλα χρυσοῦ παραδείγματα.

ΣΙ.

θεὸς Τύχη καὶ δαῖμον ἰθυντήριε,

80   τυχεῖν με πράγους οὗ δράμημ' ἐπείγεται,
λείαν ἄγραν σύλησιν ἐκκυνηγέσαι
Φοίβου κλοπαίας βοῦς ἀπεστερημένου.
τῶν εἴ τις ὀπτήρ ἐστιν ἢ κατήκοος
ἐμοί τ' ἂν εἴη προσφιλὴς φράσας τάδε

85   Φο]ί[βῳ τ'] ἄνακτι παντελὴς εὐεργέτης.

(*fragments of five lines, two by Silenus,
three by the Chorus*)

⟨ΣΙ.⟩

91   φησίν τις, ἢ [οὐδείς φησιν εἰδέναι τάδε;

84 φράσας Wilamowitz: δρασας Π   85 παντελὴς Pear-
son: προστελης Π   91 Hunt

148

⟨SI.⟩

I will bring you back your cattle; only make good your offer!

⟨AP.⟩

The finder shall have it, whoever he is; it is waiting for him!

(fragments of four lines)

⟨SI.⟩

What's this? How . . .?

⟨AP.⟩

Freedom for you and all your sons!

CHORUS OF SATYRS

(fragments of twelve lines; the Chorus make a noisy entrance, and then promise to hunt for the cattle) . . . now at our side let the god who is dear to us bring our task to fulfilment, he who has shown us these glittering samples of gold!

SI.

Goddess Success and guiding divinity! Grant me success in the quest at which my course is aimed, to track down the loot, the spoil, the plunder, the stolen cattle that Phoebus has lost! If anyone has seen them or has heard of them, let him speak out; he shall be my friend, and the lord Phoebus' greatest benefactor.

(fragments of five lines,
two by Silenus, three by the Chorus)

⟨SI.⟩

Who says he knows? Anyone, or no one? It seems high

ἔοικεν ἤδη κ[ἀμὲ πρὸς τοὖργον δραμεῖν.
ἄγ᾽ εἶα δὴ πᾶς ̣ ̣[
ῥινηλατῶν ὀσμ[αῖσι
95 αὔρας ἐάν πῃ πρ[
διπλοῦς ὀκλάζω[
ὕποσμος ἐν χρῷ [
οὕτως ἔρευναν καὶ π[
ἅπαντα χρηστὰ κα[ὶ about 11 letters τε]λεῖν.
<HMIXOPION>
100 θεὸς θεὸς θεὸς θεὸς ἔα [ἔα·
ἔχειν ἔοιγμεν· ἴσχε· μὴ ̣ ̣ρ[. . .] ̣τει.
<HMIX.>
ταῦτ᾽ ἔστ᾽ ἐκεῖνα· τῶν βοῶν τὰ βήματα.
<HMIX.>
σίγα· θεός τις τὴν ἀποι[κία]ν ἄγει.
<HMIX.>
τί δρῶμεν, ὦ τᾶν; ἢ τὸ δέον [ἄρ᾽] ἤνομεν;
105 τί; τοῖσι ταύτῃ πῶς δοκεῖ; <HMIX> δοκεῖ πάνυ·
σαφῶ[ς γ]ὰρ αὔθ᾽ ἕκαστα σημαίνει τάδε.
<HMIX.>
ἰδοῦ ἰδοῦ·
καὶ τοὐπίσημον αὐτὸ τῶν ὅπλων πάλιν.
<HMIX.>
ἄθρει μάλα·
110 αὔτ᾽ ἐστὶ τοῦτο μέτρον ἐκμε[μαγ]μ[έ]νο[ν].
<HMIX.>
χώρει δρόμῳ καὶ τα[about 11 letters] ̣ν ἔχου

92 Roberts   110 Pearson

150

time for me to set to work! Come, everyone . . . nosing the scent . . . somewhere, perhaps, a breath of wind . . . squatting double . . . follow the scent closely . . . search, and . . . everything fine, and . . . bring to an end.
(*The Chorus divides itself into three groups, who advance separately in the direction of the entrance to the cave*).

<SEMICHORUS OF SATYRS>

A god, a god, a god, a god! Hullo, hullo! I think we have them! Stop, don't . . .

<SEMICH.>

Here they are! The prints are those of the cattle!

<SEMICH.>

Quiet! A god is leading our expedition!

<SEMICH.>

What must we do, sir? Were we doing our work rightly? Well? What do our friends over there say?

<SEMICH.>

Very well, because it is clear! This is enough to prove it!

<SEMICH.>

Look, look! Again, the very imprint of their hooves!

<SEMICH.>

Look closely! Here is a moulding of the very size!

<SEMICH.>

Run hard, and . . .

...]ογμ[.....].[about 14 letters]μενος
ῥοίβδημ’ ἐάν τι τῶν [βοῶν ἐ]π’ οὖς [μόλῃ.

⟨HMIX.⟩

οὐκ εἰσακούω πω [τορῶ]ς τοῦ φθέγματος.
115 ἀλλ’ αὐτὰ μὴν ἴχ[νη τε] χὠ στίβος τάδε
κείνων ἐναργῆ τῶν βοῶν· μαθεῖν πάρα.

⟨HMIX.⟩

ἔα μάλα·
παλινστραφῆ τοι ναὶ μὰ Δία τὰ βήματα.
εἰς τοὔμπαλιν δέδορκεν· αὐτὰ δ’ εἴσιδε.
120 τί ἐστι τουτί; τίς ὁ τρόπος τοῦ τάγματ[ος;
εἰς τοὐπίσω τὰ πρόσθεν ἤλλακται, τὰ δ’ αὖ
ἐναντί’ ἀλλήλοισι συμπ[επλεγ]μένα·
δεινὸς κυκησμὸς εἶχ[ε τὸν βοη]λάτην.

⟨ΣΙ.⟩

τίν’ αὖ τέχνην σὺ τήν[δ’ ἄρ’ ἐξ]ηῦρες, τίν’ αὖ,
125 πρόσπαιον, ὧδε κεκλιμ[ένος] κυνηγετεῖν
πρὸς γῇ; τίς ὑμῶν ὁ τρόπος; οὐχὶ μανθάνω.
ἐχῖνος ὥς τις ἐν λόχμῃ κεῖσαι πεσών,
ἤ τις πίθηκος κύβδ’ ἀποθυμαίνεις τινί.
τί ταῦτα; ποῦ γῆς ἐμάθετ’; ἐν ποίῳ τόπῳ;
130 σημήνατ’· οὐ γὰρ ἴδρις εἰμὶ τοῦ τρόπου.

⟨ΧΟ.⟩

ὗ ὗ ὗ ὔ.

⟨ΣΙ.⟩

τ[ί τοῦτ’ ἰύζεις;] τίνα φοβῇ; τίν’ εἰσορᾷς;

113 ἐ]π’ Siegmann: δ]ι’ Hunt   116 punctuated by Wila-
mowitz   129 τόπῳ Wilamowitz: τρόπῳ Π

152

. . . if a noise from the cattle should reach your ear.
(*A noise is heard from offstage*)

<SEMICH.>

I can't yet hear their lowing clearly, but here are the very prints and trail of those cattle, plain to see!

<SEMICH.>

Good gracious! the footprints are reversed! They point backwards! Just look at them! What's this? What sort of order is it? The front marks have shifted to the rear, while some are entangled in two opposite directions! A strange confusion must have possessed their driver!

<SI.>

And *now* what trick have you invented? what's the game? What *is* it, I say? this new one—hunting on your bellies like that? What sort of method do you call this? It's a mystery to me! Lying on the ground like hedgehogs in a bush, or like a monkey bending over to let off at someone! What is this foolery? Where on earth did you learn it? Tell me! I never heard of such behaviour!

<CH.>

Ow! ow! ow! ow!

<SI.>

What are you howling for? Who's frightening you?

τ[ίς ἡ τάραξ]ις; τί ποτε βακχεύεις ἔχων;
ἆ[ρ’ οὗ τίς ἐστι] κέρχνος ἱμείρεις μαθεῖν;
135 τ[ί δῆτα] σιγᾶθ’, οἱ πρ[ὸ] τ[οῦ] [λαλίστ]ατοι;

<ΧΟ.>

σ[ίγα μὲν οὖν.]

<ΣΙ.>

τ[ίν’ ἔστ’ ἐκεῖθε]ν ἀπονοσ[φίζ]εις ἔχων;

<ΧΟ.>

ἄ[κουε δή.]

<ΣΙ.>

καὶ πῶς ἀκούσ[ω μηδεν]ὸς φωνὴν κλύων;

<ΧΟ.>

140 ἐμοὶ πιθοῦ.

<ΣΙ.>

ἐμ[ὸν] δίω[γμά γ’ οὐδα]μῶς ὀνήσετε.

<ΧΟ.>

ἄκουσον αὐτ[ὸ]ς νῦ[ν, πά]τερ, χρόνον τινὰ
οἵῳ ’κπλαγέντες ἐνθάδ’ ἐξενίσμεθα
ψόφῳ, τὸν οὐδεὶς π[ώπο]τ’ ἤκουσεν βροτῶν.

<ΣΙ.>

145 τί μοι ψόφον φοβ[εῖσθε] καὶ δειμαίνετε,
μάλθης ἄναγνα σώματ’ ἐκμεμαγμένα,
κάκιστα θηρῶν ὀνθ[ί’, ἐ]ν πάσῃ σκιᾷ
φόβον βλέποντες, πάντα δειματούμενοι,
ἄνευρα κἀκόμιστα κἀνελεύθερα
150 διακονοῦντες, [σώ]ματ’ εἰ[σι]δ[ε]ῖν μόνον,

133 Diggle   134 Ll.-J.   135 σιγᾶθ’ οἱ Theon:]ατ’ ὦ Π
143 οἵῳ ’κπλ. Ar. Byz.:]ῳ πλ. Π   147 ὀνθ[ί’ Walker

154

Whom are you looking at? What's the bogey that you see? Why do you keep behaving madly? Are you desirous to find millet?[a] Why are you now silent, you who used to talk so much?

< CH. >

No, be quiet!

< SI. >

What is it there that you keep turning away from?

< CH. >

Listen, do!

< SI. >

How can I listen when I hear no one's voice?

< CH. >

Do what I say!

< SI. >

A lot of help you will give me in my chase!

< CH. >

Listen yourself for a moment, father, and learn what sort of noise terrifies us here and maddens us; no mortal ever heard it yet!

< SI. >

Why does a mere noise alarm and scare you? Tell me, you damned waxwork dummies, you worthless animal dung! You see terror in every shadow, scared at everything! Useless assistants—spineless, slovenly, unenterprising! Just

[a] Lit.: are you eager to learn where there is millet seed? Millet was stored in underground storehouses called σιροί, from which we get the word silo.

καὶ γλῶσσα καὶ φαλῆτες; εἰ δέ που δέῃ,
πιστοὶ λόγοισιν ὄντες ἔργα φεύγετε,
τοιοῦδε πατρός, ὦ κάκιστα θηρίων,
οὗ πόλλ' ἐφ' ἥβης μνήματ' ἀνδρείας ὕπο
155 κεῖται παρ' οἴκοις νυμφικοῖς ἠσκημένα,
οὐκ εἰς φυγὴν κλίνοντος, οὐ δειλουμένου,
οὐδὲ ψόφοισι τῶν ὀρειτρόφων βοτῶν
πτήσσοντος, ἀλλ' α[ἰχ]μαῖσιν ἐξειργασμένου
ἃ νῦν ὑφ' ὑμῶν λάμ[πρ' ἀ]πορρυπαίνεται
160 ψόφῳ νεώρει κόλακι ποιμένων ποθέν.
τί] δὴ φοβεῖσθε παῖδες ὡς πρὶν εἰσιδεῖν,
πλοῦτον δὲ χρυσόφαντον ἐξαφίετε
ὃν Φοῖβος ὑμῖν εἶπε κἀνεδέξατο,
καὶ τὴν ἐλευθέρωσιν ἣν κατήνεσεν
165 ὑμῖν τε κἀμοί· ταῦτ' ἀφέντες εὕδετε.
εἰ μὴ 'νανοστήσαντες ἐξιχνεύσετε
τὰς βοῦς ὅπῃ βεβᾶσι καὶ τὸν βουκόλον,
κλαίοντες αὐτῇ δειλίᾳ ψοφήσετε.

⟨ΧΟ.⟩

πάτερ, παρὼν αὐτός με συμποδηγέτει,
170 ἵν' εὖ κατειδῇς εἴ τίς ἐστι δειλία.
γνώσῃ γὰρ αὐτός, ἢν παρῇς, οὐδὲν λέγων.

⟨ΣΙ.⟩

ἐγὼ παρὼν αὐτός σε προσβιβῶ λόγῳ,
κυνορτικὸν σύριγμα διακαλούμενος.
ἀλλ' εἶ' [ἐ]φίστω τριζύγ' εἰς οἶμον βάσιν,

156 δειλουμένου Nicander: δουλ- Π 158 Hunt 161 Koerte
174 [ἐ]φίστω Hunt: [ἀ]φίστω Pearson   τρίζυγ' εἰς Wila-
mowitz: τρι]ζυγης Π   οἶμον Ll.-J.: οἴμου Π

bodies and tongue and phalluses! In every crisis you profess loyalty, but fly from action. Yet your father, you worthless brutes, when young by his valour set up many a splendid trophy in the nymphs' abodes; he never yielded to flight, never lost courage, never ducked at noises made by cattle grazing on the hills; he performed feats with the spear whose lustre you now tarnish at some shepherd's latest wheedling call.[a] Scared as babies before you even see! You throw away the golden riches that Phoebus promised and guaranteed, and the freedom he agreed to give us, you as well as me. You give it all up and go fast asleep! Come back and search out where the cattle and the cowman went, or you'll be sorry—you shall make a noise out of pure cowardice![b]

〈CH.〉

Father, come here and guide me yourself! You'll soon find out if there's any cowardice! Come here, and you'll learn what nonsense you are talking!

〈SI.〉

I'll come, and win you to my way of thinking, with a cheer for all like the call of the hunter to the hounds! Come on, take your stand where the three paths meet, and I will

[a] The "feats with the spear" of which Silenus boasts are sexual triumphs; shrines dedicated to the Nymphs ("the nymphs' abodes") often contained reliefs, which might well show amorous satyrs pursuing nymphs.

[b] I.e., they will excrete out of mere terror.

157

175 ἐγὼ δ᾽ ἐν ἔργοις παρμένων σ᾽ ἀπευθυνῶ.

XO.

ὓ ὓ ὓ, ψ ψ, ἆ ἆ, λέγ᾽ ὅ τι πονεῖς.
τί μάτην ὑπέκλαγες ὑπέκριγες
ὑπό μ᾽ ἴδες; ἔχεται
ἐν πρώτῳ τίς ὅδε τρόπ[ῳ;

180 ἔχει· ἐλήλυθεν ἐλήλ[υθεν·
ἐμὸς εἶ, ἀνάγου.
δευτέρῳ τίς ὅδε .[....].της
(fragments of twenty lines)
πάτερ, τί σιγᾷς; μῶν ἀληθ[ὲς εἴπομεν;
οὐκ εἰσακούεις—ἢ κεκώφη[σαι;—ψόφον;

⟨ΣΙ.⟩

205 ἔα. ⟨ΧΟ.⟩ τί ἔστιν; ⟨ΣΙ.⟩ οὐ μενῶ. ⟨ΧΟ.⟩ μέν᾽, εἰ
θέλεις.

⟨ΣΙ.⟩

οὐκ ἔστιν, ἀλλ᾽ αὐτὸς σὺ ταῦθ᾽ [ὅπη θέλεις
ζήτει τε κἀξίχνευε καὶ πλού[τει λαβὼν
τὰς βοῦς τε καὶ τὸν χρυσόν, [ὡς ἐμοὶ δοκ]ε[ῖ
μὴ πλεῖστ[ον] ἔτι μ[έ]ν[οντα διατρίβειν] χρόνον.

⟨ΧΟ.⟩

210 ἀλλ᾽ οὔ τι μ[ή σοί] μ᾽ [ἐκλιπεῖν ἐφήσομαι
οὐδ᾽ ἐξυπελ[θεῖ]ν τ[οῦ πόνου πρίν γ᾽ ἂν σα]φῶς
εἰδῶμεν ὅσ[τις ἔνδον ἐστὶ τῆς στέγης.
(fragments of four lines)
ὁ [δ᾽ ε]ὐφ⟨ρ⟩ανε[ῖτ]αι τοῖσιν. ἀλλ᾽ ἐγὼ τάχα

178 question mark Diggle   208–9 Pearson
209 πλείον᾽ ?   217 Diggle

stand at the scene of action and set you on your way!

<CH.>

(*sundry noises of alarm and encouragement*) Say, what is your trouble? What's the good of groaning and gibbering and glowering at me? Who is this that is caught at the very first bend? You're caught! He's come, he's come! I have you! Off to jail you go! Who is this at the second . . .

(*fragments*)

Father, why are you silent? Didn't we speak the truth? Can't you hear the noise, or are you deaf?

<SI.>

Ow!

<CH.>

What's the matter?

<SI.>

(*who has now heard the noise*) I'll not stay!

<CH.>

Do stay—please!

<SI.>

Impossible! You look and search them out as you please, and catch the cattle and the gold and get rich quick! I have decided not to spend much more time waiting here!

<CH.>

I'll not allow you to desert me and sneak away from the job before we know for certain who is beneath this roof!

(*fragments of four lines*)

. . . and he will get pleasure from this. . . . but I'll quickly

φ[έρ]ων κτύπον πέδορτον ἐξαναγκάσω
πηδήμασιν κραιπνοῖσι καὶ λακτίσμασιν
220 ὥστ᾽ εἰσακοῦσαι, κεἰ λίαν κωφός τις ᾖ.

⟨ΚΥΛΛΗΝΗ⟩

θῆρες, τί τόνδε χλοερὸν ὑλώδη πάγον
ἔνθηρον ὡρμήθητε σὺν πολλῇ βοῇ;
τίς ἥδε τέχνη; τίς μετάστασις πόνων
οὓς πρόσθεν εἶχες δεσπότῃ χάριν φέρων;
225 ὕποινος αἰεί, νεβρίνῃ καθημμένος
δορᾷ χεροῖν τε θύρσον εὐπαλῆ φορῶν,
ὄπισθεν εὐίαζες ἀμφὶ τὸν θεὸν
σὺν ἐγγόνοις νύμφαισι καὶ παίδων ὄχλῳ.
νῦν δ᾽ ἀγνοῶ τὸ χρῆμα· ποῖ στροφαὶ νέαι
230 μανιῶν στρέφουσι; θαῦμα γάρ. κατέκλυον
ὁμοῦ πρέπον κέλευμ᾽ ὅπως κυνηγετῶν
ἐγγὺς μολόντων θηρὸς εὐναίου τροφῆς,
ὁμοῦ δ᾽ αναυτι[. .]. . .φωρ[. .]. .[. .]
γλώσσης ἐτειν.[. .]ις κλοπὴν [. . . . .].εναι·
235 αὖτις δ᾽ α[. . . .]τ[. . . .]. μενων[. . . . . . .]α
κηρυκ[.]. . .[. . . . .]. κηρυγμα[
καὶ ταῦτ᾽ ἀφεῖσα [σὺν] ποδῶν λακ[τίσμασιν
ἴ]λη δ[όμῳ] μου πά[.]φ.ρ[.]᾽ ἐγειτν[ία.
καὶ] ταῦτ᾽ ἂν ἄλλως ἢ κλ[.]. . . .μ[
240 . . .]ων ἀκούσασ᾽ ὧδε παραπεπαισμέν[ων

225 ὕποινος read by Maltese   226 φορῶν Diggle: φέρων
Π   227 εὐίαζετ᾽ corrected to εὐίαζες in Π   228 καὶ
παίδων Wilamowitz: καιποδων Π: κώπαδῶν Maas   230 stop
after γάρ Ll.-J.   231 ὅπως Ll.-J.: -α πως Π   238 Ll.-J.

make the ground ring with repeated jumps and kicks, and force him to hear me, however deaf he may be.

<CYLLENE>

(*emerging from the cave*) Wild creatures, why have you attacked this green and wooded hill, haunt of wild beasts, with loudest uproar? What tricks are these? What is this change from the task with which you used to please your master? Drunken always, clad in hide of fawn, bearing the light thyrsus, you used to utter that bacchic cry in the god's train, together with the nymphs of your family and the company of your children. But this I do not understand! Where are the latest whirls of your madness whirling you to? It is a mystery! I heard a cry like the call of hunters when they come near to the brood of a beast in its lair, and in the same moment . . . thief . . . your words referred to a theft . . . and to a proclamation . . . then, dropping that, (the crowd of you), with stamping of feet, . . . moved near to (my home) . . . hearing such crazy

...[...]φ.[.]η[.]....νων ὑμᾶς νοσεῖν
νο[........]ν οὐ τιθεῖτ' ἀναιτίαν.

XO.

νύμφα βαθύζωνε, π[αῦσαι χόλου
τοῦδ', οὔτε γὰρ νεῖκος ἥ[κω φέρων
245 δάου μάχας οὐδ' ἄξενό[ς τις σέθεν
γλ[ῶ]σσ' ἂν μάταιός τ' [ἀφ' ἡμῶν θίγοι.
μή με μὴ προψαλ[άξῃς κακοῖς,
ἀλλ' εὐπετῶς μοι πρ[όφανον τὸ πρᾶγ-
μ' ἐν τόποις τοῖσ[δε τίς νέρθε γᾶς ὧδ' ἀγα-
250 στῶς ἐγήρυσε θέσπιν αὐδά[ν.

⟨ΚΤ.⟩

ταῦτ' ἔστ' ἐκείνων νῦν [τρόπων πεπαίτερα,
καὶ τοῖσδε θηρῶν ἐκπύ[θοιο πλείον' ἂν
ἀλκασμάτων δ[ειλῆ]ς τε πειρατηρίων
νύμφης· ἐμοὶ γὰ[ρ οὐ]κ [ἀρεστόν ἐστ' ἔριν
255 ὀρθοψάλακτον ἐν [λ]όγο[ισ]ιν [ἱστάναι.
ἀλλ' ἥσυχος πρόφαινε καὶ μ[ή]νυ[έ μοι
ὅτου μάλιστα πράγματος χρείαν ἔχεις.

⟨XO.⟩

τόπων ἄνασσα τῶνδε, Κυλλήνης σθένος,
ὅτου μὲν οὕνεκ' ἦλθον ὕστερον φράσω·
260 τὸ φθέγμα δ' ἡμῖν τοῦθ' ὅπερ φωνεῖ φράσον,
καὶ τίς ποτ' αὐτῷ διαχαράσσεται βροτῶν.

⟨ΚΤ.⟩

ὑμᾶς μὲν αὐτοὺς χρὴ τάδ' εἰδέναι σαφῶς,

242 read by Diggle   243 Murray   244 Diehl
245 τίς σέθεν Ll.-J.: που σέθεν Murray   252 Ll.-J.

162

. . . something is wrong with you . . . you would make an innocent . . .?

CH.

Deep-girdled nymph, cease to be angry! I do not come to bring you strife of wars and enemies, nor do I think that any unfriendly foolish word from us shall reach your heart! Ah no, do not assail me with taunts, but readily disclose the secret—who is it here below the ground, who spoke to amaze us with a voice divine?

⟨CY.⟩

This is a gentler manner than the other: if you hunt like *this*, you will learn far more than by shows of strength and attempts upon a frightened nymph! I do not like loud quarrels started in argument! Now be calm and tell me clearly just what you want!

⟨CH.⟩

Queen of this region, mighty Cyllene, I will tell you later why I came. But explain to us this voice that is sounding, and tell us who among mortals is exasperating us with it!

⟨CY.⟩

You must understand this clearly, that if you reveal the

ὡς εἰ φανεῖτε τὸν λόγον τὸν ἐξ ἐμοῦ
αὑτοῖσιν ὑμῖν ζημία πορίζεται.
265 καὶ γὰρ κέκρυπται τοὖργον ἐν [θ]εῶν ἕδραις,
Ἥραν ὅπως μ[ὴ πύ]στ[ι]ς ἵξεται λόγου.
Ζ[εὺ]ς γ[ὰρ] κρυφ[αίως εἰς στέ]γην Ἀτλαντίδος
τήνδ᾽ ἦλθε Μαίας, διὰ δ᾽ ἐπαρθεν]εύσατο
(about 22 letters)   ] υ . [.]φίλας
270 . . . .]λήθη τῆς βαθυζώνου θεᾶς.
κατὰ σπέ]ος δὲ παῖδ᾽ ἐφίτυσεν μόνον.
τοῦτον δὲ] χερσὶ ταῖς ἐμαῖς ἐγὼ τρέφω·
μητρὸς γ]ὰρ ἰσχὺς ἐν νόσῳ χειμάζεται.
κἄδεστ]ὰ καὶ ποτῆτα καὶ κοιμήματα
275 πρὸς σπ]αργάνοις μένουσα λικνῖτιν τροφὴν
ἐξευθ]ετίζω νύκτα καὶ καθ᾽ ἡμέραν.
ὁ δ᾽ α]ὔξεται κατ᾽ ἦμαρ οὐκ ἐπεικότα
ἀγα]στός, ὥστε θαῦμα καὶ φόβος μ᾽ ἔχει.
οὔπω γ]ὰρ ἕκτον ἦμαρ ἐκπεφασμένος
280 τύπου]ς ἐρείδει παιδὸς εἰς ἥβης ἀκμήν,
κἀξορ]μενίζει κοὐκέτι σχολάζεται
βλάστῃ·] τοιόνδε παῖδα θησαυρὸς στέγει.
Ἑρμῆς δὲ] τοὔ[νομ᾽] ἐστὶ τοῦ πατρὸς θέσει.
δεινῇ δ᾽ ὃ πεύθει φ]θέγμα μηχανῇ βρέμ[ον
285 ἄφ[ραστ᾽ ἐκεῖνος αὐτὸ]ς ἡμέρᾳ μιᾷ
καπ . [.] . εθα[. . . . ἐξεμηχ]ανήσατο·
ἐξ ὑπτίας κ[about 11 letters] . ς ἡδονῇ

267 κρυφ[αίως Diggle   268 τήνδ᾽ ἦλθε Hunt   Μαίας
Snell   rest Page   278 Ll.-J.   280 Pearson
281–2 suppl. ex Athen. 2, 62F   283 Diggle

164

story I am going to tell, there's a punishment in store for
you yourselves. The matter is a secret, guarded in the
seats of the gods, for fear that knowledge of it should
come to Hera. Zeus came secretly to this dwelling of
Atlas' daughter, Maia, and took her virginity . . . forgetting
the deep-girdled goddess.[a] In the cave he begot one son,
whom I am nursing in my arms, since his mother's
strength is being wasted in storms of sickness. So night
and day I stay beside the cradle, and look to his infant
needs, food and drink and rest. Every day he grows, more
than seems possible, astounding; I am amazed and fright-
ened by it! Born not six days ago, he is already thrusting
forward to the full bloom of boyhood, sprouting and
shooting up with no delay. Such is the child whom our
storeroom hides! His name is Hermes, by his father's
naming. As for the voice ringing out by a strange contriv-
ance that you ask about, . . . he contrived to make it in a
single day. From the reversed . . . creature . . . the child

[a] His wife Hera.

τοιόνδε θη[*about* 11 *letters*]αι κατωδ[
ἔμμεστον α[*about* 10 *letters*] παῖς βοῆς.

<ΧΟ.>

(*fragments of six lines*)

τος πορίζειν τοιάνδε γῆρυν.

<ΚΥ.>

μή νυν ἀπίστει· πιστὰ γάρ σε προσγελᾷ θεᾶς ἔπη.

<ΧΟ.>

καὶ πῶς πίθωμαι τοῦ θανόντος φθέγμα τοιοῦτον βρέ-
μειν;

<ΚΥ.>

300 πιθοῦ· θανὼν γὰρ ἔσχε φωνήν, ζῶν δ᾽ ἄναυδος ἦν ὁ
θήρ.

<ΧΟ.>

ποῖός τις ἦν εἶδος; προμήκης ἢ ᾽πίκυρτος ἢ βραχύς;

<ΚΥ.>

βραχύς, χυτρώδης, ποικίλῃ δορᾷ κατερρικνωμένος.

<ΧΟ.>

ὡς αἰέλουρος εἰκάσαι πέφυκεν ἢ τὼς πόρδαλις;

<ΚΥ.>

πλεῖστον μεταξύ· γογγύλον γάρ ἐστι καὶ βραχυσκελές.

<ΧΟ.>

305 οὐδ᾽ ὡς ἰχνευτῇ προσφερὲς πέφυκεν οὐδ᾽ ὡς καρκίνῳ;

<ΚΥ.>

οὐδ᾽ αὖ τοιοῦτόν ἐστιν· ἀλλ᾽ ἄλλον τιν᾽ ἐξευροῦ
τρόπον.

302 χυτρώδης Hunt: -οιδης Π

166

made such a . . . pleasure . . . full of . . . sound.

<CH.>
(*fragments*)
. . . to contrive such utterance . . .

<CY.>
Don't be so disbelieving, when a goddess greets you with
words that you can trust!

<CH.>
I can't believe that so loud a sound comes from a dead
thing!

<CY.>
You must believe it! In death the creature got a voice, in
life it had none.

<CH.>
What sort of shape had it? Long? Humped? Short?

<CY.>
Short, pot-shaped, shrivelled, with a spotted skin.

<CH.>
Was it like a cat, or like a panther?

<CY.>
Vastly different! It is round and has short legs.

<CH.>
Not like a weasel, or like a crab?

<CY.>
No, not like that either; think of some other type!

167

⟨ΧΟ.⟩

ἀλλ᾽ ὡς κεράστης κάνθαρος δῆτ᾽ ἐστὶν Αἰτναῖος φυήν;

⟨ΚΥ.⟩

νῦν ἐγγὺς ἔγνως ᾧ μάλιστα προσφερὲς τὸ κνώδαλον.

⟨ΧΟ.⟩

τ[ί δ᾽ αὖ τὸ] φων[οῦ]ν ἐστιν αὐτοῦ, τοὐντὸς ἢ τοὔξω,
φράσον.

⟨ΚΥ.⟩

310 φωνεῖ μὲν αἰό]λο[ν φ]ορίνη σύγγονος τῶν ὀστρέων.

⟨ΧΟ.⟩

ποῖον δὲ τοὔνομ᾽ ἐν]νέ[πει]ς; πόρσυνον, εἴ τι πλέον
ἔχεις.

⟨ΚΥ.⟩

τὸν θῆρα μὲν χέλυν, τὸ φωνο]ῦν δ᾽ αὖ λύραν ὁ παῖς
καλεῖ.

(fragments of twelve lines)

325 καὶ τοῦτο λύπης ἔστ᾽ ἄκεστρον καὶ παραψυκτήριον
κείνῳ μόνον, χαίρει δ᾽ ἀλύων καί τι προσφων[ῶν
μέλος.
ξύμφωνον ἐξαίρει γὰρ αὐτὸν αἰόλισμα τῆς λύρας.
οὕτως ὁ παῖς θανόντι θηρὶ φθέγμ᾽ ἐμηχανήσατο.

ΧΟ.

χερ]οψάλακτός τις ὀμφὰ κατοιχνεῖ τόπου,
330 πρεπτὰ ⟨δ᾽ ἤ⟩δη τόνου φάσματ᾽ ἔγ-
χωρ᾽ ἐπανθεμίζει.

310 Marx   τῶν ὀστρέων Wilamowitz: τωστρακεων
Π: τῶν ὀστράκων Hunt   326 ἀλύων] ἀθύρων Bucherer
329 Ll.-J.   330 Diggle

‹CH.›
Well, perhaps it is like a horned beetle, one from Etna?

‹CY.›
Now you've almost guessed what the creature most resembles!

‹CH.›
What part of it makes the noise, the inside or the outside, tell me!

‹CY.›
It is the shell that rings the changes, like that of oysters.

‹CH.›
What is the name you give it? Tell me, if you know any more!

‹CY.›
The child calls the animal a tortoise and the thing that makes the sound a lyre.

(fragments of twelve lines)

And it's all he has to cure and comfort him when he's unhappy. He enjoys being crazy and singing a song; it simply transports him to ring changes on the lyre. So that is how the child invented a voice for the dead creature!

CH.
A solemn voice, made by the hand that plucks the strings, goes forth over the land! Conspicuous now are the fantasies of sound that it scatters like flowers over the

τὸ πρᾶγμα δ᾽ οἷπερ πορεύω βάδην—
ἴσθι τὸν δαίμον᾽ ὅστις ποθ᾽ ὃς
ταῦτ᾽ ἐτεχνάσατ᾽, οὐκ ἄλλος ἐστὶν κλ[οπεὺς
335 ἀντ᾽ ἐκείνου, γύναι, σάφ᾽ ἴσθι.
σὺ δ᾽ ἀντὶ τῶνδε μὴ χαλε-
φθῇς ἐμοὶ ‹μη›δὲ δυσφορήσῃς.

⟨ΚΤ.⟩

τίς ἔχει πλά]νη σε; τίνα κλοπὴν ὠνείδισας;

⟨ΧΟ.⟩

οὐ μὰ Δία σ᾽, ὦ πρέσ]βειρα, χειμάζειν [θέλω.

⟨ΚΤ.⟩

340 μῶν τὸν Διὸς παῖδ᾽ ὄ]ντα φιλήτην κα[λεῖς;

⟨ΧΟ.⟩

ὃν γ᾽ ἄσμενος λάβοιμ᾽] ἂν αὐτῇ τῇ κλοπῇ.

⟨ΚΤ.⟩

καὶ μάλα δικαίως, ε]ἴ γε τἀληθῆ λέ[γεις.

⟨ΧΟ.⟩

ὄρθ᾽ εἶπας, ὡς ἔγωγε τ]ἀληθῆ λέγ[ω.

⟨ΚΤ.⟩

τοῦτον δὲ τὰς βοῦς κεκλο]φέναι σάφ᾽ [οἶσθα σύ;

⟨ΧΟ.⟩

345 σαφῶς ἐκεῖνος κέκλοφε τάσ]δε βοῦς πάνυ,
ὡς τοὔστρακόν που τῇ δορ]ᾷ καθήρμο[σε
(about nineteen letters)]λου τεμών

332 οἷπερ Hunt: ουπερ Π 334 -άσατ᾽ Walker: -ησατ Π
337 δυσφορήσῃς Diggle: -ηθης Π 341 Hunt (ἄσμενος
Beazley) 342–3 Ll.-J. 344 end Ll.-J. 345–6 Ll.-J.

170

place! But here's the matter to which I'm slowly bringing you! You must know, lady, that whoever the god may be who invented this, none other than he is the thief, you may be sure! Do not be angry with me for saying this! Do not take it too hard!

<CY.>

What delusion possesses you now? What is this charge of theft?

<CH.>

I swear I am unwilling to distress you, honoured lady!

<CY.>

Are you calling the son of Zeus a thief?

<CH.>

Yes! I would gladly capture him red-handed!

<CY.>

And very justly, if you are speaking the truth!

<CH.>

You are right, since it is the truth that I am speaking!

<CY.>

But do you know for certain that he stole the cows?

<CH.>

I am quite certain that it was he who stole them, since he attached the shell to the hide, after cutting . . .

(four verses missing)

⟨ΚΥ.⟩

(about 11 letters)]ἄρτι μανθάνω χρόνῳ,
πονηρέ, σ᾽ ἐγχ]άσκοντα τῆμῇ μωρίᾳ.
δρᾷς δ᾽ ὑγιὲς ο]ὐδέν, ἀλλὰ παιδιᾶς χάριν.

355 σὺ δ᾽ οὖν τὸ λοιπὸ]ν εἰς ἔμ᾽ εὐδίαν ἔχων
εἴ σοι φέρει χάρ]μ᾽ ἤ τι κερδαίνειν δοκεῖς
ὅπως θέλεις κά]χαζε καὶ τέρπου φρένα·
τὸν παῖδα δ᾽ ὄ]ντα τοῦ Διὸς σαφεῖ λόγῳ
μὴ βλάπτε κιν]ῶν ἐν νέῳ νέον λόγον.

360 οὗτος γὰρ οὔτε] πρὸς πατρὸς κλέπτης ἔφυ
οὔτ᾽ ἐγγενὴς μ]ήτρωσιν ἡ κλοπὴ κρατεῖ.
σὺ δ᾽ ἄλλοσ᾽, εἴ τ]ίς ἐστι, τὸν κλέπτην σκόπει,
σκοπὴν ἄ]καρπον· τοῦδε δ᾽ οὐπάνω δόμος
δείξ]ει γένος. πρόσαπτε τὴν πονηρίαν

365 πρὸς] ὄντιν᾽ ἥκει· τῷδε δ᾽ οὐχ οὕτω πρέπει.
ἀλλ᾽ αἰὲν εἶ σὺ παῖς· νέος γὰρ ὢν ἀνὴρ
πώγωνι θάλλων ὡς τράγος κνηκῷ χλιδᾷς.
παύου τὸ λεῖον φαλακρὸν ἡδονῇ πιτνάς.
οὐκ ἐκ θεῶν τὰ μῶρα καὶ γελοῖα χρὴ

370 χ]ανόντα κλαίειν ὕστερ᾽, ὡς ἐγὼ γελῶ.

ΧΟ.

στρέφου λυγίζου τε μύθοις, ὁποίαν θέλεις
βάξιν εὕρισκ᾽ ἀπόψηκτον· οὐ
γάρ με ταῦτα πείσεις,

354 Mekler   359–61 Pearson

(four verses missing)

⟨CY.⟩

. . . At last I understand, you villain, that you are simply
grinning at me for an idiot! You're up to no good, but all
you do you do for the sake of fun! Well, for the future, if it
gives you any pleasure or any hope of profit, laugh at me
to your heart's content, enjoy yourselves at your ease so
far as I'm concerned! Only don't slander a child who can
prove that his father is Zeus; stop inventing new charges
against a newborn child! He was not born a thief on his fa-
ther's side, and theft does not prevail among his mother's
relatives.[a] Look somewhere else for your thief, if there is
one, in your fruitless search; the ancestry of this child will
be revealed by the halls above! Fix the crime where it be-
longs; to fix it upon him is not proper! You have always
been a child; grown male as you are, with your yellow
beard, you are as lascivious as a goat. Cease to expand
your smooth phallus[b] with delight! You should not make
silly jokes and chatter, so that the gods will make you shed
tears to make me laugh.

CH.

Wriggle, twist, the tales you tell! Invent what smart re-
mark you will! Of one thing you will not persuade me,

[a] But Maia was a niece of Prometheus, that master thief!
[b] Cf. Aeschylus, *Dictyulci* 788.

---

363 Ll.-J.: τουπαναι (corrected to δ᾽ οὐπαναῖ) Π   366 εἶ σὺ
Hunt: εισι Πᶜ, ει. ι Π   367 κνηκῷ Wilamowitz: κα. κωι Π

ὅπως τὸ χρῆμ᾽ οὗτος εἰργασμένος·
375 ῥινοκόλλητον ἄλλων ἔκαρ-
ψεν βοῶν που δορὰς [ἢ] ᾽πὸ τῶν Λοξίου.
μή με τᾶ[σδ᾽ ἐ]ξ ὁδοῦ βίβαζε.

(2 lyric lines of the Chorus and
1 or 2 trimeters missing)

.]δηγυνη[
380 μανιῶν .[
ὦ παμπόνη[ρ
.].ạ τάχ᾽ ὀργα[

⟨ΧΟ.⟩

τ]ἀληθὲς εἰ.[

⟨ΚΤ.⟩

]ους γαρ[

⟨ΧΟ.⟩

385 ὁ παῖς κλο[π

⟨ΚΤ.⟩

τ[ά] τοι πονη[ρά

⟨ΧΟ.⟩

κακῶς ἀκού[

⟨ΚΤ.⟩

εἰ δ᾽ ἔστ᾽ ἀλη[θ

⟨ΧΟ.⟩

389 ο]ὐ μὴ τάδ᾽ [

(fragments of two lines of the same dialogue)

375 ἔκαρψεν read by Carden: ἔκλεψεν Hunt
385 Diggle saw that 390–4 are the beginnings of these lines

174

that he who made this thing by sticking hides together
dried the skins of any other cattle than those of Loxias!
Don't try to shift me from this path!

> (*two lines, spoken by the Chorus, and
> 1 or 2 trimeters, missing*)

... madness ... you utter villain! ... quickly ... anger ...

⟨CH.⟩

The truth ...

⟨CY.⟩

...

⟨CH.⟩

The child ... theft ...

⟨CY.⟩

Villainy ...

⟨CH.⟩

Evil repute ...

⟨CY.⟩

If it is true ...

⟨CH.⟩

... not this ...

> (*fragments of two lines*)

⟨ΚΥ.⟩

397 πο[λ]λαὶ βόες νέμουσι τ[

⟨ΧΟ.⟩

πλείους δέ γ᾽ ἤδη νῦν[

⟨ΚΥ.⟩

τίς, ὦ πόνηρ᾽, ἔχει; τί πλ[

⟨ΧΟ.⟩

400 ὁ παῖς ὃς ἔνδον ἐστὶν ἐγκεκλη[μένος.

⟨ΚΥ.⟩

τὸν παῖδα παῦσαι τὸν Διὸς[κακῶς λέγων.

⟨ΧΟ.⟩

παύοιμ᾽ ἄν, εἰ τὰς βοῦς τις ἐ[ξάγοι, λόγον.

⟨ΚΥ.⟩

ἤδη με πνίγεις καὶ σὺ χα[ὶ βόες σέθεν.

⟨ΧΟ.⟩

ἀλ]λ᾽ εἴ σε πν[ίγο]υ[σ᾽, ἐ]ξέλαυν[᾽ αὐτὰς τάχα.

397 read by Siegmann   404 Ll.-J.

After this a whole column, 26 or 27 lines, is missing; so are the first three verses of the next column. But there are small fragments of the column after that, the seventeenth column of the papyrus; Apollo returns, and makes a speech containing the words μισθός ('reward') and some part of the word ἐλεύθερος ('free').

There are forty-four small fragments of the papyrus (frr. 314a and b in Radt's edition), and three small fragments preserved in quotations (frr. 315–6 and 318 Radt).

THE SEARCHERS

⟨CY.⟩

Many cattle are grazing . . .

⟨CH.⟩

But still more were . . .

⟨CY.⟩

Villain, who has them? . . .

⟨CH.⟩

The infant who is shut up in there!

⟨CY.⟩

Stop slandering the son of Zeus!

⟨CH.⟩

I'd stop, if someone would bring out those cattle!

⟨CY.⟩

You and your cattle will be the death of me!

⟨CH.⟩

If they will be the death of you, bring them out at once!

FRAGMENTS OF KNOWN PLAYS

ΙΩΝ

This play is quoted only twice, or possibly three times. It has been conjectured to be identical with the Creusa, *q.v.*

319

ἐσθλοῦ πρὸς ἀνδρὸς πάντα γενναίως φέρειν

Orion, *Florilegium* 7, 10

ἐσθλοῦ πρὸς ἀνδρὸς F. W. Schmidt: πρὸς α. ε. cod.

320

ἐν Διὸς κήποις ἀροῦσθαι
μόνον εὐδαίμονας ὁλκούς

Stobaeus, *Anthology* 4, 39, 10 (5, 904, 6 Hense)

ὁλκούς Dieterich: ὄλβους codd.

ΚΑΜΙΚΙΟΙ

In three of the four quotations the name of this play appears as Κάμικοι *(in the fourth it appears as* Κωμικοί*). But surely it was* Καμίκιοι, *as Heringa first suggested in 1748. We may compare the common corruption of the name of Aeschylus'* Αἰτναῖαι, The Women of Etna, *to* Αἶτναι, "Etnas"; *in both cases the title must have been the name of the people of the place, not the plural of the place's name. Camicus was located in what was later the territory of Acragas. After the flight of Daedalus, Minos pursued him to the west, and found that he was living at this place, under the protection of its king Cocalus.*

178

ION

319

It is the nature of a valiant man to bear all things nobly.

320

. . . that in the gardens of the gods they plough only furrows that are fruitful.

THE MEN OF CAMICUS

Everywhere he went Minos produced a spiral shell, promising a reward to whoever could contrive to thread it. When Cocalus showed that the puzzle had been solved by tying the thread to an ant, boring a hole in the shell, and getting the ant to pass through it, Minos realised that he must be sheltering Daedalus. Cocalus promised to surrender him to Minos, but first the honoured guest had to be offered the usual privilege of being given a bath by the king's daughters, and the daughters, who were fond of Daedalus, disposed of Minos by pouring over him either boiling water or boiling pitch. If G. Pugliese Carratelli

*was right in recognising the death of Minos as the subject
of a relief in one of the metopes of the archaic temple at
Foce del Sele, near Paestum, this story is attested as early
as the early sixth century. Aristophanes wrote a play*

323

ὄρνιθος ἦλθ᾽ ἐπώνυμον
πέρδικος ἐν κλεινοῖσ᾽ Ἀθηναίων πάγοις
⟨κτανών⟩

Athenaeus, *Deipnosophists* 9, 388F

1 ἐπώνυμον Holland (with ⟨κτανών⟩ after πάγοις): ἐπώνυ-
μος cod.   2 κλεινοῖσ᾽ Ἀθηναίων] κλεινοῖσι Θησειδῶν
Mekler

324

ἁλίας στραβήλου τῆσδε, τέκνον, εἴ τινα
δυναίμεθ᾽ εὑρεῖν, ⟨ὃς διείρειεν λίνον⟩

Athenaeus, *Deipnosophists* 3, 86C

2 suppl. Nauck

326

τὴν οὔτις ᾔδειν ἐκ θεοῦ κεκρυμμένην

Et. Gen. AB = Orus B 77 Alpers

τὴν ⟨δ᾽⟩ Headlam

327

πιστοί με κωχεύουσιν ἐν φορᾷ δέμας

Hesychius, *Lexicon* κ 4905 Latte = Cyril, Madrid manu-
script, ed. Naoumides, *GRBS* 9 (1968) 285 = Et. Gud. ab, ed.
Cramer, 4, 52, 19

called Cocalus; *perhaps this parodied the play of Sopho-*
cles. Valckenaer in 1763 suggested that it was a satyr play;
he may have been right. See on Daedalus *and* Minos.

323

He came after killing a man who bore the name of a bird,
Perdix, upon the famous hills of the Athenians.[a]

[a] This was Daedalus, who killed his nephew Perdix and had to
leave Athens.

324

If we could find someone to pass the linen through this
seashell . . .[a]

[a] See the prefatory note to this play.

326

. . . she whom no one knew had been hidden by a god . . .

327

Trusty [wings?] carry my body as I am borne along.

ΚΑΣ(Σ)ΑΝΔΡΑ

See fr. 897, and cf. Adespota (TrGF vol. II) fr. 5c, a quotation from a play with this title without the author's name. The prophetess Cassandra may have been a character in the Alexander, *the* Clytemnestra, *or the* Priam.

ΚΕΡΒΕΡΟΣ

This play is quoted only once, and may well be identical with the Heracles, *q.v. One of the labours imposed by Eurystheus upon Heracles was to bring up Cerberus from the underworld.*

327a

ἀλλ' οἱ θανόντες ψυχαγωγοῦνται μόνοι

John of Sardis in Aphthonius, Progymnasmata 5 (ἐν Κερβέρῳ δὲ Σοφοκλῆς ἄλλως τῇ λέξει ἐχρήσατο· φησὶ γὰρ 'ἀλλ' . . . μόνοι· ἐπὶ γὰρ τῶν διαπορθμευομένων ὑπὸ τοῦ Χάρωνος ψυχῶν λέγεται)

ΚΗΔΑΛΙΩΝ

According to one story, Cedalion was a Naxian smith to whom Hera sent her son Hephaestus to learn his trade, and Wilamowitz thought that the infancy of Hephaestus (Ἡφαίστου τροφή) was the subject of this play. But it seems likelier that the play, which was undoubtedly satyric, told how the giant Orion assaulted Merope, daughter of Oenopion, son of Dionysus and king of Chios, and was blinded by him with the help of Dionysus and his

CASSANDRA

CERBERUS

327a

But the only spirits that are led about are those of the dead.

CEDALION

satyrs. Orion's father Poseidon had given him the gift of walking on the water, and he wandered to Lemnos, where Hephaestus gave him one of his servants, Cedalion, as guide. In obedience to an oracle he was guided by Cedalion in the direction of the rising sun, and when he met it he recovered his sight. The first part of this story is clearly suitable material for a satyr play; that the second formed part of it is less probable, but the manner of Orion's recovery of his sight may have been predicted.

183

328

καὶ δή τι καὶ παρεῖκα τῶν ἀρτυμάτων
ὑπὸ τοῦ δέατος

Herodian, *On Anomalous Words* 30, 17

329

μαστιγίαι, κέντρωνες, ἀλλοτριοφάγοι

Athenaeus, *Deipnosophists* 4, 164A

330

τοῖς μὲν λόγοις τοῖς σοῖσιν οὐ τεκμαίρομαι
οὐ μᾶλλον ἢ λευκῷ ‹’ν› λίθῳ λευκῇ στάθμη.

Schol. bTW on Plato, *Charmides* 154B = Gregory of Cyprus,
cod. Leid. 2, 67

2 ‹’ν› inserted here by Postgate, before λευκῷ by Bergk

ΚΛΥΤΑΙΜΗΣΤΡΑ

*There is only one quotation, and we know nothing of
the plot; the play might be identical with the* Iphigeneia.

334

τὸν δ’ ἀνταῖον περιδινεύοντ’
οὐ ‹καθ›ορᾶτε

Erotian, *Medical Lexicon* α 46 Nachmanson

1 τὸν δ’ Heath: τὸν δὲ codd.: τόνδ’ Burges   2 περιδι-
νεύοντ’ Burges: περιδινέοντα codd.   suppl. Pearson

CEDALION

328

Then suppose I left out some of the condiments, out of
fear . . .

329

Villains, robbers, eaters of other men's food . . .

330

I can deduce nothing from your words, any more than
from a white measuring line against a white stone.

CLYTEMNESTRA

334

But you do not see (*or* do you not see . . .?) the enemy
hovering about.

ΚΟΛΧΙΔΕΣ

This play dealt with the adventures of Jason in Colchis which culminated in his capture of the Golden Fleece. A scholion on Apollonius Rhodius 3, 1040c tells us that the play contained a dialogue between Medea and Jason in which she gave him instructions regarding the task which Aeetes required him to perform. Fr. 339 was doubtless spoken by Medea to Jason, probably in the course of that dialogue, and in fr. 341 a messenger is describing to Aeetes Jason's performance of the task. From other scholia on

337

ἀπῆξε πέμφιξ Ἰονίου πέλας πόρου

Galen on Hippocrates, *Epidemics* VI 1, 29

πέμφιξ Ἰονίου πέλας πόρου Bentley (confirmed by the Arabic translation): πέμφιξιν οὐ πέλας φόρου cod.

338

κἂν ἐθαύμασα⟨ς⟩
τηλέσκοπον πέμφιγα χρυσέαν ἰδών

Galen on Hippocrates, *Epidemics* VI 1, 29

1 suppl. Hermann (confirmed by the Arabic translation)
2 τηλέσκοπον Bentley: τῇ δὲ σκοπῆ᾽ cod.

339

ἦ φῂς ὑπομνὺς ἀνθυπουργῆσαι χάριν;

Synagoge 404, 19 = Suda α 2542 = Photius 1990 Theodoridis

THE WOMEN OF COLCHIS

*Apollonius we learn that Medea's brother Apsyrtus was
a child in this play, and was killed not during the pur-
suit of the Argo by the Colchians, as in Apollonius, but in
his father's palace. From a scholion on the* Prometheus
Bound *we learn that in this play of Sophocles the story of
Prometheus was treated in a digression (see fr. 340). In
Apollonius (3, 845 f) a herb called Prometheion was given
by Medea to Jason, and this incident probably occasioned
Sophocles' mention of the Prometheus story. See on*
Σκύθαι *and* Ῥιζοτόμοι, *and cf. fr. 1135.*

337

The wind came rushing near the Ionian sea.

338

You would have wondered at the sight of the golden glow,
visible far off.[a]

 [a] Presumably this refers to the Golden Fleece.

339

Do you swear that you will return one favour for another?[a]

 [a] Medea doubtless said this to Jason.

340

ὑμεῖς μὲν οὐκ ἄρ' ἦστε τὸν Προμηθέα

Et. Gen. A = Et. Magn. 439, 2 = Orus B 77 Alpers

341

ΑΙΗΤΗΣ

ἦ βλαστὸς οὐκ ἔβλαστεν οὑπιχώριος;

ΑΓΓΕΛΟΣ

καὶ κάρτα· φρίξας γ' εὐλόφῳ σφηκώματι
χαλκηλάτοις ὅπλοισι μητρὸς ἐξέδυ.

Schol. LP on Apollonius of Rhodes 3, 1354–56a; Hesychius, *Lexicon* φ 892 (φρίξας . . . σφηκώματι)

2 κάρτα] κρᾶτα Bergk   σφηκώματι Valckenaer: σφη-
νώματι Schol. P: σφηκώμενα Schol. L: σηκώματι Hesychius
3 μητρὸς ἐξέδυ Rutgers: μὴ προσεξέδυ codd.

345

μηροῖς ὑπαίθων τὴν Διὸς τυραννίδα

Athenaeus, *Deipnosophists* 3, 602E

346

καλὸν φρονεῖν τὸν θνητὸν ἀνθρώποις ἴσα

Stobaeus, *Anthology* 3, 22, 23 (3, 589, 8 Hense)

ΚΡΕΟΥΣΑ

See on the Ion, *which may well have been the same play. We do not know the plot; but it seems likely that the play was named not after the wife of Aeneas or the Corinthian princess destroyed by Medea and by some*

340

Then you did not know that . . . Prometheus . . .

341

AEETES

Did not the brood native to the land start up?

MESSENGER

Indeed it did! They bristled with plumed helmets as with arms of bronze they came up out of their mother.

345

. . . warming with his thighs the royal might of Zeus[a] . . .

[a] Athenaeus tells us that this referred to Ganymedes.

346

It is fitting for a mortal to think like human beings.

CREUSA

called Glauce, but after the daughter of Erechtheus, wife of Xuthus and mother of Ion who figures in Euripides' Ion. *Not that it is safe to assume that the plot closely resembled that of the Euripidean play; one suspects that Sophocles presented the story in a different fashion.*

350

ταῦτ᾽ ἐστὶν ἄλγιστ᾽, ἣν παρὸν θέσθαι καλῶς
αὐτός τις αὑτῷ τὴν βλάβην προσθῇ φέρων

Stobaeus, *Anthology* 3, 4, 37 (3, 229, 1 Hense)

351

ὅστις δὲ τόλμῃ πρὸς τὸ δεινὸν ἔρχεται,
ὀρθὴ μὲν ἡ γλῶσσ᾽ ἐστίν, ἀσφαλὴς δ᾽ ὁ νοῦς

Stobaeus, *Anthology* 3, 7, 7 (3, 309, 15 Hense)

352

καλὸν μὲν οὖν οὐκ ἔστι τὰ ψευδῆ λέγειν·
ὅτῳ δ᾽ ὄλεθρον δεινὸν ἀλήθει᾽ ἄγει,
συγγνωστὸν εἰπεῖν ἐστι καὶ τὸ μὴ καλόν

Stobaeus, *Anthology* 3, 12, 4 (3, 444, 10 Hense)

353

ΧΟΡΟΣ

οὔτε γὰρ γάμον, ὦ φίλαι,
οὔτ᾽ ἂν ὄλβον ἔκμετρον
ἔνδον εὐξαίμαν ἔχειν·
φθονεραὶ γὰρ ὁδοί

Stobaeus, *Anthology* 3, 38, 26 (3, 713, 6 Hense)

354

καὶ μή τι θαυμάσῃς με τοῦ κέρδους, ἄναξ,
ὧδ᾽ ἀντέχεσθαι. καὶ γὰρ οἳ πλοῦτον μακρὸν
θνητῶν ἔχουσι, τοῦ γε κερδαίνειν ὅμως

350

The most painful thing of all happens when one could have arranged things neatly, but brings the damage over to oneself.

351

Whoever approaches danger boldly talks straight and his purpose is not shaken.

352

Telling lies is not honourable; but if the truth means grim ruin for you, even what is dishonourable may be forgiven.

353

CHORUS

I would not pray, friends, to have a marriage or a wealth beyond my measure; for the paths of envy . . .

354

And do not be surprised, my lord, if I hold on to my profit as I do! For even mortals who have great wealth grasp at

FRAGMENTS OF KNOWN PLAYS

ἀπρὶξ ἔχονται, κἄστι πρὸς τὰ χρήματα
5 θνητοῖσι τἆλλα δεύτερ'. εἰσὶ δ' οἵτινες
αἰνοῦσιν ἄνοσον ἄνδρ'· ἐμοὶ δ' οὐδεὶς δοκεῖ
εἶναι πένης ὢν ἄνοσος, ἀλλ' ἀεὶ νοσεῖν.

Stobaeus, *Anthology* 4, 31, 28 (5, 742, 1 Hense)

2 πλοῦτον μακρὸν (or βαθὺν βίον) Meineke: μακρὸν βίον
codd.

355
τί δ', ὦ γεραιέ; τίς σ' ἀναπτεροῖ φόβος;

Photius α 1614 Theodoridis

356
κάλλιστόν ἐστι τοὔνδικον πεφυκέναι,
λῷστον δὲ τὸ ζῆν ἄνοσον, ἥδιστον δ' ὅτῳ
πάρεστι λῆψις ὧν ἐρᾷ καθ' ἡμέραν

Stobaeus, *Anthology* 4, 39, 15 (5, 905, 10 Hense)

357
ἄπελθ', ἄπελθε, παῖ· τάδ' οὐκ ἀκουστά σοι

Synagoge 373, 5 = Photius α 818 Theodoridis

profit, and for human beings all other things rank after money. There are those who exalt the man who is free from sickness, but I think that no poor man is free from sickness; the poor man is always sick.

355

What is that, aged man? What fear makes you nervous?

356

The most honourable thing is to be just; the best thing is a life free from sickness; but the most delightful thing is the power each day to take hold of what one desires.[a]

   [a] This is a rendering into iambic trimeters of a famous elegiac couplet inscribed on Apollo's temple at Delphi and quoted by Aristotle, *Nicomachean Ethics* 1, 9 1099a 25.

357

Away with you, boy, away with you! You must not hear these things!

ΚΡΙΣΙΣ

Athenaeus 15, 687C tells us that this play dealt with the Judgment of Paris, in which Paris, then a shepherd, not known to be Priam's son, had to award the prize for beauty that was disputed between Hera, Athena and Aphrodite. It was a satyr play. Aphrodite, Athenaeus says, represented Pleasure, appearing anointed with myrrh and looking at herself in a mirror; Athena represented Thought and Mind, and also Excellence, anointing herself

360

καὶ δὴ φάρει τῷδ᾽ ὡς ἐμῷ καλύπτομαι

Herodian, *On Words with Two Quantities* 2, 15, 31 Lentz

ΚΩΦΟΙ

The plot of this satyr play is unknown. But we know from the ancient commentary on Nicander (on Theriaca *343–54, p. 150, 1 Crugnola) that it told the story that men informed Zeus that it was Prometheus who had given them fire, and that in return Zeus gave them immortality. But the immortality, which is conceived as a material substance, was packed on the back of an ass, which on its journey became thirsty. Trying to drink at a spring, it was prevented by the spring's guardian snake, and bought permission to drink by handing over its burden. From the play's mention of this story, some have inferred that it dealt with Prometheus, but the inference is hardly safe. The play also mentioned the Idaean Dactyls, dwarfish figures said to have invented iron and associated with the*

THE JUDGMENT

with oil and taking exercise. Hera, if as it seems safe to presume the usual story was followed, represented regal power. We find very much the same picture of the Judgment in Callimachus' Fifth Hymn (15 f) The Judgment is mentioned in the Iliad *(24, 27–30), and was described in the* Cypria. *It is a frequent theme in Euripides, on whose treatment of it see Stinton, cited in the prefatory note on the* Ἀλέξανδρος. *See on the* Ἔρις, *which may have been the same play.*

360

See, I am covering myself with this cloak as though it were my own!

THE DUMB ONES

eastern cult of the Mother of the Gods, often identified with Zeus' mother Rhea. Sometimes they are associated with Mount Ida near Troy, sometimes with Mount Ida in Crete; Sophocles placed them in the former locality. Various authorities differ as to their number, but according to Strabo Sophocles said that there were originally five male ones, and later five sisters; this would explain their name, there being five fingers on each hand. Sophocles is said to have mentioned one of them named Celmis, who was punished for having insulted Rhea. Being workers in metal, they have something in common with Prometheus, and might figure in a play about him. For the Greeks as for us, "dumb" might mean "stupid," and that may help to explain the play's mysterious title. A didascalic notice indi-

*cates that the play was produced as early as the sixties of
the fifth century; see Snell,* TrGF *I DID C 6.*

On the legend, see M.D. Reeve, Acta Academiae
Hungaricae *37 (1996–7), 245–58.*

ΛΑΚΑΙΝΑΙ

According to Proclus' summary of the Little Iliad
(Davies, Epicorum Graecorum Fragmenta, *p. 52) Odys-
seus made his way secretly into Troy, was recognised by
Helen and "made an agreement with her about the taking
of the city", and finally after killing some Trojans returned
to the ships. Later he went there again with Diomedes to
steal the Palladium, the image of Athena which the Greeks
had to get possession of if they were to take the city.*

367

στενὴν δ᾽ ἔδυμεν ψαλίδα κοὐκ ἀβόρβορον

Pollux, *Vocabulary* 9, 49 (2, 160, 1 Bethe)

ἀβόρβορον Blomfield: ἀβάρβαρον codd.

368

θεοὶ γὰρ οὔποτ᾽, εἴ τι χρὴ βροτὸν λέγειν,
ἄρξασι Φρυξὶ τὴν κατ᾽ Ἀργείους ὕβριν
ξυναινέσονται ταῦτα· μὴ μάχου βίᾳ

Priscian, *Institutions* 18, 197 (2, 302, 13 Hertz)

3 colon placed before ταῦτα by Madvig

THE LACONIAN WOMEN

Fr. 367 clearly refers to the story mentioned by Servius on Virgil, Aeneid 2, *166 that Odysseus and Diomedes got out of Troy by way of a sewer; and fr. 368 is thought to come from a speech made by one of the pair to Theano, the priestess of Athena, to persuade her to hand over the statue. The Laconian women of the title must have been attendants who had accompanied Helen to Troy from Sparta. See fr. 799.*

367

And we entered a narrow sewer, not free of mud.

368

For the gods will never approve this, if a mortal may pronounce a word, when the Phrygians have begun it with outrage against the Argives. Use no force to fight against it!

ΛΑΟΚΟΩΝ

The Sack of Troy *by Arctinus told how after the wooden horse had been brought into the city the Trojans gave themselves up to celebration, thinking that the war was over. Then two serpents appeared and devoured Laocoon, the priest of Poseidon, with one of his sons. Aeneas and his family, alarmed by the portent, then removed themselves to Mount Ida. No poet except Virgil (*Aeneid 2,

370

λάμπει δ' ἀγνιεὺς βωμὸς ἀτμίζων πυρὶ
σμύρνης σταλαγμούς, βαρβάρους εὐοσμίας

Harpocration, *Glossary to the Ten Orators* 8, 8 = Photius 279
Theodoridis = Suda α 383, etc.

371

Πόσειδον, ὃς Αἰγαίου
νέμεις πρῶνας ἢ γλαυκᾶς
μέδεις ἁλὸς ἐν βένθεσ‹σ›ιν
εὐανέμου λίμνας
ἐφ' ὑψηλαῖς σπιλάδεσσι
†στομάτων†

Aristophanes, *Frogs* 665 with Schol.

2 νέμεις Fritzsche: μέδεις Schol.: om. Aristophanes
3 ἁλὸς ἐν βένθεσι Aristophanes: om. Schol.
4–6 om. Aristophanes

LAOCOON

199 f) says that both sons were killed, though some have conjectured that because Dionysius of Halicarnassus seems to imply this Sophocles must have done so. The serpents were named Porces and Chariboea, and came from the islands called Calydnae; they were mentioned by Bacchylides fr. 9, who said that they were changed into humans. According to a papyrus commentary on a play (Trag. Adesp. fr. 721), they were sent by Apollo.

370

And fire shines on the altar in the street as it sends up a vapour from drops of myrrh, exotic scents.

371

Poseidon, you who range over the capes of the Aegean or in the depths of the gray sea rule over the windswept waters above the lofty cliffs . . .

373

ΑΓΓΕΛΟΣ

νῦν δ' ἐν πύλαισιν Αἰνέας ὁ τῆς θεοῦ
πάρεστ', ἐπ' ὤμων πατέρ' ἔχων κεραυνίου
μοτοῦ καταστάζοντα βύσσινον φάρος,
κύκλῳ δὲ πᾶσαν οἰκετῶν παμπληθίαν·
5 συνοπάζεται δὲ πλῆθός οἱ πόσον δοκεῖς,
οἳ τῆσδ' ἐρῶσι τῆς ἀποικίας Φρυγῶν

Dionysius of Halicarnassus, *History of Early Rome* 1, 48, 2;
line 3 Plutarch, *Virtue and Vice* 2, 100D

2 κεραυνίου] -άνιον Reiske   3 μότου (with that accent) Plutarch: νώτου Dionysius   4 κύκλῳ B: κυκλεῖ cett.
5 συνοπάζεται Dion. Hal. (Stephanus edition): συμπλάζεται codd. πλῆθός οἱ πόσον Herwerden: πλῆθος οὐχ ὅσον codd.
δοκεῖς οἱ Reiske: δοκεῖ σοι codd.

374

κόπου μεταλλαχθέντος οἱ πόνοι γλυκεῖς

Stobaeus, *Anthology* 3, 29, 38 (3, 635, 3 Hense)

κόπου Ellendt: πόνου codd.

375

μόχθου γὰρ οὐδεὶς τοῦ παρελθόντος λόγος

Stobaeus, *Anthology* 3, 29, 37 (3, 635, 1 Hense)

ΛΑΡΙΣΑΙΟΙ

See on Danae; *this play must have been about the
death of Acrisius. According to one story, the games at
Larissa in which Perseus was competing when he acciden-*

LAOCOON

373

MESSENGER

And now at the gates stands Aeneas, the son of the goddess, carrying on his shoulders his father with his linen robe stained with the discharge caused by the lightning,[a] and about him the whole horde of his servants. And with him follows a crowd, you cannot imagine how great, of those who are eager to take part in this migration of the Phrygians.

[a] Anchises, father of Aeneas, was struck by lightning for having boasted of his intercourse with Aphrodite.

374

When one is no longer weary, labours are delightful.

375

For one takes no account of trouble that is in the past.[a]

[a] Frr. 374 and 375 may well belong together.

THE MEN OF LARISSA

tally killed his grandfather were given by the local king, Teutamidas; according to another, they were given by Acrisius himself.

378

πολὺν δ᾿ ἀγῶνα πάγξενον κηρύσσεται,
χαλκηλάτους λέβητας ἐκτιθεὶς φέρειν,
καὶ κοῖλα χρυσόκολλα καὶ πανάργυρα
ἐκπώματ᾿, εἰς ἀριθμὸν ἐξήκοντα δίς

Athenaeus, *Deipnosophists* 11, 466B; Eustathius *Il.* 1319, 47 (lines 3–4)

1 πάγξενον Schweighäuser: -α codd.

379

Λάρισα μήτηρ προσγόνων Πελασγίδων

Geneva Scholia, *Il.* 21, 319

Πελασγίδων Diels: -δᾶν cod.

380

καί μοι τρίτον ῥίπτοντι Δωτιεὺς ἀνὴρ
ἀγχοῦ προσῆψεν Ἔλατος ἐν δισκήματι

Stephanus of Byzantium, *Ethnica* 257, 3 Meineke

381

μηδὲ τῷ τεθνηκότι
τὸν ζῶντ᾿ ἐπαρκεῖν αὐτὸν ὡς θανούμενον

Stobaeus, *Anthology* 4, 57, 10 (5, 1139, 6 Hense)

1 μηδὲ] χρὴ δὲ Gesner
2 ἐπαρκεῖν] ἐπαυχεῖν Tyrwhitt

378

And he is causing to be proclaimed a great contest, where all shall be entertained, setting out as prizes brazen cauldrons and vessels overlaid with gold, and cups of solid silver, twice sixty in all.

379

Larissa, mother of our kindred the Pelasgians . . .

380

As I threw the third time a man from Dotium called Elatus stood close to me as I hurled the quoit.[a]

[a] Very likely Perseus was the speaker.

381

. . . and the living man should not assist the dead when he is going to die himself.

ΛΗΜΝΙΑΙ Α΄ and Β΄

There were two versions of this play, or, less probably, two separate plays on the same theme. The play appears to have described the landing of the Argonauts on Lemnos while the island was ruled by the women, who had killed all the men; the story is told by Apollonius of Rhodes, 1, 609 f. The women had offended Aphrodite, who punished them by making them smell unpleasant, so that their husbands deserted them in favour of Thracian concubines.

384

ὦ Λῆμνε Χρύσης τ᾽ ἀγχιτέρμονες πάγοι

Stephanus of Byzantium, *Ethnica* 696, 16 Meineke

386

Φερητίδης τ᾽ Ἄδμητος ἠδ᾽ ὁ Δωτιεὺς
Λαπίθης Κόρωνος

Stephanus of Byzantium, *Ethnica* 257, 5 Meineke

387

ἄπλατον ἀξύμβλητον ἐξεθρεψάμην

Synagoge 413, 13 = Photius 2184 Theodoridis

388

τάχ᾽ αὐτὸ δείξει τοὖργον, οἶδ᾽ ἐγὼ σαφῶς

Schol. T on Plato, *Hippias major* 288B

τάχ᾽ Meineke: ταχὺ δ᾽ cod.   οἶδ᾽ Bergk: ὡς cod.

THE WOMEN OF LEMNOS 1 *and* 2

The women then murdered all the men except the king,
Thoas, whom his daughter Hypsipyle, who now reigned as
queen, secretly smuggled out. The women at first resisted
the landing of the Argonauts, but later joined them in a
"love-in." Hypsipyle had two sons by Jason. The subject
had featured in an Aeschylean trilogy; and the later ad-
ventures of the queen were described by Euripides in his
Hypsipyle, *of which we have considerable fragments.*

384

Lemnos and neighbouring hills of Chryse!

386

And Pheres' son Admetus and the Lapith from Dotium,
Coronus[a] . . .

[a] This probably comes from the catalogue of Argonauts which
we are told the play contained.

387

. . . the creature unapproachable, inexplicable, which I
reared.[a]

[a] Perhaps spoken of Hypsipyle by her old nurse Polyxo.

388

The action itself will soon show it, as I know for certain.

ΜΑΝΤΕΙΣ *or* ΠΟΛΤΙΔΟΣ

The story is told by both Apollodorus and Hyginus; it was also the subject of Aeschylus' Cretan Women *and Euripides'* Polyidus. *Glaucus, the young son of Minos, fell into a great jar full of honey and was suffocated. His father, not knowing what had become of him, was told by Apollo's oracle, or by the Curetes, that the child would be restored by whoever could find the aptest object of comparison to a cow which he possessed which in a single day was alternately white, red, and black. Many prophets tried but failed to do this, but the Argive Polyidus thought of the mulberry. By augury he found the child's body; Claudian,* Bellum Geticum *443 f says that he found it* avium clangore *(through the clamour of birds), which seems to be confirmed by fr. 389b. But Minos then*

Ed. pr. of P.Oxy. 2453: Turner, *P.Oxy.* xxvii (1963), with Plate III. See Ll.-J., *Gnomon* 35 (1963) 436; Carden, *PFS* 135 f, 152; Radt 338 f.

389a (=1133, 44 Radt)

ΠΟΛΤΙΔΟΣ

ὦ φ[ῶς ποθεινὸ]ν ἡλίου ̣[
ὥσ[. . . .] ̣ ̣ ̣ν τέρψιν [
νῦν [̣] ̣σκοποῦμαι χώ ̣[
ὡς ἄσμενός σ᾽ἐσεῖδον ̣[
5   οὐ γὰρ πατὴρ ἐσεῖδε π[
(scraps of seven lines)

P.Oxy. 2453 fr. 44

1 Ll.-J.

THE PROPHETS *or* POLYIDUS

demanded that he should restore it to life, and shut him up in a tomb together with the corpse. A snake appeared, which Polyidus killed; another snake then approached it with a particular herb and brought it back to life. Polyidus then tried the herb on Glaucus, with success. Minos insisted that before he left he should teach his art to Glaucus, but just before leaving he told Glaucus to spit into Polyidus' mouth, and in this way the boy lost the gift.

Turner's suggestion that this was a satyr play was based on an uncertain restoration of fr. 389b; but it may well be right. It would help to explain the title Μάντεις, *since a chorus consisting of prophets would be more surprising than a chorus of satyrs pretending to be prophets in the hope of gaining a reward.*

Fr. 389a and b come from the same papyrus as fr. 1130; see also fr. 133.

389a

POLYIDUS

O longed-for light of the sun . . . how . . . delight. . . . I now look on. . . . With what joy did I behold you. . . . For no father ever beheld. . . .[a]

[a] The sentence probably ran something like this: For no father ever beheld an only son returning after long absence with such joy.

389b (=1133, 45 Radt)

]…[…]ειλ.[
  ]νορος [
  ]..αυλαγενη[
  ].ελουσα.φιπ…[
  ]λα δὲ τῶν αἰθερίων [
  ]οῦσσα πλᾶξις οἰωνῶν [
  π]οικίλος κέκλαγγεν [
  ].ῳ κρόκῳ λοπίζων [
  ].ων κατὰ σηκὸν οικε.[
  ].´.τις ἁμι. [γ]ενέτωρ [
  ]οικος ἔξω.[.]ο.ων[

5

10

P. Oxy. 2453, fr. 45

390

ὁρῶ πρόχειρον Πολυΐδου τοῦ μάντεως

Et. Gud. = *Lexicon of Cyril* (*Anecd. Paris.* 4, 188, 25 = Et. Gen. AB)

391

οὐκ ἔστιν εἰ μὴ Πολυΐδῳ τῷ Κοιράνου

See on 390

392

Ξάνθας Φαμενὸς <καὶ> Τειρεσίου
παῖς

Herodian, *On Anomalous Words* 8, 27

Ξάνθας Radt: Ξανθὰς cod.   <καὶ> Nauck

389b

(5 f) . . . the beating of the wings . . . of birds of the air . . .
subtly varied, has rung out[a] . . . yolk . . . shelling (an egg)
. . . in the precinct . . . father . . . house . . .

[a] See the prefatory note to this play.

390

I see ready to hand the . . . of the prophet Polyidus.

391

It is . . . except to Polyidus the son of Coeranus.

392

Phamenus the son of Xantha and Tiresias . . .

393

ψυχῆς ἀνοῖξαι τὴν κεκλημένην πύλην

Epimerismi Homerici (*Anecdota Oxoniensia* 1, 226, 5)

κεκλημένην Sauppe: κεκλημένην cod.

395

πρῶτον μὲν ὄψῃ λευκὸν ἀνθοῦντα στάχυν,
ἔπειτα φοινίξαντα γογγύλον μόρον,
τέλος δὲ γῆρας λαμβάνει σφ' Αἰγύπτιον

Synagoge 361, 19 = Photius 514 Theodoridis

3 τέλος δὲ Nauck: ἔπειτα codd.

397

οὗτοι ποθ' ἅψει τῶν ἄκρων ἄνευ πόνου

Stobaeus, *Anthology* 3, 29, 25 (3, 632, 2 Hense)

ἅψει O. Schneider: ἥξει codd.

398

ἦν μὲν γὰρ οἰὸς μαλλός, ἦν δ' ⟨ἀπ'⟩ ἀμπέλου
σπονδή τε καὶ ῥὰξ εὖ τεθησαυρισμένη·
ἐνῆν δὲ παγκάρπεια συμμιγής, ὀλαὶ
λίπος τ' ἐλαίας καὶ τὸ ποικιλώτατον
5 ξουθῆς μελίσσης κηρόπλαστον ὄργανον

Porphyry, *On Abstinence* 2, 19 (148, 17 Nauck); Clement of Alexandria, *Miscellanies* 4, 2, 6, 2 (2, 250, 15 Stählin); Schol. MTAB on Eur., *Phoenissae* 114 (line 5)

1 suppl. Tucker   3 ὀλαὶ M. L. West: ὅλαις (with that accent) codd.

393

To open the closed door of the mind . . .

395

First you will see a crop in flower, all white; then a round mulberry that has turned red; lastly old age of Egyptian blackness takes it over.[a]

[a] See the prefatory note to this play.

397

You will never attain to the heights without labour.

398

For there was the fleece of a sheep, there was a libation from the vine and grapes carefully treasured, and there was a mixture of all kinds of fruit, barley and the juice of the olive and the fabric of moulded wax, cunningly made by the tawny bee.

399

ὁ πρόσθεν ἐλθὼν ἦν ἀραῖός μοι νέκυς

Hesychius, *Lexicon* α 6947 Latte

400

καὶ δεῖμα προσπεσὸν τόδ᾽ ἀνταίας θεοῦ

Erotian, *Medical Lexicon* α 46 Nachmanson

προσπεσὸν τόδ᾽ Ll.-J.: προσπέοντα codd.

ΜΕΛΕΑΓΡΟΣ

In telling the story of Meleager in the ninth book of the Iliad (527 f), Homer mentions (575) that the embassy sent to Meleager by the elders of Calydon urging him to defend the city consisted of the leading priests (θεῶν ἱερῆας ἀρίστους). A scholion on this passage tells us that because of this Sophocles made the chorus in his play Meleager *consist of priests; and this suggests that in a general way Sophocles followed Homer's version of the story. One wonders whether like Phrynichus fr. 6 Snell and Aeschylus,* The Libation-Bearers *603 f, but unlike Homer, Sophocles used the story that Meleager's mother*

401

συὸς μέγιστον χρῆμ᾽ ἐπ᾽ Οἰνέως γύαις
ἀνῆκε Λητοῦς παῖς ἑκηβόλος θεά

Lucian, *Symposium* 25

399

The first that came was a corpse that brought a curse on me.[a]

[a] It is conjectured that this refers to the first of the two snakes (see prefatory note above); the guilt felt by Polyidus was presumably removed when the snake was restored to life.

400

And this terror of the adverse goddess that had fallen upon me . . .

MELEAGER

Althaea caused his death by throwing on the fire the brand that had to be preserved if he was to survive. Phrynichus had told that story in his Women of Pleuron, *and Aeschylus may have told it in his* Atalanta. *Did Atalanta figure in Sophocles' play? Fr. 1111, from which we learn that Sophocles called Atalanta* φίλανδρος, *fond of men, might suggest it. Both Euripides and the Roman tragedian Accius wrote plays called* Meleager; *the resemblance of fr. 402 to Accius V 2* (pro se quisque cum corona clarum conestat caput) *may indicate that his play was based on that of Sophocles.*

401

A boar, a mighty creature, was let loose by Leto's far-darting daughter against the fields of Oeneus.

FRAGMENTS OF KNOWN PLAYS

402

στεφάνοισι κρᾶτα καταμπυκοῖς

Photius 1256 Theodoridis

στεφάνοισι . . . καταμπυκοῖς Reitzenstein: -ουσι . . .
-πύκοις cod.

ΜΕΜΝΩΝ

See on Αἰθίοπες

ΜΙΝΩΣ

See on Δαίδαλος, Θησεύς, Καμίκιοι

407

οὐκ ἔστι τοῖς μὴ δρῶσι σύμμαχος τύχη

Clement of Alexandria, *Miscellanies* 6, 2, 10, 7 (2, 430, 1
Stählin)

ΜΟΥΣΑΙ

See on Θαμύρας

407a

ψέλια, τιάρας καὶ σισυρνώδη στολήν

Pollux, *Vocabulary* 10, 186 (2, 246, 5 Bethe)

ψέλια Pearson: ψαλίδας codd.

MELEAGER

402

You cover your head with a wreath.[a]

[a] See the prefatory note above.

MEMNON

See on The Ethiopians

MINOS

See on Daedalus, Theseus, Men of Camicus

407

Fortune does not fight on the side of those who take no action.

THE MUSES

See on Thamyras

407a

. . . armlets, Persian caps, and the short-sleeved coat[a] . . .

[a] It is possible that this fragment really belongs not to the *Muses,* but to the *Mysians.*

FRAGMENTS OF KNOWN PLAYS

ΜΥΣΟΙ

See on The Sons of Aleus; *this play is likely to have belonged to the trilogy about Telephus. Aristotle mentions a tragedy in which occurred the famous silence of Telephus throughout his journey from Tegea, where he had incurred pollution by killing his uncles, all the way to*

409

ὡς τοῖς κακῶς πράσσουσιν ἡδὺ καὶ βραχὺν
χρόνον λαθέσθαι τῶν παρεστώτων κακῶν

Stobaeus, *Anthology* 3, 26, 4 (3, 610, 7 Hense)

410

ἄμοχθος γὰρ οὐδείς· ὁ δ᾽ ἥκιστ᾽ ἔχων
μακάρτατος

Stobaeus, *Anthology* 4, 34, 22 (5, 833, 7 Hense)

411

Ἀσία μὲν ἡ σύμπασα κλῄζεται, ξένε,
πόλις δὲ Μυσῶν Μυσία προσήγορος

Strabo, *Geography* 8, 3, 31 p. 356C

412

πολὺς δὲ Φρὺξ τρίγωνος ἀντίσπαστά τε
Λυδῆς ἐφυμνεῖ πηκτίδος συγχορδία

Athenaeus, *Deipnosophists* 4, 183E; id., 14, 635B

2 συγχορδία Musurus: -αι codd.

THE MYSIANS

Mysia. Aeschylus and Euripides both wrote plays about Telephus, and some have argued that the play Aristotle speaks of cannot be that of Sophocles, because of fr. 411; but obviously Telephus would have spoken after he got there.

409

. . . since for the unfortunate it is delightful even for a short time to forget the woes that are with them.

410

No one is without troubles, and he who has the least is the most fortunate.

411

The whole country is called Asia, stranger, and the Mysians' community is called Mysia.

412

. . . and there is many a Phrygian trigonon, and the harmonious tuning of the Lydian pectis resounds with doubly twanged notes.[a]

[a] The trigonon and the pectis are both a kind of harp; see Maas and Snyder, *Stringed Instruments of Ancient Greece* 147 f and 150 f.

ΜΩΜΟΣ

There are six quotations from this play, one of which shows that it was a satyr play. We do not know what its plot was, but it is a fair surmise that it involved the story, told in the early epic Cypria, *that Zeus wished to reduce the population of the earth, and at first thought of doing so by means of thunderbolts or of a flood, but changed his mind and decided to go down to earth and beget a beauti-*

ΝΑΥΠΛΙΟΣ ΚΑΤΑΠΛΕΩΝ *and* ΝΑΥΠΛΙΟΣ ΠΥΡΚΑΕΥΣ

Nauplius was the son of Poseidon by Amymone, one of the daughters of Danaus, and was by his wife Clymene the father of Palamedes. Palamedes, often said to have been the inventor of the alphabet, of numbers, and of other useful devices, was the main rival of Odysseus as a man of cunning, and was hated by him because he had unmasked the pretence of madness by which Odysseus had tried to avoid taking part in the expedition to Troy. Odysseus trumped up a charge against him and caused him to be put to death (see on the Palamedes), *and the dead man's father, Nauplius, came to the Greek camp to demand justice. When his demand was refused, he first used his celebrated skill as a navigator to sail round the homes of the various Greek heroes and encourage their wives to commit adultery. The wives of Agamemnon, Diomedes and Idomeneus responded to his suggestions, with unfortunate consequences for their husbands when they returned home. When the Greeks were sailing home from Troy, Nauplius lighted a beacon on Cape Caphereus,*

MOMUS

ful daughter over whom men would fight, with the desired result. According to a scholion on Homer, Iliad 1, 5 *Zeus took this decision on the advice of Momos, the personification of fault-finding, who had criticised his original proposal. One wonders if the encounter with Leda, resulting in the birth of Helen, which was the consequence of Zeus' decision, figured in the play.*

NAUPLIUS SAILS IN *and*
NAUPLIUS LIGHTS A FIRE

at the southern tip of Euboea, near some of the most dangerous rocks of the Mediterranean. Thinking this to indicate a safe refuge, a number of the Greeks sailed their ships on to the rocks and perished. There is a story that Nauplius himself finally met his end as the victim of some other wrecker; for another story about him, see on the Aleadae. *A fragmentary hypothesis on papyrus seems to summarise the* καταπλέων: *it is printed below as fr. 434a.*

Four quotations (frr. 425–428) name the καταπλέων, *three (429–431) the* πυρκαεύς, *and six simply the* Ναύπλιος. *Possibly there was only one play, but probably there were two. Some think that the* καταπλέων *dealt with Nauplius' visit to the Greek camp to demand justice; others that it described his voyage around Greece to corrupt his enemies' wives. But the title* πυρκαεύς *seems to indicate that that play was about Nauplius' activities as a wrecker, and fr. 435, and perhaps 433 and 434 also, support this notion. See on* The Madness of Odysseus *and the* Palamedes.

FRAGMENTS OF KNOWN PLAYS

425

Ζεῦ παυσίλυπε καὶ Διὸς σωτηρίου
σπονδὴ τρίτου κρατῆρος

Schol. BD on Pindar, *Isthm.* 6, 10a (3, 251, 20 Drachmann);
Schol. T on Plato, *Charmides* 167A (p. 116 Greene); Schol. T on
Plato, *Philebus* 66D (p. 55 Greene) = Schol. A on Plato, *Rep.*
583B (p. 269 Greene); Hesychius, *Lexicon* τ 1450

426

ἀλλ' ἀσπιδίτην ὄντα καὶ πεφαργμένον

Stephanus of Byzantium, *Ethnica* 135, 6 Meineke

πεφαργμένον Dindorf: πεφραγ- codd.

427

ὡς ἀσπιδοῦχος ἢ Σκύθης τοξεύμασιν;

Stephanus of Byzantium, *Ethnica* 135, 4 Meineke

429

καὶ πεσσὰ πεντέγραμμα καὶ κύβων βολαί

Eustathius, *Od.* 1397, 27 (=Suetonius, Περὶ παιδιῶν fr. 1, 12
p. 65 Taillardat); Pollux, *Vocabulary* 9, 97 (2, 174, 20 Bethe);
Hesychius, *Lexicon* π 2020, etc.

431

κάτω κρέμανται, σπίζα τὼς ἐν ἔρκεσιν

Herodian, *On Anomalous Words* 31, 19 Dindorf

⟨καὶ⟩ κάτω ⟨κάρα⟩ Bergk   τὼς Walker: τέως cod.

425

Zeus who gives relief from pain and you, libation of the mixing-bowl to Zeus Preserver!

426

. . . but being a shield-bearer and in armour . . .

427

As a shield-bearer or like a Scythian with bow and arrow?

429

. . . and draughts-boards with five lines and castings of the dice . . .

431

They hang downwards, like a finch caught in a net.

FRAGMENTS OF KNOWN PLAYS

432

ΝΑΥΠΛΙΟΣ

οὗτος δ' ἐφηῦρε τεῖχος Ἀργείων στρατῷ,
σταθμῶν, ἀριθμῶν καὶ μέτρων εὑρήματα
τάξεις τε ταύτας οὐράνιά τε σήματα.
κἀκεῖν' ἔτευξε πρῶτος, ἐξ ἑνὸς δέκα
5 κἀκ τῶν δέκ' αὖθις ηὗρε πεντηκοντάδας
καὶ χιλιοστῦς, καὶ στρατοῦ φρυκτωρίαν
ἔδειξε κἀνέφηνεν οὐ δεδειγμένα.
ἐφηῦρε δ' ἄστρων μέτρα καὶ περιστροφάς,
ὕπνου φύλαξι πιστὰ σημαντήρια
10 νεῶν τε ποιμαντῆρσιν ἐνθαλασσίοις
ἄρκτου στροφάς τε καὶ κυνὸς ψυχρὰν δύσιν

Achilles, *Introduction to Aratus* 1 (p. 27, 5 Maass)

2 σταθμῶν Salmasius: στάθμη δ' V¹, στάθμην δ' V²L The
line was deleted by Pearson
6 καὶ¹ Scaliger: ὃς   codd. χιλιοστῦς Nauck: ὃς χίλι'
εὐθὺς ὃς codd.   καὶ² Gomperz: ὃς codd.
9 φύλαξι πιστὰ Nauck: φυλάξεις στιθόα M: φυλάξει
στιθοα V¹: φυλάξει θόα V²
10 νεῶν Blomfield: ναῶν codd.   ποιμαντῆρσιν Heath:
πυ- V¹: πη- V²M

433

ἐπεύχομαι δὲ Νυκτὶ τῇ κατουλάδι

Photius Galeanus 150, 9; Schol. LP on Ap. Rhod. 4, 1695
(325, 20 Wendel)

222

432

NAUPLIUS

And it was he[a] who devised the wall for the army of the Argives; his was the invention of weights, numbers and measures; he taught them to marshal armies thus and how to know the heavenly signs. He was the first, too, who showed how to count from one to ten and so to fifty and to a thousand; he showed the army how to use beacons, and revealed things that earlier were hidden. He discovered how to measure terms and periods of the stars, trustworthy signs for those who watched while others slept, and for the shepherds of ships at sea he found out the turnings of the Bear and the chilly setting of the Dogstar.

[a] Palamedes. The Platonic Socrates remarks (*Republic* 522D) that Agamemnon did not know even how to count his feet until Palamedes taught him how to do so.

433

And I pray to Night that conceals all things.

434

τῷ γὰρ κακῶς πράσσοντι μυρία μία
νύξ ἐστιν, εὐπαθοῦντα δ᾽ ἡμέρα φθάνει

Stobaeus, *Anthology* 4, 40, 3 (5, 920, 13 Hense)

2 εὐπαθοῦντα Meineke: εὖ παθόντα codd.   δ᾽ ἡμέρα
φθάνει Gomperz (φθάνει Heath): ἡτέρα θανεῖν M: εἴθ᾽ ἑτέρα
θανεῖν A

434a

Ed. pr. H. M. Cockle, *P.Oxy.* 52 (1984) No. 3653, fr. 1, 1–6 p.
31 (cf. Radt, *TGrF* iii, p. 575; Sutton, *ZPE* 61 (1986) 15 f.; Luppe,
C.R. 36 (1986) 22)

Να]ύπλιος, ὃς τὴν κρίσιν ἀθετεῖ [*about* 16 *letters*]
..[..].ς ὑπάρχειν τούτ[.].. μὲν [*about* 15 *letters*] καὶ
πρὸς αὐτοὺς καλῶς ὁμιλῆ[σαι *about* 13 *letters*] κελεύει.
κατοδυρομένου δ᾽ Οἴα[κος *about* 10 *letters* Ναύ]πλιος
ἀποπλεῖ τοῖς Ἕλλησιν α[*not more than* 14 *letters*]

ΝΑΥΣΙΚΑΑ *or*
ΠΛΥΝΤΡΙΑΙ

Athenaeus, Deipnosophists *1, 20F and Eustathius,* Od.
1553, 64 f. (cf. Il. *381, 10) say that Sophocles himself
played the part of Nausicaa, and won great credit for the
skill which he showed in the game of ball played by her
and her attendant maidens (cf.* Od. *6, 99 f.). No author
describes the plot of the play, which was presumably
based upon the sixth book of the* Odyssey. *Casaubon and
others have guessed that it was a satyr play, feeling that
the subject was hardly serious enough for tragedy. It was*

434

For to the unhappy man one night is equal to ten thou-
sand, but the fortunate man is taken by surprise by day.

434a

Nauplius, who rejects the judgment . . . and to have
friendly intercourse with them . . . orders. But when
Oeax[a] lamented . . . Nauplius sailed off . . . the Greeks . . .

[a] Oeax was another son of Nauplius, who had been at Troy
with Palamedes.

NAUSICAA or
THE WOMEN WASHING CLOTHES

*in fact treated by the Old Comedy poet Philyllius (PCG
VII p. 378 f.) and the Middle Comedy poet Eubulus
(PCG V p. 229). But others have felt that the incursion of
satyrs, from whom Odysseus would have rescued the girls,
would not have been appropriate. On tragedians as actors
in their own plays see Pickard-Cambridge,* The Dramatic
Festivals of Athens, *2nd ed., revised by Gould and Lewis,
1968, 93; but it is not impossible that the story of Sopho-
cles' success as Nausicaa may have originated from one of
the comedies that dealt with this subject. See on frr. 819,
827 and 861.*

439

πέπλους τε νῆσαι λινογενεῖς τ' ἐπενδύτας

Pollux, *Vocabulary* 7, 45 (2, 64, 9 Bethe)

τε νῆσαι Canter: τάννσαι FS: τε νίσαι A

440

τὸ κῦμά με
παρῆ‹λθεν, εἶτα δ'› ἥσυχ' ἀναροιβδεῖ πάλιν

Photius 1645 Theodoridis; cf. Hesychius, *Lexicon* α 4553
Latte ἀναροιδοῖ ('sic recte legit Schow': Radt) . . . καὶ Σοφοκλῆς
ἐν Ναυσικάᾳ ἀντὶ τοῦ ἀναρρίπτει

1 τὸ κῦμά Ll.-J.: ὄχημά cod.: ‹τὸ κῦμ'› ὄχημά μοι Pearson
2 παρῆ‹λθεν, εἶτα δ'› ἥσυχ' ἀναροιβδεῖ Ll.-J.: παρήσυχα
ἀναρροιβδεῖ cod.

NIOBH

In the last book of the Iliad *Achilles reminds Priam of
the story of Niobe, who boasted to the goddess Leto that
she herself was the mother of many children, whereas
Leto had only two. But Leto's two children were Artemis
and Apollo, and they killed all the children of Niobe. Per-
petually weeping for her children, Niobe was turned to
stone; she was identified with a rock upon Mount Sipylus
in Lydia, down which streams of water perpetually ran.
Niobe was the daughter of the Lydian king Tantalus (see
on the* Tantalus) *and wife of Amphion, who with his
brother Zethus built the walls of Thebes; in Sophocles'
play the children died at Thebes, but after their death
their mother returned to her native land.*

439

. . . to weave robes and tunics made of linen . . .

440

The wave passed me by, and then slowly sucked me back.[a]

[a] If the bold supplement which I have printed is correct, Odysseus is describing the occurrence recorded at *Od.* 5, 424–431.

NIOBE

The hypothesis and the fragments of text found on papyri are assigned to Sophocles' Niobe only on circumstantial evidence. But since in Aeschylus' play of that name the children had been killed before the play began (see my Appendix to the LCL edition of Aeschylus, p. 556 f), and Euripides wrote no play about this subject, the assignation is virtually certain, since two papyrus texts of a play by one of the minor tragedians would have been unlikely to survive.

Different authorities differ over the number of Niobe's children, but according to the tragedians there were seven boys and seven girls. The boys were evidently killed first, while hunting, probably on Mount Cithaeron. Their deaths were evidently described, probably by a messenger

*(see fr. 442). Fr. 443 seems to describe a fight, perhaps
a fight with an animal; one of the boys appealed for help
to a homosexual lover (see fr. 448). Their father Amphion
tried to avenge their deaths, but he too was shot down. Fr.
441a shows that some at least of the girls were killed on
stage, apparently by Artemis shooting from the roof, with*

Ed. pr. of fr. 441aa: H. M. Cockle, in *The Oxyrhynchus Papyri* 52 (1984) No. 3653, fr. 1, 7, p. 31 f.

Ed. pr. of fr. 441a: Lobel, *The Oxyrhynchus Papyri* 37 (1971), 15 f.

Ed. pr. of frr. 442–445: Grenfell and Hunt, *New Classical Fragments and other Greek and Latin Papyri* (1897) 14.

Ed. pr. of fr. 445a: Grenfell and Hunt, *The Hibeh Papyri* I (1906) 40. 44.

See Pearson ii 94–101; Barrett ap. Carden, 171–235; Radt, 363–373; Radt, *TrGF iii (Aeschylus)* (1985) 575–6; Sutton, *ZPE* 62 (1985) 15–18; Luppe, *CR* 36 (1986) 122

441aa

Ὅσων δέδορκεν ὄψ[ὶς ἡλίου τέκνα
⟨κάλλιστα πάντων τέτοκε Ταντάλου κόρη
Νιόβη, σύνευνος Διογενοῦς Ἀμφίονος⟩

2–3 ex. gratia suppl. Ll.-J.

P. Oxy. 3653, fr. 1

       Νιόβη ο[ὖ ἀρ[χὴ] ἥδε·
      ].‥ις ἡλίου τέκνα. ἡ δ᾽ ὑπόθεσις·
Νιόβη τοὺς παῖδα]ς περισσότερον στέρξασα πολλά-
10 κις τὴν γονὴν τὴν ἰ]δίαν ἀμείνονα τῆς Λητοῦς ἔφησεν.
ἀποπέμπουσα] δὲ ἐπὶ θήραν τοὺς ἄρρενας μετὰ

Apollo directing her. Fr. 444 seems to indicate that one girl
survived; in several versions of the story the one girl who
survived was Chloris, later wife of Neleus and mother of
Nestor. After the killings Amphion's brother Zethus made
his appearance; perhaps he took Niobe back to Lydia. One
may guess that Niobe's petrification was predicted, per-
haps by a god speaking from the machine.

441aa

The most beautiful children of all that the sun's eye looks
upon are those of the daughter of Tantalus, Niobe, the
wife of Amphion, son of Zeus.

fr. 1

Niobe, which began with this line: The most . . . son of
Zeus. The plot is as follows: Niobe had an excessive love
for her children and often said that her own progeny was
better than that of Leto. While sending the boys off to

φίλων τινῶν πάλ]ιν ἐμεγαλορημ[όν]ησεν
ὡς παναρίστων ὑ]πάρχουσα μήτη[ρ] τῶνδε κατὰ τὰς
(remains of seven lines)

fr. 2

(remains of 20 lines)
]πυθόμενος δὲ ταῦτα ὁ Ἀμφίων ὠν(ε)ίδι-
σε τὸν θεὸν προκαλ]ῶν κατὰ πρόσωπον εἰς μάχην
καταν-
τῆσαι παραγε]νηθέντος δὲ τοῦ θεοῦ καθοπλισάμε-
νος τὸν βίον τοξ]ευθεὶς μετήλλαξεν. Ἀπόλλων δ' ἐνε-
25 κέλευσε καὶ τῇ Ἀρτέ]μιδι καὶ τὰς κατ' οἶκον κόρας
ἐτόξευσεν
..........]σδα[...].ιν τὴν ὑπεροχὴν τοῖς θεοῖς
..........π]αραγενόμενος δὲ Ζῆθος Νιόβην μὲν

fr. 1 9 Parsons   10–11 Ll.-J   12 Ll.-J.   ἐμεγα-
λορημ[όν]ησεν legit Parsons   13 Ll.-J.
fr. 2 22 Parsons   23 Diggle
24 -νος Rea   τὸν βίον Ll.-J.   25 Parsons

441a
(remains of two lines)
]ουσα.αιδος ἠχώ.
⟨ΑΠΟΛΛΩΝ⟩
ὁρ]ᾷς ἐκείνην τὴν φοβουμένην ἔσω,
5 τ]ὴν ἐν πιθῶνι κἀπὶ κυψέλαις κρυφῇ
μό]νην καταπτήσσουσαν; οὐ τενεῖς ταχὺν
ἰὸ]ν κατ' αὐτὴν πρὶν κεκρυμμένην λαθεῖν;

hunt with some friends she boasted of them again, saying that she was the mother of the best of all children . . .

(*remains of seven lines*)

fr. 2

(*remains of 20 lines*)

When he heard of this Amphion reproached the god and challenged him to combat, but when the god came he took up arms against him and was shot dead. And Apollo egged on Artemis and . . . she shot the girls in the palace, so as to show that superiority belonged to the gods. And Zethos appeared and . . . Niobe . . .

441a

(*remains of three lines*)

⟨APOLLO⟩

Do you see that frightened one inside, the one who is cowering alone, trying to hide, in the tun-store and by the bins? Will you not aim a swift arrow at her, before she can hide out of sight?

⟨ΧΟΡΟΣ⟩

ἀπαπαπαῖ ἐέ.
βραχύ τι τοὖν μέσῳ διοίσει γονᾶς
10 μόρος ἀπ’ ἀρσένων ἀδαμάτοις κόραις.
ἐπὶ μέγα τόδε φλ[ύει κα]κόν.

6–7 Barrett, Austin, Kannicht   11 Barrett

442

⟨ΧΟ.⟩
      ]ε.εμανιαδ[
⟨ΝΙΟΒΗ⟩

ὄλω]λα Φοίβου τῆς θ’ ὁμοσπόρο[υ κότῳ.
τί μ’] ἐξελαύνεις δωμάτων; τ[ί οὐ πικρῷ
5 κατ]αστοχάζῃ πλευρὸν εἰς ἐμ[ὸν βέλει;

⟨ΧΟ.⟩
      ]...α τὴν πολύστονον.[
εἰσδῦσ’] ἐκεῖσε τῇδ’ ἐπουρίσω πόδα;

⟨ΝΙ.⟩
οἴχομαι,] ἐς δὲ μυχαλὰ Τάρταρα τ[έκνων φροῦδον
ἄγαλμα· π]οῖ πόδα καταπτήξω;

⟨ΚΟΡΗ⟩
10   ]α, λίσσομαι, δέσποιν[ά σε
      ]αι τόξα, μηδέ με κτά[νῃς.

⟨ΧΟ.⟩
      ἀθ]λία κόρη [
      (remains of five lines)

2–3 Barrett   5 κατ]αστοχάζῃ Barrett: -ιζει Π   9
Barrett (π]οῖ Carden)   10 Diggle   11, 12 Blass

NIOBE

<CHORUS>

Woe, ah, ah! By only a short space of time will the death of the family be different for the unmarried girls than what it was for the boys! This calamity is swelling to great magnitude![a]

[a] The gods will have been on the roof, shooting down into the palace.

442
(remains of two lines, probably lyrics by the Chorus)

<NIOBE>

I am undone by the anger of Phoebus and his sister! Why are you driving me from the palace? Why do you not aim your cruel arrow at my side?

<CH.>

. . . her of many sorrows. Am I to slip inside and waft her steps this way?

<NI.>

I am lost! The children who were my pride are gone to the caverns of Tartarus! Where shall I cower?

<DAUGHTER>

. . . I beg you, queen . . . do not shoot an arrow and kill me!

<CH.>

. . . unhappy girl . . .

FRAGMENTS OF KNOWN PLAYS

444

(remains of two lines)

⟨χο.?⟩

κλύεις; ἀλύει συμφοραῖς] τ᾽ ἐνθουσιᾳ.

]

5 ὦ παρ᾽ ἐλπίδας θέαμα κ]αὶ λόγων ὑπέρτερον·
ἐκ δόμων γὰρ ἥδ᾽ ἀίσ]σει, πῶλος ὡς ὑπὸ ζυγοῦ,
ἧς πάθαις ἐδυσφο]ροῦμεν ἀρτίως καὶ συγγ[όνων.
ποῖ φέρῃ; τί δ᾽ ὦ ταλαίπ]ω[ρ᾽] αὖ φοβῇ νέον; μ[ένε.

suppl. Barrett

446

I καὶ Σοφοκλῆς ἐν Νιόβῃ ἑπτά φησιν αὐτὰς εἶναι καὶ
⟨ἑπτὰ⟩ τοὺς ἄρρενας.
II Niobe secundum Homerum duodecim filios habuit,
Sophocles autem dicit eam quattuordecim habuisse.

I Schol. MTAB on Euripides, *Phoenissae* 159 (I, 271, 3
Schwartz)   II Lactantius Placidus on Statius, *Thebaid* 6, 124
(306, 6 Jahnke)

447

ἦ γὰρ φίλη 'γὼ τῶνδε τοῦ προφερτέρου

Porphyrius, *Homeric Questions* ad *Il.* 5, 533 (83, 29 Schrader)

448

τῶν μὲν γὰρ τοῦ Σοφοκλέους Νιοβιδῶν βαλλομένων
καὶ θνησκόντων ἀνακαλεῖταί τις οὐδένα βοηθὸν
ἄλλον οὐδὲ σύμμαχον ἢ τὸν ἐραστήν· ὦ . . . ἀμφ᾽
ἐμοῦ στεῖλαι.

Plutarch, *Amatorius* 17, 760D

234

444

(remains of two lines)

‹CH.›

Do you hear? She is wandering, distraught by her sorrows! . . .

O sight unhoped for and beyond words! For she is darting from the palace, like a colt released from the yoke, she whose sorrows with those of her sisters lately distressed us! Where are you rushing? What is the cause of your new terror, unhappy one? Wait![a]

[a] The girl in question is probably Chloris, the one who survived (see prefatory note).

446

I Sophocles in the *Niobe* says that there were seven daughters and seven sons.

II According to Homer Niobe had twelve children, but Sophocles says that she had fourteen.

447

Indeed, I was dear to him who is mightier than they.[a]

[a] This was surely said by Niobe, with reference to Zeus, who according to one story was the father of her father Tantalus.

448

In Sophocles when the sons of Niobe are being shot and killed, one of them calls on no other to come to his rescue and fight for him but his male lover: "O . . . place about me . . . !"

FRAGMENTS OF KNOWN PLAYS

ΝΙΠΤΡΑ

Brunck's guess that this play was identical with the Ὀδυσσεὺς Ἀκανθοπλήξ has long been generally accepted. Cicero (see fr. 461a) tells us that Pacuvius in his Niptra brings on the wounded Odysseus lamenting, and contrasts that lamentation with the "very tearful" lamentation described by Sophocles. Scholars have assumed that the painful wound which caused Odysseus to lament was the fatal wound inflicted by Telegonus, his son by Circe, with the spear made of the spine of a roach. Telegonus had set out to find his father, arrived in Ithaca and became involved in a fight, and killed his father in ignorance of his identity. But Pacuvius in his play (see fr. 461a below) also described the washing of someone's feet by Eurycleia "just as I used to wash Odysseus' feet" in a way that recalls the famous episode in Book 19 of the Odyssey. How can these things have been presented in the same play? Several theories have been put forward; people have thought that Odysseus returned incognito from

451a

τὴν παρουσίαν

τῶν ἐγγὺς ὄντων

Photius Galeanus 400, 1 = Sud. π 707 Adler

THE FOOTWASHING

*one of his journeys later than the actions described in
the* Odyssey *and was recognised all over again, or that
Pacuvius somehow contrived to mix together the events of
two separate plays of Sophocles. But suppose that the
wound that caused Odysseus to lament was not his death
wound, but a wound inflicted before the washing of his
feet by Eurycleia. The suitor Ctesippus threw a calf's foot
at the disguised Odysseus (Od. 20, 287 f); in Homer Odys-
seus dodges this missile, but it might easily have dealt him
a painful blow. Again, Odysseus might have been repre-
sented as sustaining some wound during the battle with
the suitors. Why should not Pacuvius have heightened the
excitement of his play by having Odysseus suffer some
painful injury at the hands of the suitors whom he exter-
minated? We have only to make this assumption to avoid
the notion that Sophocles seems to have written two plays,
one about the washing of Odysseus' feet by Eurycleia and
the other about his death. See fr. 960.*

451a

. . . the presence of those who are near by.

ΟΔΥΣΣΕΥΣ ΑΚΑΝΘΟΠΛΗΞ

See on Νίπτρα *and see fr. 861.*

453

ποδαπὸν τὸ δῶρον ἀμφὶ φαιδίμοις ἔχων
ὤμοις . . .;

Schol. CAE on Dionysius Thrax, *Grammar* 12 (239, 24 Hilgard)

454

ὤμοις ἀθηρόβρωτον ὄργανον φέρων

Schol. HV on *Od*. 11, 128 (2, 486, 16 Dindorf)

455

Δωδῶνι ναίων Ζεὺς ὁ Νάιος βροτῶν

Stephanus of Byzantium, *Ethnica* 248, 2 Meineke

ὁ νάιος Wilamowitz: ὁμί[ ]ος cod.

456

τὰς θεσπιῳδοὺς ἱερέας Δωδωνίδας

Stephanus of Byzantium, *Ethnica* 248, 18 Meineke

458

εἰ μέν τις οὖν ἔξεισιν· εἰ δὲ μή, λέγε

Schol. MP on *Il*. 1, 135–7; Eustath. *Il*. 66, 30

ODYSSEUS WOUNDED BY THE SPINE

See on The Footwashing *and see fr. 861.*

453

Where does the gift come from that you have upon your famous shoulders?[a]

[a] Tiresias in the *Odyssey* tells Odysseus that after he has killed the suitors he must travel, carrying an oar, until he finds men who do not know the sea, and he will know that he has reached them when someone says that he is carrying a winnowing-fan upon his famous shoulder (11, 126–8). Why is the oar called a gift? The word may be corrupt.

454

Carrying on my shoulders a machine for winnowing[a] . . .

[a] See note on fr. 453.

455

Zeus living at Dodona,[a] whom mortals call Zeus of the temple . . .

[a] Dodona in Epirus was the site of a famous oracle of Zeus, whose priestesses were called Peleiades (Doves).

456

. . . the prophesying priestesses of Dodona . . .

458

Perhaps someone will come out; but if not, say . . .

460

νῦν δ' οὔτε μ' ἐκ Δωδῶνος οὔτε Πυθικῶν
γυ⟨άλων⟩ τις ἂν πείσειεν

Stephanus of Byzantium, *Ethnica* 247, 16 Meineke

1 ἐκ Bernardus: εἰς cod.   2 suppl. Bernardus

461

καὶ τὸν ἐν Δωδῶνι παῦσον δαίμον' εὐλογούμενον

John of Alexandria, *On Accents* p. 11, 28 Dindorf

Dindorf was probably right in thinking this to be a trochaic
tetrameter; but cf. *O.C.* 495–6.

461a

Non nimis in 'Niptris' ille sapientissimus Graeciae saucius
lamentatur, vel modice potius: 'pedetemptim' inquit 'ite
et sedato nisu, ne succussu arripiat maior dolor' (Pacuvius
256–8 Ribbeck). Pacuvius hoc melius quam Sophocles;
apud illum enim perquam flebiliter Ulixes lamentatur in
volnere.

Cicero, *Tusculan Disputations* 2,49

ΟΔΥΣΣΕΥΣ ΜΑΙΝΟΜΕΝΟΣ

According to the author of the Cypria *and other later
authorities, Odysseus tried to evade participation in the
Trojan expedition by feigning madness, but his stratagem
was exposed by Palamedes. According to Apollodorus,
Palamedes made as if to kill the infant Telemachus;*

460

But as things are no one from Dodona[a] or the hollows of
Pytho could persuade me . . .

[a] See note on fr. 455; Pytho is a name for Delphi.

461

. . . and put a stop to the praises of the god at Dodona!

461a

In the *Niptra* the wisest man in Greece laments not exces-
sively when he is wounded, but moderately. "Go step by
step," he says, "and slowly, so that you do not shake me
and worse pain comes upon me!" In this Pacuvius does
better than Sophocles, because in his play Ulysses la-
ments over his wound with many tears.

THE MADNESS OF ODYSSEUS

*according to Hyginus and others Odysseus tried to prove
himself mad by ploughing the sand, but Palamedes placed
the infant in the way of the plough. We do not know how
Sophocles handled the story. See on the two Nauplius
plays and on the* Palamedes.

462

πάντ᾽ οἶσθα, πάντ᾽ ἔλεξα τἀντεταλμένα·
μῦθος γὰρ Ἀργολιστὶ συντέμνων βραχύς

Schol. BD on Pindar, *Isthm.* 6, 87a (3, 257, 26 Drachmann)

2 συντέμνων Dindorf: -ει codd.

ΟΙΝΕΥΣ

"The evidence for this title is meagre and inconclusive," wrote Pearson (I, p. 121); but see on fr. 1130.

ΟΙΝΟΜΑΟΣ

Oenomaus, king of Pisa in Elis, either because he himself was in love with her or because an oracle had told him that the man who married her would kill him, obliged any suitor of his beautiful daughter Hippodameia to take her with him in a chariot and try to get as far as the Isthmus of Corinth. Oenomaus himself would pursue him, in a chariot drawn by horses given him by Ares, and if he overtook him killed him. In this way twelve or thirteen suitors perished, and their heads were nailed to the front of the king's palace. But Pelops, the son of Tantalus, had as a boy been the lover of Poseidon. From him he obtained tireless horses, and a chariot that could travel over sea as well as land. Pindar in his First Olympian Ode *attributes Pelops' victory to Poseidon's help; but in other versions of the story he obtains it by bribing Myrtilus, Oenomaus' charioteer, to remove the linchpins from the wheelboxes of his master's chariot. To prevent Myrtilus from claiming*

242

462

You know all, I have told you all the commands; for my words are brief, after the Argive fashion.

OENEUS

OENOMAUS

his reward—in one version of the story it was to take the form of erotic favours from the bride—Pelops hurled him from his chariot into the sea. Both in Sophocles' Electra *(504) and Euripides'* Orestes *(990) the misfortunes of the house of Pelops are said to have begun with Myrtilus' dying curse. Since Pelops was a legendary founder of the Olympic games, the sculptures of the eastern gable of the Temple of Zeus at Olympia show the moment before the race; the face of Oenomaus has a look of great malevolence, and a crouching figure is identified by some as Myrtilus.*

We do not know how Sophocles handled this legend, but he surely used some version of the story about Myrtilus, which is clearly suitable material for a tragedy. The play was revived as late as the middle of the fourth century; the future orator Aeschines made an unfortunate appearance as Oenomaus, later mocked by Demosthenes in his oration on the crown (18, 180).

471

ἡ μὲν ὡς ῐ θάσσονα,
ἡ δ᾽ ὡς ῐ τέτοκε παῖδα

Apollonius Dyscolus, *On Pronouns* 55, 20 Schneider; Schol. T
on *Il.* 22, 410 (2, 398, 13 Maass)

1 ὡς ῐ Dindorf: ὡσεὶ codd.   2 ὡς ῐ Dindorf: ὥσι Schol.
Hom.: ως ει Ap. Dysc.   τέτοκε Cobet: τέξοι Schol. Hom.:
τεκοι Ap. Dysc.

472

ὅρκου δὲ προστεθέντος ἐπιμελεστέρα
ψυχὴ κατέστη· δισσὰ γὰρ φυλάσσεται,
φίλων τε μέμψιν κεἰς θεοὺς ἁμαρτάνειν

Stobaeus, *Anthology* 3, 27, 6 (3, 612, 1 Hense)

1 προστεθέντος Gesner: προ- codd.

473

Σκυθιστὶ χειρόμακτρον ἐκκεκαρμένος

Athenaeus, *Deipnosophists* 9, 410B; cf. Hesychius, *Lexicon* σ
1157 Schmidt

473a

ἰδίως τὸν Ἀνταῖόν φησι (Pindarus) τῶν ξένων τῶν
ἡττωμένων τοῖς κρανίοις ἐρέφειν τὸν τοῦ Ποσειδῶ-
νος ναόν· τοῦτο γὰρ ἱστοροῦσι Διομήδην τὸν Θρᾷκα
ποιεῖν, Βακχυλίδης δὲ (20) Εὔηνον ἐπὶ τῶν Μαρπήσ-
σης μνηστήρων, οἱ δὲ Οἰνόμαον, ὡς Σοφοκλῆς.

Schol. BD on Pindar, *Isthm.* 4, 92 a (3, 236, 5 Drachmann)

471

The one said that her son was faster, the other that hers
was.

472

But when an oath is taken in addition, the mind is more
attentive; for it guards against two things, the reproach of
friends and offence against the gods.

473

. . . scalped for a napkin in Scythian fashion.[a]

[a] Cf. Herodotus 4, 52: "The Scythians skinned the heads of
the enemies they captured and used them as napkins."

473a

Pindar's story that Antaeus roofed a temple of Poseidon
with the heads of strangers he had vanquished is peculiar
to him. The same story is told of the Thracian Diomedes;
Bacchylides says that Evenus did the same thing with the
suitors of Marpessa, and others, including Sophocles, tell
it of Oenomaus.

474

ΙΠΠΟΔΑΜΕΙΑ

τοίαν Πέλοψ ἴυγγα θηρατηρίαν
ἔρωτος, ἀστραπήν τιν᾽ ὀμμάτων, ἔχει·
ᾗ θάλπεται μὲν αὐτός, ἐξοπτᾷ δ᾽ ἐμέ,
ἴσον μετρῶν ὀφθαλμόν, ὥστε τέκτονος
5 παρὰ στάθμην ἰόντος ὀρθοῦται κανών

Athenaeus, *Deipnosophists* 13, 564B

1 τοίαν Πέλοψ ἴυγγα Valckenaer (ἴυγγα iam Musurus): τοιάνδ᾽ ἐν ὄψει λύγγα cod.   3 ᾗ θάλπεται Papageorgiu: ἤθ᾽ ἄλλεται cod.

475

διὰ ψήκτρας σ᾽ ὁρῶ
ξανθὴν καθαίρονθ᾽ ἵππον αὐχμηρᾶς τριχός

Pollux, *Vocabulary* 10, 55 (2, 205, 13 Bethe)

476

⟨εἰ γὰρ⟩ γενοίμαν αἰετὸς ὑψιπέτας
ὡς ἀμποταθείην ὑπὲρ ἀτρυγέτου
γλαυκᾶς ἐπ᾽ οἶδμα λίμνας

Aristophanes, *Birds* 1337–9: cf. Schol. RVEΓ on v. 1337 ἐν τοῖς Καλλιστράτου ταῦτα ἐξ Οἰνομάου τοῦ Σοφοκλέους

1 suppl. White   2 ἀμπ- Shilleto: ἂν π- codd.   Kock inserted αἰθέρος after ὑπὲρ

474

HIPPODAMEIA

Such is the magic charm of love, a kind of lightning of the eyes, that Pelops has; by this he himself is warmed and I am inflamed; he scans with responsive vision as closely as the craftsman's straight-driven plumbline clings to its level.

475

I see you cleaning off the dirty hair of the bay horse with the curry-comb.

476

Would that I could become a high-flying eagle, so that I could fly beyond the barren ether over the waves of the gray sea!

477

λήθουσι γάρ τοι κἀνέμων διέξοδοι
θήλειαν ὄρνιν, πλὴν ὅταν τόκος παρῇ

Diogenes Laertius, *Lives of Eminent Philosophers* 4, 35; Plutarch, *Table Talk* 8, 1, 3, 718A

1 λήθουσι] πλήθουσι Plutarch
2 πλήν ‹γ᾽› Blaydes   τόκος παρῇ] παρῇ τόκος Plutarch

ΠΑΛΑΜΗΔΗΣ

According to the early epic Cypria, *Palamedes was drowned by Diomedes and Odysseus while fishing. But Sophocles is likelier to have used the story that gold was found buried in his tent, and he was unjustly condemned for having taken bribes from the enemy. It is hard to guess what female person may have been given the instruction in fr. 478; perhaps the servant who according to a scholion on Euripides,* Orestes *432 was paid to hide the gold in*

478

εὔφημος ἴσθι μοῦνον ἐξορμωμένη

Ammonius, *On Similar and Different Words* 249 (ed. Nickau, p. 65, 16); Erennius Philo, *Lexicon Parisinum* 96 Nickau

OENOMAUS

477

For the female bird does not notice the passage of the winds except when she is near to giving birth.[a]

[a] Aristotle in his *History of Animals* mentions more than one story of birds being impregnated by the wind.

PALAMEDES

Palamedes' tent may have been a female in this play. With fr. 479 compare fr. 432; they may well have come from the same play. The existence of the Palamedes *is explicitly attested by Eustathius, but the play may have had a double title. See on* Nauplius Sails In *and* Nauplius Lights a Fire, *and also on* The Madness of Odysseus; *one cannot rule out the possibility that these plays belonged to a tetralogy with a continuous theme. See fr. 855.*

478

Only keep silent as you set out![a]

[a] See prefatory note above.

479

οὐ λιμὸν οὗτος τῶνδ᾽ ἀπῶσε, σὺν θεῷ
εἰπεῖν, χρόνου τε διατριβὰς σοφωτάτας
ἐφηῦρε φλοίσβου μετὰ κόπον καθημένοις,
πεσσοὺς κύβους τε, τερπνὸν ἀργίας ἄκος;

Eustathius, *Il.* 228, 1; vv. 3–4 Eustathius, *Od.* 1397, 7 =
Suetonius, *On Games* fr. 1, 1 (ed. Taillardat, 64)

1 τῶνδ᾽ Scaliger: τόνδ᾽ cod.

ΠΑΝΔΩΡΑ *or* ΣΦΥΡΟΚΟΠΟΙ

Hesiod, Works and Days *60–105, and also* Theogony
*570–589, tells how Zeus punished men for Prometheus'
theft of fire by causing the first woman to be created,
endowed with various gifts by various gods, and sent to
Epimetheus, brother of Prometheus. This woman, called
Pandora, 'All-Gifted', because of the gifts given her by the
gods, in the* Theogony *is herself men's punishment for the
theft of fire. In the* Works and Days *she opens the jar in
which all kinds of evils were contained, so that they escape
and have ever since been wandering over the earth. Only
Hope remained in the jar; whether that means that men
have it or that they do not have it is debated.*
*This story must have been the subject of the play, and
the title indicates that the satyrs who formed its chorus
were engaged in hammering, so that they must have been
working for Hephaestus, who figured in several satyric
dramas. Several vases seem to confirm this conjecture.*

479

Was it not he who drove famine away from them, be it said with reverence towards the god, and he who discovered the cleverest ways of passing time for them when they were resting after their struggle with the waves, draughts and dice, a pleasant remedy against idleness?

PANDORA *or* THE HAMMERERS

Proclus in his commentary on Hesiod says that Prometheus "received the jar of evils from the satyrs and entrusted it to Epimetheus, warning Pandora not to receive it," and this statement may reflect the play of Sophocles, though some scholars prefer to connect it with Aeschylus' play Prometheus the Firekindler *(see my Appendix to the LCL Aeschylus, p. 562 f). Some believe that the satyrs were engaged in modelling Pandora, as if she were a statue later endowed with life; but Hesiod says that Pandora was made from clay, and fr. 482 seems to indicate that Sophocles did the same. Still, satyrs working for the time being for Hephaestus may have carried hammers. Some scholars think that their hammering was done to allow her to rise up out of the earth; one legend made men come from the earth, Pandora is found as a name for an earth goddess, and several vases show men or satyrs wielding mallets while a female figure emerges from the earth. But fr. 482 seems hard to reconcile with this idea.*

251

482

καὶ πρῶτον ἄρχου πηλὸν ὀργάζειν χεροῖν

Erotian, *Medical Lexicon* fr. 10 (p. 101, 22) Nachmanson

πηλὸν Foesius: πῖλον codd.

483

καὶ πλῆρες ἐκπιόντι χρύσεον κέρας
τρίψει γέροντα μαλθακῆς χλαίνης ὕπο

Athenaeus, *Deipnosophists* 11, 476B

1 ἐκπιόντι] -τα Adam   2 γέροντα Adam: γέμοντα cod.
χλαίνης ὕπο Tucker: ὑπολαινης codd.: ὑπ᾽ ὠλένης Musurus

ΠΗΛΕΥΣ

Achilles in the Iliad *and the ghost of Achilles in the*
Odyssey *express the fear that the aged Peleus may be un-*
able to protect himself against his neighbours, and Euripi-
des in his Trojan Women *makes Neoptolemus sail home*
from Molossia because Peleus has been driven out by
Acastus, the son of Pelias. A full account of Peleus' trou-
bles which is given by Dictys (Diary of the Trojan War 6,
7–9) has been conjectured to summarise the plot of Sopho-
cles' play. Neoptolemus is driven off course by the storm
and arrives in Molossia, where he hears that Peleus has
been expelled from his kingdom by Acastus, and sends out
two agents who confirm this report. Neoptolemus sails
with his fleet to rescue him, but his ships come to grief on
the rocky coast of the Sepiades, and most of them are lost.
He himself manages to get ashore, and finds Peleus, who
has been hiding in a cave and anxiously looking out for a
relieving expedition. The sons of Acastus, Menalippus and

482

And first begin to mould the clay with your hands![a]

[a] Hemsterhuis conjectured that this was spoken by Athena to Prometheus.

483

And when he has drunk off a golden horn full of wine, she will massage the old one[a] under the soft blanket.

[a] I.e., the penis.

PELEUS

Pleisthenes, arrive in the neighbourhood while hunting, and Neoptolemus, pretending to be a native of Iolcos, tells them of his own death, and takes advantage of their invitation to join in the hunt to kill them both. Their servant Cinyras comes to look for them, and is also killed, after having revealed that Acastus himself is on his way to join them. Pretending to be Mestor, a son of Priam whom he had taken prisoner, Neoptolemus tells Acastus that his enemy is tired after his voyage and is sleeping in a cave. Here he is intercepted by Thetis, who has come to look for Peleus. After rebuking Acastus for his actions against the family of Peleus, Thetis tells Neoptolemus to spare him, and Acastus in gratitude hands over the kingdom to Neoptolemus. This sounds very like the plot of a tragedy in which Thetis was the god from the machine, and we know of no tragedy that it suits better than the Peleus *of Sophocles. See on* The Women of Phthia.

253

FRAGMENTS OF KNOWN PLAYS

487

Πηλέα τὸν Αἰάκειον οἰκουρὸς μόνη
γεροντἀγωγῶ κἀναπαιδεύω πάλιν·
πάλιν γὰρ αὖθις παῖς ὁ γηράσκων ἀνήρ

Clement of Alexandria, *Miscellanies* 6, 2, 19, 5 (2, 438, 3
Stählin); v. 2: Schol. on Aristophanes, *Knights* 1098; Trypho, *On
Tropes* 8; Cocondrius, *On Tropes* 3

488

τὸ μὴ γὰρ εἶναι κρεῖσσον ἢ τὸ ζῆν κακῶς

Stobaeus, *Anthology* 4, 53, 11 (5, 1101, 3 Hense)

489

ὁμορροθῶ, συνθέλω,
συμπαραινέσας ἔχω

Aristophanes, *Birds* 851 with Schol.

490

ἴτω δὲ Πυθιὰς βοά

Aristophanes, *Birds* 857, with Schol. VE ad loc.

corrected by Nauck: ἴτω ἴτω ἴτω δὲ Πυθιὰς βοὰ τῷ θεῷ
codd.

491

βοάσομαί τἄρα τὰν ὑπέρτονον
βοάν· ἰώ, πύλαισιν ἤ τις δόμοις;

Aristophanes, *Clouds* 1154 f. with Schol. V: given to Euripi-
des, *Peleus* by Schol. RERs

PELEUS

487

I alone keep the house and tend the old age of Peleus, son
of Aeacus, and retrain him; for as a man grows old he be-
comes a child once more.

488

For it is better not to exist than to live in misery.

489

I pull together with you, I share your wish, I have given
my consent!

490

Let the Pythian cry go up![a]

[a] This means the paean, sung in honour of Apollo, sung in
battles, at symposia or in celebration.

491

Then I shall utter the high-pitched cry! Ho, is there any-
one at the gate or in the house?

FRAGMENTS OF KNOWN PLAYS

492

βασιλεὺς χώρας τῆς Δωτιάδος

Stephanus of Byzantium, *Ethnica* 257, 8 Meineke

493

μὴ ψεῦσον, ὦ Ζεῦ· μή μ' ἕλῃς ἄνευ δορός

Schol. R on Aristophanes, *The Women at the Thesmophoria* 870

494

καὶ ξηραλοιφῶν εἵματος διὰ πτυχῶν

Harpocration, *Glossary to the Ten Orators* 216, 1

ΠΟΙΜΕΝΕΣ

This play dealt with the beginning of the Trojan War. The shepherds who formed its chorus sighted the approaching Greek army; there was mention of the death at Hector's hands of Protesilaus, the first Greek warrior to be killed, and of Achilles' success in enabling the Greeks to land, at the same time killing the formidable hero Cycnus. He was a son of Poseidon, whose skin was impervious to spear or sword, but Achilles killed him with a stone. Her-

497

ἱστορεῖ δὲ Σοφοκλῆς ἐν Ποιμέσιν ὑπὸ τοῦ Ἕκτορος ἀναιρεθῆναι τὸν Πρωτεσίλεων.

Schol. on Lycophron 530 (190, 21 Scheer)

PELEUS

492

. . . king of the land of Dotion[a] . . .

[a] Dotion was in Thessaly, not far from Iolkos, the domain of Acastus.

493

Do not deceive me, Zeus! Do not kill me without a weapon!

494

. . . and anointing himself with powder through the folds of his tunic[a] . . .

[a] Athletes rubbed themselves either with oil mixed with water or with powder; see E. N. Gardner, *Athletics of the Ancient World* 78.

THE SHEPHERDS

*mann inferred from the character of some of the frag-
ments that this was a satyr play; but if this play is really
named in the tragic hypothesis in P.Oxy. 2256, fr. 3 (text in
my Appendix to LCL Aeschylus, p. 595 f; Kannicht, TGrF
I, 2nd ed., pp.44–45 and Radt, TGrF III, T 70 give up-to-
date discussions of the problems) this cannot be correct. If
The Shepherds is really named in that place, it must have
been an early play of Sophocles, produced not later than
the sixties of the fifth century. See frr. 859 and 917.*

497

Sophocles in *The Shepherds* relates that Protesilaus was killed by Hector.

FRAGMENTS OF KNOWN PLAYS

498

ΕΚΤΩΡ

ἡδὺ ξανῆσαι καὶ προγυμνάσαι χέρα

Photius Galeanus 307, 17 = Suda ξ 14 Adler

500

οὐ χαλκός, οὐ σίδηρος ἅπτεται χροός

Aristarchus, *Commentary on Herodotus* 1, 215, 2 (*Amherst Papyrus 12 II 13*)

501

ΚΥΚΝΟΣ

καὶ μή <σ᾽> ὑβρίζων αὐτίκ᾽ ἐκ βάθρων ἕλω,
ῥυτῆρι κρούων γλουτὸν ὑπτίου ποδός

Hesychius, *Lexicon* ρ 537 Schmidt; v. 2 Photius Galeanus 493, 13

1 suppl. Dindorf

502

ἑωθινὸς γάρ, πρίν τιν᾽ αὐλιτῶν ὁρᾶν,
θαλλὸν χιμαίραις προσφέρων νεοσπάδα
εἶδον στρατὸν στείχοντα παρ᾽ ἁλίαν ἄκραν

Harpocration, *Glossary to the Ten Orators* 210, 1; Athenaeus, *Deipnosophists* 13, 587A

1 αὐλιτῶν Casaubon: αὐλητῶν codd.   2 χιμαίραις Brunck: -αι Athen.: χίλια vel χιλίαις Harpocr.   νεοσπάδα Casaubon: νέος παῖδα Athen.: νεόπαιδα Harpocr.   3 παρ᾽ ἁλίαν Musurus: παραλίαν codd.   ἄκραν Athen.: πέτραν Harpocr.

258

498

HECTOR

It is pleasant to get some exercise and to give one's arm
some practice.

500

Not bronze, not iron can touch his skin.

501

CYCNUS

. . . and in case I do you violence and wreck you utterly,
striking your buttocks with the flat of my foot for whip . . .

502

For at dawn, before any of the farmhands saw it, as I was
bringing newly plucked branches to the goats, I saw the
army marching beside the cape that runs into the sea.

FRAGMENTS OF KNOWN PLAYS

503

ἔνθ᾽ ἡ πάροικος πηλαμὺς χειμάζεται
πάραυλος Ἑλλησποντίς, ὡραία θέρους
τῷ Βοσπορίτῃ· τῇδε γὰρ θαμίζεται

Athenaeus, *Deipnosophists* 7, 319A; v. 2: Hesychius, *Lexicon*
π 723 Schmidt

2 πάραυλος] πάροικος Athen.   3 τῇδε Ellendt: τῷδε
codd.

504

κημοῖσι πλεκτοῖς πορφύρας φθείρει γένος

Schol. VΘ on Aristophanes, *Knights* 1150a (II) (I 2, 245, 1
Mervyn Jones / Wilson)

πλεκτοῖς Küster: -αῖς δὲ VΘ: -αῖς Ald. φθείρει] θηρᾷ
Tucker: αἱρεῖ Degani

505

τούτοις γὰρ ὄντες δεσπόται δουλεύομεν,
καὶ τῶνδ᾽ ἀνάγκη καὶ σιωπώντων κλύειν

Plutarch, *Life of Agis* 1, 3 (ὅπερ οἱ Σοφοκλέους βοτῆρες ἐπὶ
τῶν ποιμνίων λέγουσιν)

506

τειχέων καὶ δὴ τοὺς Ποσιδείους
θριγκοὺς . . . ἀποσεισαμένη

Herodian, *On Anomalous Words* 11, 2

1 τειχέων Dindorf: τυχῶν cod.   Ποσιδείους Dindorf:
-ειδίους cod.   2 lacuna indicated by Radt

503

. . . where the neighbouring young tunny spends the winter, living close by in the Hellespont, in season in the summer for the native of the Bosporus; for it is there that it is often found.

504

In woven creels he destroys the race of the murex.

505

For though we are their masters, we are slaves to them, and we must listen to them even though they do not speak.[a]

[a] A shepherd is speaking of his flock.

506

. . . having had shaken down already the cornice of the walls built by Poseidon[a] . . .

[a] The subject of the sentence must have been Troy.

507

×–] τριταῖος ὥστε πῦρ ἀφί[ξεται
κρυμὸν φέρων γναθμοῖσιν ἐξ ἀμφημέρου

Schol. on Nicander, *Theriaca* 382 in P.Oxy. 2221 I 23; v. 2:
Suda α 1695 Adler

1 suppl. Kassel   2 γναθμοῖσιν Schol. Nicand.: γνά-
θοισιν Suda

508

λόγῳ γὰρ ἕλκος οὐδὲν οἶδά που χανόν

Schol. on Sophocles, *Ajax* 581 (p. 140 f., Christodoulou) =
Suda θ 480 Adler

ΠΟΛΥΞΕΝΗ

This play, like the Hecuba *of Euripides, dealt with the
appearance of the ghost of Achilles, and with the sacrifice
of Polyxena in obedience to the ghost's demand. It surely
began with the appearance of the ghost (fr. 523); "Longi-
nus" 15, 7 (p. 23, 7 Russell) praises Sophocles for the
"brilliant visualization" which he achieved "on the occa-
sion of the departure of the Greeks when Achilles spoke to
them over his tomb as they were taking off." According to*

507

The tertian fever will arrive like a fire, succeeding the quotidian, bringing a chill to the jaws.

508

For I know of no wound that a word has caused to gape.

POLYXENA

the epic Nostoi, *the ghost warned the Greeks to postpone their departure, prophesying its disastrous consequences, and this may have happened in the play of Sophocles. Fr. 522 shows that the play presented the quarrel between Agamemnon and Menelaus which resulted in the departure of the latter while the former stayed behind in order to try to propitiate Athena by means of sacrifice. See fr. 887.*

522

ΜΕΝΕΛΑΟΣ

σὺ δ' αὖθι μίμνων που κατ' Ἰδαίαν χθόνα
ποίμνας Ὀλύμπου συναγαγὼν θυηπόλει

Strabo, *Geography* 10, 3, 14 p. 470C (εἰσὶ μὲν οὖν λόφοι
τέτταρες Ὄλυμποι καλούμενοι τῆς Ἴδης κατὰ τὴν Ἀνταν–
δρίαν . . . ὁ δ' οὖν Σοφοκλῆς ποιήσας τὸν Μενέλαον ἐκ τῆς
Τροίας ἀπαίρειν σπεύδοντα ἐν τῇ Πολυξένῃ, τὸν δ' Ἀγα–
μέμνονα μικρὸν ὑπολειφθῆναι βουλόμενον τοῦ ἐξιλάσασθαι
τὴν Ἀθηνᾶν χάριν, εἰσάγει λέγοντα τὸν Μενέλαον· σὺ κτλ.

1 που κατ' Xylander: τοῦ κατ', τὴν κατ' codd.

523

ΨΥΧΗ ΑΧΙΛΛΕΩΣ

ἀκτὰς ἀπαίωνάς τε καὶ μελαμβαθεῖς
λιποῦσα λίμνης ἦλθον, ἄρσενας χοὰς
Ἀχέροντος ὀξυπλῆγας ἠχούσας γόους

Apollodorus, *On the Gods* 20 (*FGrH* 244 F 102a 2), accord-
ing to Porphyry in Stobaeus, *Anthology* 1, 49, 50 (1, 419, 1
Wachsmuth)

1 ἀκτὰς Jacobs: ὦ τὰς codd.   2–3 The words ἦλθον
ἄρσενας χοὰς, written in the manuscripts after γόους, were
transposed by Jacobs   3 ἠχούσας Grotius: ἠχοῦσα codd.

524

⟨ΑΓΑΜΕΜΝΩΝ⟩

οὐ γάρ τις ἂν δύναιτο πρωράτης στρατοῦ
τοῖς πᾶσιν εἶξαι καὶ προσαρκέσαι χάριν.
ἐπεὶ οὐδ' ὁ κρείσσων Ζεὺς ἐμοῦ τυραννίδι

522

MENELAUS

Do you remain here somewhere in the land of Ida and
round up the flocks of Olympus[a] for a sacrifice!

[a] Strabo in quoting this fragment mentions that the Trojan
Mount Ida had four peaks, each of which was called an Olympus.

523

GHOST OF ACHILLES

I have come, leaving the shores of the lake, far from re-
joicing and deep in darkness, the resounding waters of
Acheron that echo wailing that accompanies fierce blows.[a]

[a] These were surely the opening words of the prologue; com-
pare the opening words of Euripides' *Hecuba*, also spoken by a
ghost. "Blows" refers to the beating of the head by mourners.

524

⟨AGAMEMNON⟩

For the helmsman of an army could not give in to all and
render favours to all. Indeed, not even Zeus, whose royal
power is mightier than mine, is approved by mortals

FRAGMENTS OF KNOWN PLAYS

οὔτ᾽ ἐξεπομβρῶν οὔτ᾽ ἐπαυχμήσας φίλος,
5 βροτοῖς ⟨δ᾽⟩ ἂν ἐλθὼν ἐς λόγον δίκην ὄφλοι.
πῶς δῆτ᾽ ἔγωγ᾽ ἂν θνητὸς ἐκ θνητῆς τε φὺς
Διὸς γενοίμην εὖ φρονεῖν σοφώτερος;

Stobaeus, *Anthology* 4, 8, 13 (4, 299, 3 Hense)

2 πᾶσιν εἶξαι Wecklein: πᾶσι δεῖξαι codd.
5 ⟨δ᾽⟩ ἂν ἐλθὼν Dobree: ἀνελθὼν codd.   ἐς λόγον
δίκην Dobree: ἐς δίκην λόγων codd.   ὄφλοι Heath: ὄφλαι
codd.   6 ἔγωγ᾽ ἂν θνητὸς ἐκ Hense: ἐγὼ θνητός γ᾽ ἂν
(ὢν A) ἐκ codd.

525

ἀπ᾽ αἰθέρος δὲ κἀπὸ λυγαίου νέφους

Schol. L (206, 17 Wendel) and Schol. P (207 Schaefer) on
Apollonius of Rhodes 2, 1120

526

χιτών σ᾽ ἄπειρος, ἐνδυτήριον κακῶν . . .

Et. Gen. AB (Et. Magn. 120, 47)

ΠΡΙΑΜΟΣ

*Only two authorities quote the play, and we know
nothing of its plot; see on* Ἀλέξανδρος, Κασσάνδρα, *and*
Φρύγες.

either when he sends rain or when he sends drought, but if they could call him to account he would lose his case. How then can I, the mortal son of a mortal mother, be cleverer than Zeus?

525
... but from the upper air and from the gloomy cloud[a] ...

[a] Did the ghost prophesy the storm that struck the Achaean fleet on the way back from Troy?

526
A shirt without an egress, a garment of evil[a] ...

[a] This must refer to the cloth like a garment without neck- or arm-holes which Clytemnestra threw over Agamemnon (Aeschylus, *Agam.* 1382); evidently the ghost prophesied the murder.

PRIAM

See on Alexander, Cassandra *and* The Phrygians

FRAGMENTS OF KNOWN PLAYS

ΠΡΟΚΡΙΣ

*Procris was daughter of Erechtheus, king of Athens,
and wife of Cephalus, son of Deion or Deioneus or else
son of Hermes by the Athenian princess Herse. It seems
that originally one Cephalus was carried off by Eos, the
goddess of the dawn, but another married Procris; but in
some authorities the two Cephali are merged, as in Ovid,*
Metamorphoses *7, 690–892. There is a story that
Cephalus tested his wife's virtue, which according to some
legends was indeed doubtful, by going away for eight*

ΡΙΖΟΤΟΜΟΙ

*All that we know for certain about the plot of this play
comes from fr. 534, which describes Medea's cutting of the
herbs needed for her magic. It is therefore surprising that
Welcker's guess that the play dealt with her murder of
Jason's uncle Pelias should have found general accep-
tance. That story provided the subject of Euripides' early
play, the* Daughters of Pelias. *Medea restored the youth of
her husband's aged father Aeson by cutting him up and
boiling him in a pot together with certain herbs; in*

534

ἡ δ᾽ ἐξοπίσω χερὸς ὄμμα τρέπουσ᾽
ὀπὸν ἀργινεφῆ στάζοντα τομῆς
χαλκέοισι κάδοις δέχεται . . .

* * *

. . . αἱ δὲ καλυπταὶ
5   κίσται ῥιζῶν κρύπτουσι τομάς,

268

PROCRIS

years and then returning in disguise and making love to her. A better known story is that when exhausted after hunting he used to call on "Nephele," the word for a cloud, to come and refresh him, and that his wife, believing this to be the name of a rival, concealed herself nearby in order to surprise them. But Cephalus, hearing a noise and thinking that a beast was lurking in the bushes, hurled his javelin, and his wife was killed. It seems likely that this story figured in the play; but there is only one quotation, and we know nothing of the plot.

THE ROOT-CUTTERS

another version, it was not Aeson but an aged ram which she subjected to this process. She advised the daughters of Pelias to do the same for their father; but after they had cut him up, Medea broke her promise to provide the necessary magic. Welcker may have been right; but for all we know the action took place while the Argonauts were in Colchis, where Medea used the herb Prometheion to protect Jason during his ordeal. If so, the play may have been identical with the Women of Colchis; *see on that play, and also on the* Scythians.

534

And she, looking back as she did so, caught the white, foamy juice from the cut in bronze vessels . . . And the hidden boxes conceal the cuttings of the roots, which she,

ἃς ἥδε βοῶσ᾽ ἀλαλαζομένη
γυμνὴ χαλκέοις ἧμα δρεπάνοις

Macrobius, *Saturnalia* 5, 19, 8 (1, 326, 14 Willis)

535

ΧΟΡΟΣ

Ἥλιε δέσποτα καὶ πῦρ ἱερόν,
τῆς εἰνοδίας Ἑκάτης ἔγχος,
τὸ δι᾽ Οὐλύμπου ‹προ›πολοῦσα φέρει
καὶ γῆς ναίουσ᾽ ἱερὰς τριόδους,
5 στεφανωσαμένη δρυὶ καὶ πλεκταῖς
ὠμῶν σπείραισι δρακόντων

Schol. LP on Apollonius of Rhodes, 3, 1214 f. (253, 10 Wendel; Schaefer, *Ap. Rh. Argonautica* 2, 1813, 263)

3 suppl. Pearson   5 πλεκταῖς Valckenaer: πλείστοις
P: -τους L   6 ὠμῶν Meursius: ὤμῳ codd.   σπείραισι
Scaliger: -ήμασι P: -ουσι L

ΣΑΛΜΩΝΕΥΣ

*Salmoneus, son of Aeolus and father of Tyro, a
Thessalian who became king in Elis, figures in more than
one story (see on the Tyro). But since this play was a satyr*

uttering loud ritual cries, naked,[a] was severing with bronze sickles.

[a] The nudity was part of the ritual. Medea's ritual cry was one usually uttered by men, but it would be a mistake to emend the word to the name of a cry usually uttered by women.

535

CHORUS

O Sun our lord and sacred fire, the spear of Hecate of the roads, which she carries as she attends her mistress[a] in the sky and as she inhabits the sacred crossroads of the earth, crowned with oak-leaves and the woven coils of savage dragons!

[a] Hecate regularly attends a greater goddess, Artemis, Demeter, or Persephone; see Richardson on *Homeric Hymn to Demeter* 440.

SALMONEUS

play, it seems likely that it dealt with his imitation of Zeus' thunder and lightning, mentioned in Ajax the Locrian *fr. 10c and by Virgil,* Aen. *6, 586 f.*

537

τάδ᾽ ἐστὶ κνισμὸς καὶ φιλημάτων ψόφος·
τῷ καλλικοσσαβοῦντι νικητήρια
τίθημι καὶ βαλόντι χάλκεον κάρα

Athenaeus, *Deipnosophists* 11, 487D

3 χάλκεον Blaydes: χαλκεῖον cod.

538

καὶ τάχ᾽ ἂν κεραυνίαις
πέμφιξι βροντὴ καὶ δυσοσμίᾳ βάλοι

Galen on Hippocrates, *Epidemics* libr. VI comm. 1, 29 ed.
Wenkebach-Pfaff (Corp. Med. Gr. 5, 10, 2, 2; p. 47, 25)

1 κεραυνίαις Ll.-J.: -αύνια cod.   2 βροντὴ Pfaff: -ῆς
cod.   δυσοσμίᾳ Deichgräber: -ας cod.   βάλοι Bentley:
λάβοι cod.

539

πέμφιγι πᾶσιν ὄψιν ἀγγελῶ πυρός

Galen on Hippocrates, *Epidemics* libr. VI comm. 1, 29 (see on
fr. 538)

πᾶσιν Wenkebach (rendering the Arabic translation): πᾶσαν
cod.   ὄψιν ἀγγελῶ Wenkebach: ὀψιαγέλων cod.

537

These things are a titillation and the smack of kisses! I
award them as prizes for the best player at kottabos and
the one who has hit the brazen head.[a]

[a] Kottabos was a game played at Greek drinking-parties, in
which the player threw wine-lees at a long pole with a small disc
balanced on the top, or at a large bowl; see Sparkes, *Archaeology*
13 (1960) 202 f. Cf. fr. 277.

538

And perhaps the thunder will strike ⟨you⟩ with the blasts
of its bolt and with an evil stench.

539

With the blast I shall announce the appearance of the fire
to all.

ΣΙΝΩΝ

The post-Homeric epics The Little Iliad *and* The Sack of Troy *both told the story of Sinon, recounted by Virgil in the second book of the* Aeneid *(57 f). Pretending to be a companion of Palamedes whom the departing Greeks had intended to sacrifice, but who had escaped, Sinon won the confidence of the Trojans, and told them that the Wooden Horse had been made as an offering to Athena. If the Trojans destroyed it, the goddess would punish them; but if*

ΣΙΣΥΦΟΣ

There is only one quotation, and that may well be due to a confusion with one of Aeschylus' two plays about the crafty king of Corinth.

ΣΚΥΘΑΙ

Like the Κολχίδες *and the* Ῥιζοτόμοι, *this play dealt with the voyage of the Argonauts, in all probability with the return voyage. The corrupt fragment 546 would appear to show that Medea's brother Apsyrtus was a child at the time of the action. This suggests that Sophocles did not, like Apollonius, use the version that made Apsyrtus the leader of the expedition sent by Aeetes to pursue Medea, but the alternative story that Medea took him with her and delayed the pursuers by killing him, cutting him up, and throwing the pieces of his body into the sea so that the Colchians would be obliged to stop to pick them*

SINON

they brought it into their city, they would one day invade Greece and enjoy a great triumph. According to one story, Sinon was a first cousin of Odysseus. It has been conjectured that Virgil was influenced by this play in his account of Sinon, particularly in the speeches with which Sinon deceived the Trojans. None of the four quotations is more than one word long.

SISYPHUS

THE SCYTHIANS

up. Some authors place the murder of Apsyrtus off the coast of Scythia, and according to one story his remains were buried at Tomi, which could be called part of Scythia. This would account for the play's name, a name presumably taken from its chorus. A scholion on Apollonius 4, 284 (fr. 547) says that Sophocles made the Argonauts return by the route they had come by, so that he did not, like Pindar, make them sail down the Phasis into Oceanus and thus arrive in Libya. Did the Women of Colchis, the Root-Cutters and the Scythians form a connected trilogy? It seems possible.

546

οὐ γὰρ ἐκ μιᾶς
κοίτης ἔβλαστον, ἀλλ' ὁ μὲν Νηρηίδος
†τέκνον ἄρτι βλάστεσκε, τὴν δ'†
Εἰδυῖα πρίν ποτ' Ὠκεανοῦ τίκτει κόρη

Schol. LP on Apollonius of Rhodes, 4, 223–30a (271, 29 Wendel; Schaefer, *Ap. Rhod. Argonautica* 2, 1813, 283)

3 βλάστεσκε LV: βλαστάνεσκε P   τὴν δ' P: ἦν L
4 κόρη τίκτεν codd., transposed by Bergk: τίκτει Bothe

549

κρημνούς τε καὶ σήραγγας ἠδ' ἐπακτίας
αὐλῶνας

Athenaeus, *Deipnosophists* 5, 189C

ΣΚΥΡΙΟΙ

Brunck and Welcker believed that this play, like the Men of Scyros *of Euripides, dealt with the fetching of Achilles from Scyros to Troy. But Tyrwhitt in 1794 had argued from fr. 557 that it dealt rather with the fetching of Neoptolemus, which had been described in the* Little Iliad, *and this view has been generally accepted. Since the person addressed by Neoptolemus in fr. 557 is an old man (line 4), it seems that as in the* Philoctetes *Neoptolemus was fetched by Odysseus and his father's aged tutor, Phoenix. Philostratus Minor, Pictures 1b, 2 f tells us that Neoptolemus' mother Deidameia and his grandfather*

546

For they[a] were not born of the same union, but he was the child of a Nereid . . . lately . . ., but her Eiduia, daughter of Ocean, bore some time before.

[a] Medea and her brother Apsyrtus, both children of Aeetes, had different mothers.

549

. . . the cliffs and hollows and creeks along the shore . . .

THE MEN OF SCYROS

Lycomedes wished to prevent him from going to Troy, and that while in charge of the flocks by the seashore, and feeling frustrated at being confined to the island, he encountered Phoenix; this may well be relevant to this play. Fr. 555b (scraps of 25 lines, including half of each of nine consecutive lines) has been thought to indicate that there was a plan to send Neoptolemus off to Chalcodon, king of Euboea, to keep him out of the war. In fact the text of the papyrus fragment cannot be supplemented with any confidence, but it supports the notion that his departure must have been opposed by his relations on the island. The young hero himself was probably keen to sail to Troy.

554

φιλεῖ γὰρ ἄνδρας πόλεμος ἀγρεύειν νέους

Stobaeus, *Anthology* 4, 10, 22 (4, 333, 4 Hense)

555

Ed. pr. of P.Oxy. 2077, Hunt, Part 17, 1927, 30 f. Cf. Pfeiffer, *Philologus* 88 (1933) 1 f = *Ausgewählte Kleine Schriften* (1960) 85 f, who identified the play, observing that fr. 555 coincides with part of the papyrus; Page, *GLP* no. 5, p. 20; Carden 94 f; Radt 420 f.

ἢ ποντοναύτας τῶν ταλαιπώρων νέμω,
οἷς οὔτε δαίμων οὔτε τις θνητῶν βροτῶν
πλούτου ποτ᾽ ἂν νείμειεν ἀξίαν χάριν·
[λεπταῖς ἐπὶ ῥοπῇσιν ἐμπολ]ὰ[ς μ]ακρὰς
5 [ἀεὶ παραρρίπτοντες] οἱ πολύφθ[οροι]
[ἢ ἔσωσαν ἀκέρδα]ναν ἢ διώλεσαν.
ὅμως δὲ θαυμάζω] τε κἀπαινῶ βροτοὺς
τολμῶντας αἰεὶ] χειρὶ τῇ δυστλήμονι
τὸν σπάνιον ἀλγεινόν τε πο]ρσύνειν βίον.

vv. 1–6: Stobaeus, *Anthology* 4, 17, 3 (4, 400, 10 Hense); vv. 4–9: P.Oxy. 2077, fr. 1

1 ποντοναύτας Ll.-J.: -ναῦται codd.   νέμω Ll.-J.: βροτῶν cod.   2 θνητῶν F. W. Schmidt: θεῶν cod.   βροτῶν Ll.-J.: νέμων cod.   7 Page   8–9 Ll.-J.

556

οὐδὲν γὰρ ἄλγος οἷον ἡ πολλὴ ζόη

Stobaeus, *Anthology* 4, 50, 63 (5, 1043, 15 Hense)

ζόη Porson: ζωή codd.

554

For war likes to hunt down men who are young.

555

Truly I count mariners among unhappy mortals—they to whom neither god nor mortal men can ever give their due reward in wealth! Ever risking their distant enterprises on slender chances, amid many ruinous wanderings they either keep or lose their profits! But I revere and praise those mortals who constantly find the courage to earn a scarce and painful living with their much-enduring hands.

556

For there is no pain like long life.

557

‹ΝΕΟΠΤΟΛΕΜΟΣ ›

ἀλλ' εἰ μὲν ἦν κλαίουσιν ἰᾶσθαι κακὰ
καὶ τὸν θανόντα δακρύοις ἀνιστάναι,
ὁ χρυσὸς ἧσσον κτῆμα τοῦ κλαίειν ἂν ἦν.
νῦν δ', ὦ γεραιέ, τοῦτ' ἀνηνύτως ἔχει,
5 τὸν ἐν τάφῳ κρυφθέντα πρὸς τὸ φῶς ἄγειν·
κἀμοὶ γὰρ ἂν χάριν γε δακρύων πατὴρ
ἀνῆκτ' ἂν εἰς φῶς.

Stobaeus, *Anthology* 4, 56, 17 (5, 1127, 1 Hense)

4 τοῦτ' Blaydes: ταῦτ' codd.   5 τὸν ἐν Bergk: τὸν (τὸ A)
μὲν codd.   6 χάριν γε δακρύων πατὴρ Blaydes: πατήρ γε
δακρύων χάριν codd.

ΣΥΝΔΕΙΠΝΟΙ

The play is usually called Σύνδειπνοι, *though
Athenaeus in quoting fr. 565 says that it comes from the*
Ἀχαιῶν Σύνδειπνον (The Achaeans Dine Together).
Toup's conjecture that this was the same as the Ἀχαιῶν
Σύλλογος (The Assembly of the Achaeans), *q.v., was
generally accepted until the publication in 1907 from a
Berlin papyrus of what in Pearson's edition appears as
fr. 142 (= Euripides, fr. 149 Austin = fr. 727c. Kannicht);
and now that the publication in 1957 of P.Oxy. 2460 = fr.
727a Kannicht has shown that this comes from Euripi-
des,*Telephus, *it would appear that Toup was right. In the*

557

⟨NEOPTOLEMUS⟩

Why, if it were possible to heal troubles by weeping, and to raise up the dead by tears, gold would be a less precious possession than lamentation! But as things are, aged man, it is impossible to bring up to the light him who is hidden in the tomb. Why, if tears could have done it, my father would have been brought up to the light!

THOSE WHO DINE TOGETHER

Cypria *the Achaeans on the way to Troy put in to Tenedos, and there Achilles quarrelled with Agamemnon, considering himself to have been slighted in not being invited or in being invited late to a dinner. Fr. 565 has suggested to some that it was a satyr play. It is hard to see how a chorus of satyrs could have figured in a play about this subject, but it is conceivable that their presence was occasioned by the supplying of wine for the dinner by order of Dionysus or some person connected with him. Agamemnon and Achilles must have been reconciled; fr. 562 suggests that Thetis appeared as the god from the machine.*

FRAGMENTS OF KNOWN PLAYS

562

ΘΕΤΙΣ

λιποῦσα μὲν
Νηρηίδων ὤρουσα πόντιον χορόν

Anonymous, *On Tropes* = Schol. on Dionysius Thrax 1 (460, 3 Hilgard)

2 π. χ. ὤρ. Νηρ. codd.: transposed by Wilamowitz

563

φορεῖτε, μασσέτω τις, ἐγχείτω βαθὺν
κρατῆρ'· ὅδ' ἀνὴρ οὐ πρὶν ἂν φάγῃ καλῶς
ὅμοια καὶ βοῦς ἐργάτης ἐργάζεται

Athenaeus, *Deipnosophists* 15, 685F

564

οὔτοι γένειον ὧδε χρὴ διηλιφὲς
φοροῦντα κἀντίπαιδα καὶ γένει μέγαν
γαστρὸς καλεῖσθαι παῖδα, τοῦ πατρὸς παρόν

Athenaeus, *Deipnosophists* 15, 678F

565

ἀλλ' ἀμφὶ θυμῷ τὴν κάκοσμον οὐράνην
ἔρριψεν οὐδ' ἥμαρτε· περὶ δ' ἐμῷ κάρᾳ
κατάγνυται τὸ τεῦχος οὐ μύρου πνέον·
ἐδειματούμην δ' οὐ φίλης ὀσμῆς ὕπο

Athenaeus, *Deipnosophists* 1, 17C. Cf. Aeschylus fr. 180 Radt; both probably come from satyr plays.

562

THETIS
I made haste, leaving the Nereids dancing in the sea.

563

Bring the stuff, let someone knead cakes, fill a deep mixing bowl! This man, like a working ox, does not work well till he has eaten!

564

When you are a young man of great family with luxuriant beard, you ought not to be called the son of your stomach, when you could be called that of your father![a]

[a] Thersites to Ajax? Odysseus to Achilles?

565

But in his anger he hurled at me the stinking chamber pot, nor did he miss; and the vessel, which did not smell of myrrh, broke about my head, and I was shocked by the unpleasing smell.

FRAGMENTS OF KNOWN PLAYS

566

ΟΔΥΣΣΕΥΣ

ἤδη τὰ Τροίας εἰσορῶν ἐδώλια
δέδοικας; . . .

ΑΧΙΛΛΕΥΣ

(διαγανακτεῖ καὶ ἀποπλεῖν λέγει)

ΟΔ.

ἐγῷδ᾽ ὃ φεύγεις· οὐ τὸ μὴ κλύειν κακῶς;
ἀλλ᾽ ἐγγὺς Ἕκτωρ ἐστίν· οὐ μένειν καλόν;

Plutarch, Friends and Flatterers 36, 74A

2 question mark Pearson   3, 4 question marks Ll.-J.

567

ὦ πάντα πράσσων, ὡς ὁ Σίσυφος πολὺς
ἔνδηλος ἐν σοὶ πάντα χὠ μητρὸς πατήρ

Schol. LG on Sophocles, Ajax 190 (20, 11 Papageorgiu)

2 πάντα χὠ Vater: πανταχοῦ L: πάντα χ G¹

568

λάθα Πιερίσιν στυγερὰ
κἀνήρατος· ὦ δύνασις
θνατοῖς εὐποτμοτάτα μελέων,
ἀνέχουσα βίου βραχὺν ἰσθμόν

Stobaeus, Anthology 3, 26, 1 (3, 609, 6 Hense)

1 Πιερίσιν Grotius: Πιερίδων codd.   2 κἀνήρατος Jebb:
καὶ ἀνάρατος SMA: καὶ ἀνάρετος Trincavelli   ὦ δύνασις
Schneider: ᾠδυνάσεις codd.   3 θνατοῖς Grotius: θανάτοις
codd.

284

566

ODYSSEUS

Are you afraid already at the sight of the buildings of Troy?

ACHILLES

(expresses distress and says that he wants to leave)

OD.

I know what you wish to flee from! Is it not from ill-repute! But Hector is near! Does not honour demand that you remain?

567

(*to Odysseus*) You who are up to everything, how clearly in all things does one see in you much of Sisyphus and of your mother's father![a]

[a] Odysseus, son of Laertes, was said by his enemies to be the bastard son of the cunning Sisyphus; his mother Anticleia was the daughter of the equally cunning Autolycus.

568

Oblivion is hateful to the Pierians and is unlovely! O power of songs, thing happiest for mortals, you who maintain the narrow channel of their life![a]

[a] Memory (Mnemosyne) was said to be the mother of the Muses, who were associated with Pieria, near Mount Olympus. Life is visualised as a narrow channel between the great oceans of the periods before birth and after death.

ΤΑΝΤΑΛΟΣ

The punishment in Hades of Tantalus, the wealthy king of Lydia and father of Niobe, at one time honoured by the gods, is mentioned as early as the eleventh book of the Odyssey. *Different accounts are given of his offence;* Pindar in the First Olympian Ode *says that at a banquet*

572

ΧΟΡΟΣ

βιοτῆς μὲν γὰρ χρόνος ἐστὶ βραχύς,
κρυφθεὶς δ᾿ ὑπὸ γῆς κεῖται θνητὸς
τὸν ἅπαντα χρόνον

Stobaeus, *Anthology* 4, 53, 1 (5, 1097, 3 Hense); om. codd. MA

2 κρυφθεὶς δ᾿ Grotius: κρυφθεῖσα cod. S

573

Ἑρμῆς ἐδήλου τήνδε χρησμῳδὸν φάτιν

Lexicon Messanense f. 282v 13 ed. Rabe

ΤΕΥΚΡΟΣ

In the Ajax (1007 f) *Teucer expresses his fear that when he returns home to Salamis his father Telamon will cast him out for not having prevented the suicide of his brother. Later authors tell us that this fear was realised, and that Teucer sailed away and founded Salamis in Cyprus. The most famous allusion is in* Horace, Odes *1, 7, but Teucer's foundation of Salaminian Cyprus is mentioned as early as Pindar. Fr. 576 shows that Oileus, father*

TANTALUS

*given to the gods he served up the flesh of his son Pelops,
and he is also said to have received from Pandareus, who
had stolen it, the golden dog which Zeus had sent to guard
a temple in Crete, and then to have lied about it when
Hermes came to recover it. But we know nothing of the
plot of this play.*

572

CHORUS

For the time of life is short, and once a mortal is hidden
beneath the earth he lies there for all time.

573

Hermes revealed this message of the oracle.

TEUCER

*of the Locrian Ajax, was a character, and a chance allu-
sion in Aristotle's* Rhetoric *(1416a 36) shows that surpris-
ingly Odysseus was another; the part played by Odysseus
in the* Ajax *suggests that he may have turned up to plead
for Teucer with Telamon. Pacuvius wrote a* Teucer *which
has been conjectured to have been based upon the play of
Sophocles. The quotation in the* Clouds *(fr. 578) shows
that the play was produced before 423 B.C. See on the*
Eurysaces; *and see TrGF ii (Adespota) fr. 569.*

576

τοὺς δ' ἂν μεγίστους καὶ σοφωτάτους φρενὶ
τοιούσδ' ἴδοις ἂν οἷός ἐστι νῦν ὅδε,
καλῶς κακῶς πράσσοντι συμπαραινέσαι·
ὅταν δὲ δαίμων ἀνδρὸς εὐτυχοῦς τὸ πρὶν
5 πλάστιγγ' ἐρείσῃ τοῦ βίου παλίντροπον,
τὰ πολλὰ φροῦδα καὶ καλῶς εἰρημένα

Stobaeus, *Anthology* 4, 49, 7 (5, 1018, 18 Hense)

5 πλάστιγγ' Ellendt: μάστιγ' codd.

577

⟨ΤΕΛΑΜΩΝ⟩
ὡς ἄρ', ὦ τέκνον, κενὴν
ἐτερπόμην σου τέρψιν εὐλογουμένου
ὡς ζῶντος· ἡ δ' ἄρ' ἐν σκότῳ λαθοῦσά με
ἔσαιν' Ἐρινὺς ἡδοναῖς ἐψευσμένον

Stobaeus, *Anthology* 4, 54, 9 (5, 1114, 14 Hense)

3 λαθοῦσά] λήθουσά Papageorgiu

578

οὐρανοῦ δ' ἄπο
ἤστραψε, βροντὴ δ' ἐρράγη δι' ἀστραπῆς

Schol. VEG on Aristophanes, *Clouds* 583

576

But you might see the greatest and wisest men to be like this man is now, in offering good comfort to one who is unfortunate; but when the daemon of a man who formerly enjoyed good fortune swings the balance of life to the other side, most of their sayings, good as they are, have vanished.[a]

[a] This passage is quoted by Stobaeus as from the *Oedipus*; but it is found in neither of Sophocles' plays of that name, and since Cicero, *Tusculan Disputations* 3, 71, who gives a free translation of this passage, tells us that in Sophocles these words referred to Oileus, who had tried to console Telamon after the death of Ajax, Grotius conjectured with much probability that "Oedipus" was a mistake for "Oileus," the name of that play having been wrongly substituted for *Teucer* because the lines referred to that person. Oileus was the father of the Locrian Ajax; see on the play named after the latter.

577

⟨TELAMON⟩

So the delight was empty which I felt, my son, when I heard you praised as though you were alive; and in the darkness, unknown to me, the Erinys beguiled me with false pleasure in my delusion.

578

And from heaven came lightning, and through its flash burst thunder.

FRAGMENTS OF KNOWN PLAYS

ΤΗΛΕΦΟΣ, ΤΗΛΕΦΕΙΑ

See on Ἀλεάδαι, Μυσοί, Εὐρύπυλος

ΤΗΡΕΥΣ

In the Odyssey *the father of the nightingale is Pandareus and her son is Zethus, but in Hesiod she is daughter of Pandion, who was king of Athens. In Aeschylus'* Suppliant Women *she is wife of Tereus, but the earliest full account of her story that we know of is that of this play. A hypothesis published in 1974 (P.Oxy. 3013) seems to have been closely followed by Tzetzes. Other accounts conform in general to this, but it is hazardous to try to use the* Tereus *of Accius or Ovid's* Metamorphoses *in attempts at detailed reconstruction.*

Procne, daughter of Pandion, king of Athens, is married to the Thracian king Tereus; some authors say that she was given to him as a reward for his help in war. After a time she is lonely, and asks Tereus to travel to Athens and bring her sister Philomela to Thrace to keep her company. On the way Tereus rapes the sister, and to avoid detection cuts out her tongue. According to some versions

581

τοῦτον δ' ἐπόπτην ἔποπα τῶν αὑτοῦ κακῶν
πεποικίλωκε κἀποδηλώσας ἔχει
θρασὺν πετραῖον ὄρνιν ἐν παντευχίᾳ·

290

TELEPHUS

TELEPHUS, TELEPHEIA

See on The Sons of Aleus, The Mysians, Eurypylus

TEREUS

Tereus had pretended that she had died on the journey, but in fact she had got away and was hiding somewhere in the wilds. There she wove a picture of what had happened into a tapestry, and contrived to send it to her sister. Procne revenged herself on her husband by killing their son Itys—the name sometimes appears as Itylus—and serving him up to his father as a meal. Tereus having learned the truth pursued the two women with a sword, but the gods intervened, changing Tereus into a hoopoe, Philomela into a swallow, and Procne into a nightingale, who never ceases to lament her son. The Roman poets made Procne the swallow and Philomela the nightingale, and most later poets have followed them. The play was produced before 414 B.C., for it was made fun of in Aristophanes' Birds, in which Tereus, in his hoopoe form, plays a not unimportant part. See fr. 890. For attempts to reconstruct the plot, see D. Fitzpatrick, CQ 51 (2001), 90–101.

581

Him, the hoopoe who looks upon his own misery,[a] he has adorned with varied colours and has displayed as a bird of

---

[a] There is an untranslatable pun here between *epops*, the hoopoe, and *epoptes*, someone who looks over or surveys.

ὃς ἦρι μὲν φανέντι διαπαλεῖ πτερὸν
5   κίρκου λεπάργου· δύο γὰρ οὖν μορφὰς φανεῖ
παιδός τε χαὐτοῦ νηδύος μιᾶς ἄπο·
νέας δ᾽ ὀπώρας ἡνίκ᾽ ἂν ξανθῇ στάχυς,
στικτή νιν αὖθις ἀμφινωμήσει πτέρυξ·
ἀεὶ δὲ μίσει τῶνδ᾽ ἀπαλλαγεὶς τόπων
10   δρυμοὺς ἐρήμους καὶ πάγους ἀποικιεῖ

Aristotle, *History of Animals* 633a 17, who attributes the fragment to Aeschylus; cf. Pliny, *Natural History* 10, 86; Welcker assigned it to Sophocles. There is no indication that Aeschylus ever wrote about this subject. The style and language seem more like those of Sophocles, and Aristotle's memory may well have played him false.

4 φανέντι Nauck: φαίνοντ(α)ι codd.   διαπαλεῖ Gilbert: διαπάλλει or διαβάλλει codd.   9 τῶνδ᾽ ἀπαλλαγεὶς τόπων Heath: τῶνδ᾽ ἀπ᾽ ἄλλον εἰς τόπον codd.   10 ἀποικιεῖ Dindorf: ἀποικίσει codd.

582

Ἥλιε, φιλίπποις Θρῃξὶ πρέσβιστον σέλας

Schol. A on *Il.* 15, 705 (4, 145, 30 Erbse)

1 σέλας] σέβας Bothe

583

⟨ΠΡΟΚΝΗ⟩

νῦν δ᾽ οὐδέν εἰμι χωρίς· ἀλλὰ πολλάκις
ἔβλεψα ταύτῃ τὴν γυναικείαν φύσιν,
ὡς οὐδέν ἐσμεν. αἱ νέαι μὲν ἐν πατρὸς
ἥδιστον, οἶμαι, ζῶμεν ἀνθρώπων βίον·
5   τερπνῶς γὰρ ἀεὶ παῖδας ἀνοία τρέφει.

the rocks, bold in his full panoply. When spring appears
he shall spread the wing of a white-feathered hawk; for he
shall show two forms from a single womb, the young one's
and his own. And when the harvest is new and the corn is
threshed, again a dappled wing will guide him. But ever in
hatred he will get clear of these places and will make his
home in lonely woods and mountains.

582

O Sun, light greatly honoured by the horse-loving
Thracians . . .

583

⟨PROCNE⟩

But now I am nothing on my own. But I have often
regarded the nature of women in this way, seeing that we
amount to nothing. In childhood in our father's house we
live the happiest life, I think, of all mankind; for folly
always rears children in happiness. But when we have

ὅταν δ᾽ ἐς ἥβην ἐξικώμεθ᾽ ἔμφρονες,
ὠθούμεθ᾽ ἔξω καὶ διεμπολώμεθα
θεῶν πατρῴων τῶν τε φυσάντων ἄπο,
αἱ μὲν ξένους πρὸς ἄνδρας, αἱ δὲ βαρβάρους,
10 αἱ δ᾽ εἰς ἀγηθῆ δώμαθ᾽, αἱ δ᾽ ἐπίρροθα.
καὶ ταῦτ᾽, ἐπειδὰν εὐφρόνη ζεύξῃ μία,
χρεὼν ἐπαινεῖν καὶ δοκεῖν καλῶς ἔχειν

Stobaeus, *Anthology* 4, 22, 45 (4, 517, 15 Hense)

3 ἐν Valckenaer: γὰρ SMA: γὰρ ἐν B   5 παῖδας F.W.
Schmidt: πάντας codd.   6 ἔμφρονες Dobree: εὔφρονες
codd.   10 ἀγηθῆ Scaliger: ἀληθῆ SMA: ἀήθη B

584

πολλά σε ζηλῶ βίου,
μάλιστα δ᾽ εἰ γῆς μὴ πεπείρασαι ξένης

Stobaeus, *Anthology* 3, 39, 12 (3, 724, 5 Hense)

2 μάλιστα Brunck: κάλλιστα codd.

585

ἀλγεινά, Πρόκνη, δῆλον· ἀλλ᾽ ὅμως χρεὼν
τὰ θεῖα θνητοὺς ὄντας εὐπετῶς φέρειν

Stobaeus, *Anthology* 4, 44, 58 (5, 972, 4 Hense)

586

σπεύδουσαν αὐτήν, ἐν δὲ ποικίλῳ φάρει

Herodian, *On Words with Two Quantities* 2, 16, 3 Lentz =
On Anomalous Words 36, 24 Dindorf

294

understanding and have come to youthful vigour, we are pushed out and sold, away from our paternal gods and from our parents, some to foreign husbands, some to barbarians, some to joyless homes, and some to homes that are opprobrious. And this, once a single night has yoked us, we must approve and consider to be happiness.

584

I envy you for many features of your life, but most of all because you have no experience of any foreign land.

585

This is painful, Procne, that is clear; but none the less we are mortals and must put up with what the gods send us.

586

. . . as she was hurrying herself, and in a coloured coat . . .

587

φιλάργυρον μὲν πᾶν τὸ βάρβαρον γένος

Stobaeus, *Anthology* 3, 10, 25 (3, 414, 3 Hense)

588

θάρσει· λέγων τἀληθὲς οὐ σφαλῇ ποτε

Stobaeus, *Anthology* 3, 13, 21 (3, 457, 8 Hense)

589

ἄνους ἐκεῖνος· αἱ δ' ἀνουστέρ<ως> ἔτι
ἐκεῖνον ἠμύναντο <πρὸς τὸ> καρτερόν.
ὅστις γὰρ ἐν κακοῖσι θυμωθεὶς βροτῶν
μεῖζον προσάπτει τῆς νόσου τὸ φάρμακον,
5 ἰατρός ἐστιν οὐκ ἐπιστήμων κακῶν

Stobaeus, *Anthology* 3, 20, 32 (3, 545, 6 Hense)

1 suppl. Pflugk   2 suppl. Bamberger

590

ΧΟΡΟΣ

θνητὴν δὲ φύσιν χρὴ θνητὰ φρονεῖν,
τοῦτο κατειδότας, ὡς οὐκ ἔστιν
πλὴν Διὸς οὐδεὶς τῶν μελλόντων
ταμίας ὅ τι χρὴ τετελέσθαι

Stobaeus, *Anthology* 3, 22, 22 (3, 589, 3 Hense)

1 transposed by Grotius: θνητὰ φρ. χ. θνητὴν φ. codd.

TEREUS

587

For the whole race of barbarians loves money.

588

Have no fear! If you speak the truth you will never come to grief.

589

He is mad! But they acted still more madly in punishing him by violence. For any mortal who is infuriated by his wrongs and applies a medicine that is worse than the disease is a doctor who does not understand the trouble.[a]

[a] These look like the words of a god from the machine, commenting on the action.

590

CHORUS

Human nature must think human thoughts, knowing that there is no master of the future, of what is destined to be accomplished, except Zeus.[a]

[a] These must have been the concluding words of the play; compare the final words of the *Ajax* or of Euripides' *Medea*.

591

⟨ΧΟ.⟩

ἓν φῦλον ἀνθρώπων, μί᾽ ἔδειξε πατρὸς
καὶ ματρὸς ἡμᾶς ἀμέρα τοὺς πάντας· οὐδεὶς
ἔξοχος ἄλλος ἔβλαστεν ἄλλου.
βόσκει δὲ τοὺς μὲν μοῖρα δυσαμερίας,
5   τοὺς δ᾽ ὄλβος ἡμῶν, τοὺς δὲ δουλεί-
    ας ζυγὸν ἔσχεν ἀνάγκας.

Stobaeus, *Anthology* 4, 29, 12 (5, 706, 4 Hense); 1–2 ἓν . . .
ἀμέρα: Favorinus, *On Exile* col. IX 22 (385, 25 Barigazzi)

592

ΧΟ.

ἀλλὰ τῶν πολλῶν καλῶν
τίς χάρις, εἰ κακόβουλος
φροντὶς ἐκτρίψει τὸν εὐαίωνα πλοῦτον;

* * *

τὰν γὰρ ἀνθρώπου ζόαν
5   ποικιλομήτιδες ἆται
    πημάτων πάσαις μεταλλάσσουσιν ὥραις

vv. 1–3: Plutarch, *On Reading the Poets* 4, 21B; vv. 4–6:
Stobaeus, *Anthology* 4, 34, 39 (5, 837, 8 Hense)

3 ἐκτρίψει Herwerden: ἐκτρέφει codd.
4 γὰρ Bergk: δ᾽ codd.   ζόαν Dindorf: ζωὰν codd.

591

⟨CH.⟩

Mankind is one tribe; one day in the life of father and
mother brought to birth all of us; none was born superior
to any other. But some are nurtured by a fate of misfor-
tune, others of us by prosperity, and others are held down
by the yoke of compulsion that enslaves us.

592

CH.

But what pleasure comes from the many splendid things,
if thought that gives bad counsel is to destroy the wealth
that makes life happy?

. . . For the life of men is transformed by the cunning
wiles of ruinous error that bring calamities at all seasons.

593

⟨XO.⟩

ζώοι τις ἀνθρώπων τὸ κατ᾽ ἦμαρ ὅπως
ἥδιστα πορσύνων· τὸ δ᾽ ἐς αὔριον αἰεὶ
τυφλὸν ἕρπει

Stobaeus, *Anthology* 4, 34, 40 (5, 837, 12 Hense)

3 τυφλὸς Friedländer

ΤΡΙΠΤΟΛΕΜΟΣ

The Eleusinian hero Triptolemus, according to some accounts the inventor of the plough, was sent round the earth by Demeter in a chariot drawn by flying dragons to spread the blessings of agriculture. Several of the fragments clearly refer to this mission. We know from fr. 598 that Demeter herself gave Triptolemus instructions about his journey. These fragments have reminded scholars of the speeches full of geographical details in the Io scene of the Prometheus Bound, *and fr. 597 closely resembles line 815 of that play. Pliny,* Natural History *18, 65 says that the* Triptolemus *was produced "about 145 years before the death of Alexander," and since he died in 323 B.C., that means in about 468 B.C. If that is correct, it must have been one of the earliest plays of Sophocles, perhaps part of the earliest tetralogy of all. It has often been supposed that Sophocles was influenced by Aeschylus; but if, as many scholars nowadays believe, the* Prometheus Bound *was not by Aeschylus, then its author may have been influ-*

593

〈CH.〉

Let any man procure as much pleasure as he can as he lives his daily life; but the morrow comes ever blind.

TRIPTOLEMUS

enced by Sophocles. But in any case geographical cata-logues may have been not uncommon in tragedy.

We do not know the plot of the play, but there are sev-eral stories about Triptolemus which may have supplied it. In one of these stories Triptolemus is identified with the child of Metaneira whom Demeter was trying to make im-mortal when its mother interrupted her (see the Homeric Hymn to Demeter*), and he was compensated for the loss of immortality by being made the pioneer of agriculture. One of the many different persons stated to have been his father is the Eleusinian hero Celeus. But in one story Celeus was not his father, but plotted to kill him out of jealousy, only the goddess intervened and made Celeus hand over the kingdom to Triptolemus. He was also said to have been in danger from some of the persons encoun-tered on his mission, such as the Scythian king Lyncus and the Thracian king Charnabon, mentioned in fr. 604. See frr. 804, 837.*

596

δράκοντε θαιρὸν ἀμφιπλὶξ εἰληφότε

Et. Magn. 395, 11; Rufus of Ephesus, *On the parts of a human being* 108; Pollux, *Vocabulary* 2, 172; Suda α 3031, etc.

δράκοντε Jungermann: -α Et. Magn. εἰληφότε Et. Magn., Ruf. Ephes.: -ες Pollux, etc.

597

⟨ΔΗΜΗΤΗΡ⟩

θοῦ δ' ἐν φρενὸς δέλτοισι τοὺς ἐμοὺς λόγους

Schol. ABCDEQ on Pindar, *Ol.* 10, 1e (1, 309, 1 Drachmann)

θοῦ δ' ἐν Pfeiffer: οὐδ' αὖ A: σὲ δ' ἐν cett. σὺ δὲν Meineke, quo accepto ad finem γράφου addidit Zuntz.

598

ΔΗ.

τὰ δ' ἐξόπισθε χειρὸς ἐς τὰ δεξιὰ
Οἰνωτρία τε πᾶσα καὶ Τυρσηνικὸς
κόλπος Λιγυστική τε γῆ σε δέξεται

Dionysius of Halicarnassus, *History of Early Rome* 1, 12, 1

600

et fortunatam Italiam frumento canere candido

Pliny, *Natural History* 18, 65 ut . . . Sophocles poeta in fabula Triptolemo frumentum Italicum ante cuncta laudaverit, ad verbum tralata sententia, 'et fortunatam . . .'

TRIPTOLEMUS

596

Two dragons twined around the axle[a] . . .

[a] This corresponds exactly with what we see on vases showing Triptolemus in his chariot.

597

⟨DEMETER⟩

And place my words in the tablets of your mind![a]

[a] See prefatory note.

598

DE.

And the regions lying behind you on the right, the whole of Oenotria[a] and the Tyrrhenian Gulf[b] and the Ligurian land shall receive you.

[a] This word denotes the western seaboard of Italy from the Straits of Messina as far north as the gulf of Paestum.
[b] This means the sea off the coast of Latium and Etruria.

600

. . . and that fortunate Italy is white with shining corn.

602

Καρχηδόνος δὲ κράσπεδ᾽, ⟨ἣν⟩ ἀσπάζομαι

Schol. A on Euripides, *Trojan Women* 221 (2, 354, 18 Schwartz)

suppl. Bergk

604

καὶ Χαρναβῶντος, ὃς Γετῶν ἄρχει τὰ νῦν

Herodian, *On Anomalous Words* 9, 25 (2, 915, 3 Lentz)

ὃς Γετῶν K.O. Müller: ὅτι τῶν ὅς γε cod.

605

ἦλθεν δὲ Δαὶς θάλεια, πρεσβίστη θεῶν

Hesychius, *Lexicon* δ 104 Latte

θάλεια Küster: θήλεια codd.   πρεσβίστη] -ῃ (i.e., to Demeter) v. Blumenthal

606

οὐδ⟨ἐν⟩ ἡ τάλαινα δοῦσα τοῦ ταριχηροῦ γάρου

Pollux, *Vocabulary* 6, 65 (2, 19, 10 Bethe); Athenaeus 2, 67C (τοῦ . . . γάρου)

suppl. Meineke

611

ἀπυνδάκωτος οὐ τραπεζοῦται κύλιξ

Pollux, *Vocabulary* 10, 79 (2, 213, 8 Bethe); Schol. on *Il.* 11, 634; Demetrius, *On Style* 114, etc.

TRIPTOLEMUS

602

. . . and the skirts of Carthage, which I greet . . .

604

. . . and Charnabon, who at present rules the Getae[a] . . .

[a] See prefatory note; the Getae were a Thracian tribe.

605

And there came rich Banquet, greatly honoured among the gods.

606

The wretch gave none of the pickled caviare.[a]

[a] Caviare is perhaps too polite a name for *garum*, which was made from the salted livers of fish, often the Spanish mackerel, and whose modern descendant "looks like anchovy sauce, and has an evil but appetizing smell" (D'Arcy Thompson, *A Glossary of Greek Fishes*, p. 121).

611

A cup without a bottom is not put on the table.[a]

[a] This line is censured by Demetrius, *On Style* 114 as frigid, on the ground that "the matter is trivial, and does not justify such an orotund expression." But the line passed into a proverb, which surely proves that it has some merit.

FRAGMENTS OF KNOWN PLAYS

ΤΡΩΙΛΟΣ

*Troilus, the very young and handsome son of Priam,
was killed by Achilles in an ambush, when in order to
exercise his horses he had ridden to the temple of Apollo
Thymbraeus, which was outside the walls of Troy. The
scene appears on several vases, and Troilus is often
accompanied by his sister Polyxena. According to one
story, Achilles saw her on this occasion and fell in love
with her. We are ignorant of the plot of the play, though it*

618

ἔγημεν ὡς ἔγημεν ἀφθόγγους γάμους,
τῇ παντομόρφῳ Θέτιδι συμπλακείς ποτε

Schol. BDP on Pindar, *Nem.* 3, 60 (3, 51, 17 Drachmann)

παντομόρφῳ Casaubon: παντα- BP: ποντο- D

619

τὸν ἀνδρόπαιδα δεσπότην ἀπώλεσα

Schol. BEFGQ on Pindar, *Pyth.* 2, 121c (2, 51, 7 Drachmann)

620

σκάλμῃ γὰρ ὄρχεις βασιλὶς ἐκτέμνουσ᾽ ἐμούς

Pollux, *Vocabulary* 10, 165 (2, 239, 7 Bethe)

621

πρὸς ναρὰ καὶ κρηναῖα χωροῦμεν ποτά

Orion, *Etymologies* 110, 1 Sturz; Et. Gud. 408, 60 Sturz; Et.
Gen. AB = Et. Magn. 597, 43

TROILUS

*is clear that an eunuch who was Troilus' paidagogos was
one of the characters. There was a story that according to
an oracle Troy could not be taken so long as Troilus was
alive, which might explain why Achilles took the trouble
to ambush so young and harmless a person. The older
Troilus who was involved with Cressida is an invention of
the Middle Ages, the name Cressida being a corruption of
the name Chryseis. If an inscription (*TrGF *I DID A 2b78)
is rightly restored, this play was produced in 418* B.C.

618

He married as he married, a wedding without speech,
wrestling with Thetis who took every shape.[a]

[a] This obviously refers to Peleus, the father of Achilles, whose
encounter with Thetis is described by Pindar, *Nem.* 4, 63 f.

619

I lost the man-boy who was my master.[a]

[a] The speaker must be the eunuch who was Troilus' paida-
gogos; cf. fr. 620.

620

For the queen, cutting off my testicles with a knife . . .

621

We are going to the running waters of the springs.

FRAGMENTS OF KNOWN PLAYS

ΤΥΜΠΑΝΙΣΤΑΙ

We do not know the subject of this play. Welcker's conjecture that it dealt with the story of Phineus is based on very inadequate evidence. The Thracian king Phineus married first Cleopatra, the daughter of Boreas, the North Wind, by the Athenian princess Oreithyia. His second wife, who put out the eyes of his sons by his first marriage, or else falsely accused them of having tried to rape her, so that their father blinded them, was Idaea, daughter of Dardanus. We know from a scholion on the

636

φεῦ φεῦ, τί τούτου χάρμα μεῖζον ἂν λάβοις,
τοῦ γῆς ἐπιψαύσαντα κᾷθ᾽ ὑπὸ στέγῃ
πυκνῆς ἀκοῦσαι ψακάδος εὐδούσῃ φρενί;

Stobaeus, *Anthology* 4, 17, 12 (4, 402, 13 Hense); v. 1: Plutarch, *Life of Aemilius Paullus* 1, 3; vv. 2–3: Cicero, *Letters to Atticus* 2, 7, 4 κἂν (instead of κᾷθ᾽) . . . φρενί

2 κὀθ᾽ Meineke: καὶ Stobaeus: κᾷν Cicero

637

ἡμεῖς δ᾽ ἐν ἄντροις, ἔνθα Σαρπηδὼν πέτρα

Herodian, *On Anomalous Words* 9, 8 Dindorf (2, 914, 9 Lentz)

ἄντροις Bergk: ἄστροις cod.

638

Κόλχος τε Χαλδαῖός τε καὶ Σύρων ἔθνος

Stephanus of Byzantium, *Ethnica* 680, 12 Meineke

THE DRUMMERS

Antigone *(fr. 645, on line 981) that Eidothea was mentioned in the* Drummers; *fr. 637 mentions the cave to which Boreas carried Oreithyia, and fr. 643 may refer to a legend about Oreithyia's family in Athens, but this evidence does not amount to much. Drums figured in the worship of Dionysus and of Cybele, which was popular in Thrace, where Phineus lived, and the chorus may have consisted of worshippers of these deities, who in Thrace were regarded as mother and son. If the play did deal with Phineus, it may have been identical with the* Phineus, *q.v. See fr. 956.*

For an attempt to reconstruct the action of this play and the two plays about Phineus, see Innocenza Giudice Rizzo, Inquieti 'commerci' tra uomini e dei: Timpanisti, Fineo A e B di Sofocle *(Studia Archaeologica dell'Erma di Bretschneider 117, Rome, 2002).*

636

Ah, ah, what greater joy could you obtain than this, that of reaching land and then under the roof hearing the heavy rain in your sleeping mind?

637

And we in the caves, where the Sarpedonian rock is[a] . . .

[a] Boreas carried off Oreithyia to the neighbourhood of this peak of Mount Haemus, in Thrace.

638

The Colchian and the Chaldaean and the race of the Syrians . . .

ΤΥΝΔΑΡΕΩΣ

There are only two quotations, and no evidence bearing on the plot of the play. Tyndareus, son of Oebalus or of Perieres, was king of Sparta. He was at one time driven into exile by his brother Hippocoon, but was restored to his throne by Heracles, after a memorable battle. His wife Leda, the daughter of Thestius, gave birth to two sons, Castor and Polydeuces, and two daughters, Helen and Clytemnestra. According to the usual story, Helen and Polydeuces were the children of Zeus, Clytemnestra and Castor the children of Tyndareus. Tyndareus entertained

646

οὐ χρή ποτ᾽ εὖ πράσσοντος ὀλβίσαι τύχας
ἀνδρός, πρὶν αὐτῷ παντελῶς ἤδη βίος
διεκπεραθῇ καὶ τελευτήσῃ δρόμον.
ἐν γὰρ βραχεῖ καθεῖλε κὠλίγῳ χρόνῳ
5 πάμπλουτον ὄλβον δαίμονος κακοῦ δόσις,
ὅταν μεταστῇ καὶ θεοῖς δοκῇ τάδε.

Stobaeus, *Anthology* 4, 41, 3 (5, 928, 5 Hense)

3 διεκπεραθῇ Nauck: -περανθῇ codd.   δρόμον Headlam: βίον codd.

647

ἀμβλυφαεῖ δ᾽ ὄμμ᾽ ὑπὸ γήρως

Photius 1165 Theodoridis

ἀμβλυφαεῖ] -ὲς Wilamowitz

TYNDAREUS

the many suitors of his daughter Helen, and persuaded them to swear that if she was abducted they would come to the aid of her husband. It has been argued that the fragments indicate that the play was about the sad old age of Tyndareus. But there is no evidence that his old age was sad, though in Euripides' Orestes *he reproaches Orestes with the killing of Clytemnestra, and he may have been represented as surviving after the end of the earthly life of Castor and Polydeuces. See on the plays about Helen.*

646

When a man prospers one should never call his fortune good before his life has been completed and he has run his course. For with little effort and in a moment of time the gift of an adverse fortune ruins the happiness brought by vast wealth, when the gods decree that things must change.

647

The eye grows dim with age.

ΤΥΡΩ Α΄ ανδ Β΄

Tyro, the daughter of Salmoneus (see on the Salmoneus), who became the wife of her father's brother Cretheus, fell in love with the Thessalian river Enipeus, and often visited the bank of the stream. Poseidon in the likeness of the river god took her, and she gave birth to twins, Pelias and Neleus. The twins were exposed, and brought up by a herdsman. Tyro was blamed by her father for her pregnancy, and was brutally ill-treated by her stepmother Sidero. But her sons, now grown to manhood, rescued her and pursued her enemy. Sidero took refuge at the altar of Hera, and had just reached the altar when Pelias cut her down, thus incurring the enmity of the goddess. The true identity of the sons was revealed near the end of the play by means of the cradle in which

648

λευκὸν ⟨γὰρ⟩ αὐτὴν ὧδ᾽ ἐπαίδευσεν γάλα

Erotian, *Medical Lexicon* π 32 Nachmanson (Σοφοκλῆς ἐν Πελίᾳ: Engelmann assigned it to the *Tyro*)

⟨γὰρ⟩ Cobet   ὧδ᾽ Schneider: ὅδ᾽ codd.

649

P. Hibeh 10 (ed. Grenfell and Hunt, *Hibeh Papyri* I, 1906, p. 17); assigned to the *Tyro* by Blass, ap. ed. pr.; Pearson ii 275–8; Page, *GLP* no. 25; Carden, pp. 161–170; Kannicht and Snell, *TrGF (Adespota)* 626 (ii p. 181 s.)

TYRO 1 *and* 2

*they had been exposed. Later, Neleus moved to Messenia,
and became the father of Nestor. Pelias ruled in Iolcos,
and sent his nephew Jason to recover the Golden Fleece.*

*Since what is recorded about Tyro does not appear to
provide material for more than one tragedy, it seems likely
that the second play named after her was a revised version
of the first. The second must have been earlier than 414,
since it is quoted in Aristophanes'* Birds *(fr. 654).*

*The grounds for assigning P.Hibeh 3 (fr. 649) to this
play are slight; the mention of the Alpheus, which flows
through Elis, where Salmoneus ruled, in fr. d and the
prayer to Poseidon in fr. f do not amount to much. If this
guess is right, the chorus consisted of women (frr. a–c 26).*

648

The nurture of the white milk made her like this.[a]

[a] This alludes to Tyro's complexion. Her name comes from
the word for cheese, and Sidero's name from the word for iron.
Cf. fr. 658.

649

frr. a–c

26 εὔνους δὲ καὶ τάσδ᾽ εἰσορᾷς πεν[θητρί]ας

fr. d

37 φό]βος τις αὐτὴν δεῖμά τ᾽ ἔννυχον πλανᾷ
    (about 8 letters)] ...εν τῷδε κοινωνεῖ τάδε
    (about 10 letters) καλ]λίρουν ἐπ᾽ Ἀλφειοῦ πόρον

fr. f

52 ...].ας ἀρωγὸν πατέρα λίσσομα[ι μολεῖν
    ἄν]ακτα πόντου μητρί

supplements by ed. pr.

653

μὴ σπεῖρε πολλοῖς τὸν παρόντα δαίμονα·
σιγώμενος γάρ ἐστι θρηνεῖσθαι πρέπων

Stobaeus, *Anthology* 4, 45, 2 (5, 993,10 Hense) (Τυροῦς β΄)
1 πολλοῖς] ἐς ἄλλους F.W. Schmidt: ἐπ᾽ ἄλλοις?

654

τίς ὄρνις οὗτος ἔξεδρον χώραν ἔχων;

Schol. VΓ on Aristophanes, *Birds* 275 (ἐκ τοῦ Σοφοκλέους
β΄ Τυροῦς)

TYRO

frr. a–c

And these mourning women whom you see are friendly.[a]

> [a] The speaker is telling his interlocutor that they may speak freely in the presence of the Chorus.

fr. d 37–39

Some fear, some nocturnal terror is making her distracted.[a] . . . these . . . accompany this . . . to the fair-flowing stream of Alpheus . . .

> [a] If this fragment is really from the *Tyro*, one may guess that Sidero, like Clytemnestra in the *Electra*, has had a warning dream.

fr. f 52–53

I pray my father, the lord of the sea, to come to help my mother.[a]

> [a] The son of Poseidon who is praying his father to help his mother may be Pelias or Neleus.

653

Do not spread abroad to many your prevailing fortune; it is fitter to keep silent about it as you lament it.

654

What is this bird in an unaccustomed quarter?[a]

> [a] The word translated "quarter" is a technical term in augury.

658

αὕτη δὲ μάχιμός ἐστιν ὡς κεκλημένη
σαφῶς Σιδηρώ, καὶ φρονοῦσα τοὔνομα
οὐκ οἴεται δύσκλειαν ἐκ τούτου φέρειν

Aristotle, *Rhetoric* 2, 23, 1400 b 16 and Schol. (ed. Rabe), p. 146, 26

1 κεκλημένη Cobet: κεχρημένη Ar. et Schol.   2 φρο-
νοῦσα Cobet ('sapiens nomen' in the Latin versions): φοροῦσα
Aristotle and Schol.   3 omitted by Aristotle

659

ΤΥΡΩ

κόμης δὲ πένθος λαγχάνω πώλου δίκην,
ἥτις συναρπασθεῖσα βουκόλων ὕπο
μάνδραις ἐν ἱππείαισιν ἀγρίᾳ χερὶ
θέρος θερισθῇ ξανθὸν αὐχένων ἄπο,
πλαθεῖσα δ' ἐν λειμῶνι ποταμίων ποτῶν
ἴδῃ σκιᾶς εἴδωλον αὐγασθεῖσά που
κουραῖς ἀτίμως διατετιλμένης φόβην.
φεῦ, κἂν ἀνοικτίρμων τις οἰκτίρειέ νιν
πτήσσουσαν αἰσχύνῃσιν οἷα μαίνεται
πενθοῦσα καὶ κλαίουσα τὴν πάρος χλιδήν

Aelian, *On the Nature of Animals* 11, 18

5 πλαθεῖσα Reiske: σπασθεῖσα codd.   6 αὐγασθεῖσά
που Meineke: αὐγασθεῖσ' ὑπὸ codd.   φόβην Wakefield:
-ης codd.   8–10 Kassel suspects that these lines were spo-
ken by another person   10 χλιδήν Brunck: φόβην codd.

658

She is combative, like one who is truly called Sidero, and since she has the mind of such a one she does not think her name brings her discredit.[a]

[a] See note on fr. 648.

659

TYRO

And it is my lot to mourn my hair, like a foal, whom herdsmen have seized in the horses' stables with rough grip, and who has had the yellow mane reaped from her neck; and when she comes to the meadow to drink the water of the river, reflected in the water she sees her image, with her hair shamefully hacked off. Ah, even a pitiless person might pity her, cowering beneath the outrage, as she madly laments and bewails the luxuriant hair she had before![a]

[a] The last sentence may have been spoken by another character.

FRAGMENTS OF KNOWN PLAYS

660

προσβῆναι μέσην
τράπεζαν ἀμφὶ σῖτα καὶ καρχήσια

Athenaeus, *Deipnosophists* 11, 475A (Σοφοκλῆς Τυροῖ . . .
πρὸς τὴν τράπεζαν φάσκων προσεληλυθέναι τοὺς δράκοντας
καὶ γενέσθαι περὶ τὰ σιτία καὶ τὰ καρχήσια); Macrobius, *Saturnalia* 5, 21, 6 (337, 16 Willis)

1 προσβῆναι Hartung: προστῆναι Athen.

661

πόλλ᾽ ἐν κακοῖσι θυμὸς εὐνηθεὶς ὁρᾷ

Stobaeus, *Anthology* 3, 20, 29 (3, 544, 14 Hense)

662

μήπω μέγ᾽ εἴπῃς, πρὶν τελευτήσαντ᾽ ἴδῃς

Stobaeus, *Anthology* 4, 41, 21 (5, 934, 4 Hense), etc.

663

τίκτουσι γάρ τοι καὶ νόσους δυσθυμίαι

Stobaeus, *Anthology* 4, 35, 13 (5, 860, 1 Hense)

664

γῆρας διδάσκει πάντα καὶ χρόνου τριβή

Stobaeus, *Anthology* 4, 50, 6 (5, 1021, 14 Hense)

665

ἄκων δ᾽ ἁμαρτὼν οὔτις ἀνθρώπων κακός

Stobaeus, *Anthology* 4, 5, 12 (4, 199, 18 Hense)

660

. . . to approach the middle of the table near the food and
the cups . . .

661

When you are in trouble, you see much if you can calm
your anger.

662

Make no pronouncement till you have seen his end![a]

[a] Cf. fr. 646.

663

For sicknesses too are caused by depressions.

664

Old age and the wearying effect of time teach all things.

665

No human being who does wrong by accident is evil.

666

σίτοισι παγχόρτοισιν ἐξενίζομεν

Athenaeus, *Deipnosophists* 3, 99F

σίτοισι Porson: οἱ τοῖσι cod.

667

πολλῶν δ' ἐν πολυπληθίᾳ πέλεται
οὔτ' ἀπ' εὐγενέων ἐσθλὸς οὔτ' ἀχρείων
γόνος ἀεὶ κακός· βροτῶν δὲ πιστὸν οὐδέν

Stobaeus, *Anthology* 4, 29, 29 (5, 715, 10 Hense)

1 πολλῶν] λαῶν Nauck   3 γόνος ἀεὶ Ll.-J.: τὸ λίαν
codd.   βροτῶν Heath: -ῷ codd.

668

Διονύσου τοῦ ταυροφάγου

Schol. RVE on Aristophanes, *Frogs* 357 (Κρατίνου τοῦ
ταυροφάγου)

ΥΒΡΙΣ

*We are altogether ignorant of the plot of this satyr
play; but it is worth remarking that according to one story
Hybris was the mother of Pan by Zeus. Hybris would be a*

670

Λήθην τε τὴν <τὰ> πάντ' ἀπεστερημένην,
κωφήν, ἄναυδον

Stobaeus, *Anthology* 3, 26, 3 (3, 610, 4 Hense)

1 suppl. Wagner

TYRO

666

We entertained . . . with every kind of provender.

667

Among the multiplicity of the many the descendant of noble men is not always good and that of useless people is not always bad; nothing about mortals can be trusted.

668

. . . bull-eating Dionysus[a] . . .

[a] With this in mind, Aristophanes, *Frogs* 357 applied the same epithet to the comic poet Cratinus.

HYBRIS

suitable name for a nymph, and the birth of Pan would be an appropriate subject for a satyr play, just as the birth of Hermes is the subject of The Searchers. *See fr. 809.*

670

And Forgetfulness that is deprived of all things, dumb, speechless . . .

FRAGMENTS OF KNOWN PLAYS

ΥΔΡΟΦΟΡΟΙ

Plot unknown; the play by Aeschylus of the same name,
Semele *or* The Water-Carriers, *dealt with the birth of Dionysus. Bergk conjectured that it was a satyr play.*

672

ὄχοις Ἀκεσταίοισιν ἐμβεβὼς πόδα

Photius Galeanus 366, 12; Suda o 1029 Adler

ΦΑΙΑΚΕΣ

There are only two quotations, and we have no means of knowing the plot. One would hardly expect another play about Phaeacians besides the Nausicaa. *Pearson tried to find a way out by suggesting that the play may have dealt with the visit of the Argonauts to Phaeacia that*

ΦΑΙΔΡΑ

The play evidently dealt with the same subject as the surviving second Hippolytus *of Euripides. Phaedra, daughter of Minos and wife of Theseus, fell in love with her stepson, Hippolytus, son of Theseus by the Amazon whom he had captured, and on being rejected by him killed herself, leaving behind a false accusation that he had offered her violence which led his father Theseus to lay on him a curse that resulted in his death. We do not know how Sophocles treated the subject, nor the chronological relation of his play to the two different* Hippolytus *plays of Euripides; attempts to reconstruct Sophocles' plot from the summary of the myth given by Asclepiades of Tragilus in the scholia on the* Odyssey *or from Seneca's*

THE WATER-CARRIERS

672

... with his foot upon the Acestan chariot[a] ...

[a] Acesta is the same as Egesta, in the *Aeneid* the site of a Trojan settlement in Sicily ruled by Acestes; since it was famous for its mules, the allusion may be to a mule-car.

THE PHAEACIANS

is described by Apollonius of Rhodes in the fourth book of his Argonautica*. But it is not impossible for the same play to have, or at least to be referred to by, three titles. See on* Thyestes *and* Odysseus Wounded by the Spine, *and see fr. 861.*

PHAEDRA

Phaedra *are unconvincing. It is clear that the chorus consisted of women (fr. 679), and that at the beginning of the action Theseus was in Hades, having accompanied his friend Pirithous in his attempt to carry off Persephone (frr. 686–7), a circumstance that might be held to extenuate Phaedra's behaviour. If fr. 693a is rightly assigned to this play, Phaedra had a female counsellor who at one point offered her advice of which she strongly disapproved. This may well have been a nurse, and like the nurse in Euripides'* Hippolytus *she may have made a proposition to Hippolytus on her behalf against the orders of her mistress. For discussion of the tragedies of Sophocles, Euripides and Seneca on this subject, see Barrett,*

Euripides, Hippolytos *(1964, corr. ed. 1966) and Zwierlein,* Senecas Phaedra und ihre Vorbilder (Abh. der Mainzer Akademie, *1987).*

677

οὐ γὰρ δίκαιον ἄνδρα γενναῖον φρένας
τέρπειν, ὅπου γε μὴ δίκαια τέρψεται

Stobaeus, Anthology 3, 17, 2 (3, 490, 1 Hense) ; Orion, Florilegium 6,7

2 γε μὴ Schneidewin: μὴ καὶ Stob.: γε Orion   τέρψεται]
-πεται Orion

678

ἀπέπτυσε⟨ν⟩ λόγους

Hesychius, Lexicon a 5993 Latte

679

σύγγνωτε κἀνάσχεσθε σιγῶσαι· τὸ γὰρ
γυναιξὶν αἰσχρὸν σὺν γυναῖκα δεῖ στέγειν

Stobaeus, Anthology 4, 23, 16 (4, 575, 14 Hense)

2 γυναῖκα Meineke: γυναικὶ A

680

αἴσχη μέν, ὦ γυναῖκες, οὐδ᾽ ἂν εἷς φύγοι
βροτῶν ποθ᾽, ᾧ καὶ Ζεὺς ἐφορμήσῃ κακά·
νόσους δ᾽ ἀνάγκη τὰς θεηλάτους φέρειν

Stobaeus, Anthology 4, 44, 50 (5, 970, 9 Hense)

677

For it is not right that a noble man should take pleasure when the pleasure is not right.

678

He scornfully rejected the proposal.

679

Be sympathetic and maintain silence! For a woman should cover up what brings shame on women.[a]

[a] Evidently Phaedra is asking the Chorus not to reveal her secret.

680

Not one mortal, women, could escape shameful actions, upon whom Zeus brought troubles; and we have to bear the sicknesses sent by the gods.

681

τὸ⟨ν⟩ δ' εὐτυχοῦντα πάντ' ἀριθμήσας βροτῶν
οὐκ ἔστιν ὄντως ὄντιν' εὑρήσεις ἕνα

Stobaeus, *Anthology* 4, 41, 40 (5, 939, 12 Hense)

1 suppl. Grotius   ἀριθμήσας Grotius: -ῆσαι codd.
2 ὄντως Gesner: οὗτος codd.

682

οὕτω γυναικὸς οὐδὲν ἂν μεῖζον κακὸν
κακῆς ἀνὴρ κτήσαιτ' ἂν οὐδὲ σώφρονος
κρεῖσσον· παθὼν δ' ἕκαστος ἂν τύχῃ λέγει

Stobaeus, *Anthology* 4, 22, 80 (4, 527, 15 Hense)

3 ἂν Campbell: ὧν codd.

683

οὐ γάρ ποτ' ἂν γένοιτ' ἂν ἀσφαλὴς πόλις
ἐν ᾗ τὰ μὲν δίκαια καὶ τὰ σώφρονα
λάγδην πατεῖται, κωτίλος δ' ἀνὴρ λαβὼν
πανοῦργα χερσὶ κέντρα κηδεύει πόλιν

Stobaeus, *Anthology* 4, 1, 5 (4, 2, 7 Hense); Schol. on Lucian,
Lexiphanes 10 (199, 19 Rabe)

684

Ἔρως γὰρ ἄνδρας οὐ μόνους ἐπέρχεται
οὐδ' αὖ γυναῖκας, ἀλλὰ καὶ θεῶν ἄνω
ψυχὰς ταράσσει κἀπὶ πόντον ἔρχεται·

681

If you go through them all, you will not find a single mortal who is fortunate in all things.

682

And so a man could acquire no plague worse than a bad wife nor any treasure better than a right-minded one; and each man tells the tale according to his own experience.

683

For no city can be safe in which justice and good sense are trampled under foot, and a clever talker criminally grasps a goad and guides the city.

684

For Love comes not only upon men and women, but troubles the minds even of the gods in the sky, and moves over

καὶ τόνδ᾽ ἀπείργειν οὐδ᾽ ὁ παγκρατὴς σθένει
5 Ζεύς, ἀλλ᾽ ὑπείκει καὶ θέλων ἐγκλίνεται

Stobaeus, *Anthology* 4, 20, 24 (4, 440, 16 Hense); vv. 1–3
Clement of Alexandria, *Miscellanies* 6, 2, 14, 7 (2, 434, 9 Stählin),
who assigns it to Euripides

685

ἀλλ᾽ εἰσὶ μητρὶ παῖδες ἄγκυραι βίου

Synagoge 338, 15 Bekker = Photius α 191 Theodoridis

686

A

ἔζης ἄρ᾽, οὐδὲ γῆς ἔνερθ᾽ ᾤχου θανών;

B

οὐ γὰρ πρὸ μοίρας ἡ τύχη βιάζεται.

Stobaeus, *Anthology* 1, 5, 13 (1, 77, 3 Wachsmuth)

687

ἔσαινεν οὐρᾷ μ᾽ ὦτα κυλλαίνων κάτω

Hesychius, *Lexicon* κ 4513 Latte

ἔσαινεν Salmasius: ἔσταιεπ᾽ cod.   οὐρᾷ μ᾽ Hiller: οὐραν
(sic) cod.   ὦτα Salmasius: ὦτι cod.   κυλλαίνων κάτω
Salmasius: κυαλάννων καὶ τὸ cod.

687a

γλώσσης ἀπαυστὶ στάζε μυξώδης ἀφρός

Photius α 2288 Theodoridis

στάζε Tsantsanoglu: στάζει cod.

the sea. And not even the all-powerful Zeus can keep him off, but he too yields and willingly gives way.

685
But to a mother children are the anchors of her life.

686

A

So you were alive, and though beneath the earth you were not dead?

B

No, for fate does not do violence to a man before his time.[a]

[a] The second speaker is presumably Theseus; see prefatory note.

687
He fawned upon me with his tail, with his ears back.[a]

[a] Theseus is probably speaking about Cerberus.

687a
An unclean foam dripped continually from its mouth.[a]

[a] The omission of the augment shows that this comes from a messenger speech; it probably comes from the description of the monstrous bull that scared Hippolytus' horses, thus causing his death.

693a

A

ἄπειμι τοίνυν· οὔτε γὰρ σὺ τἄμ᾽ ἔπη
τολμᾷς ἐπαινεῖν οὔτ᾽ ἐγὼ τοὺς σοὺς τρόπους.

B

ἀλλ᾽ εἴσιθ᾽· οὔ σοι μὴ μεθέψομαί ποτε,
οὐδ᾽ ἢν σφόδρ᾽ ἱμείρουσα τυγχάνῃς· ἐπεὶ
πολλῆς ἀνοίας καὶ τὸ θηρᾶσθαι κενά.

S., *Electra* 1050–1054; vv. 1050–1 are assigned to Sophocles, *Phaedra* by Stobaeus, *Anthology* 3, 2, 29; 1050–4 are assigned to that play by Ll.-J. (see *Sophoclea* 62).

ΦΘΙΩΤΙΔΕΣ

Aristotle, Poetics *1456a 1 says that this was a tragedy of character; but we know nothing of the plot. But Phthia was the home of Peleus, and some have argued that the*

694

νέος πέφυκας· πολλὰ καὶ μαθεῖν σε δεῖ
καὶ πόλλ᾽ ἀκοῦσαι καὶ διδάσκεσθαι μακρά

Stobaeus, *Anthology* 2, 31, 16 (2, 204, 18 Wachsmuth)

695

γέρων γέροντα παιδαγωγήσω σ᾽ ἐγώ

Aulus Gellius, *Attic Nights* 13, 19, 3

PHAEDRA

693a

A

Then I shall go away; for you cannot bring yourself to approve my words, and I cannot approve your behaviour.

B

Well, go! I shall never follow you, however much you may desire it; since it is utter folly to embark on a vain quest.[a]

[a] These lines seem to have been interpolated into the *Electra* (1050–54); Stobaeus says that the first two come from the *Phaedra*, and very likely all of them do, since they have no relevance in the place where they are found. They seem to come from a conversation between Phaedra and her confidante and go-between, perhaps a nurse, as in the *Hippolytus*; in that case, Phaedra is probably the second speaker.

THE WOMEN OF PHTHIA

play was the same as the Peleus, *q.v., and others that it was the same as the* Hermione, *q.v. It has also been conjectured that the play dealt with episodes from Peleus' early life.*

694

You are young; you have much to learn and much to listen to, and need long schooling.[a]

[a] Perhaps this was addressed to the young Neoptolemus.

695

I shall lead you like a child, one old man leading another.[a]

[a] This line is identical with Euripides, *Bacchae* 193; in this play it may have been spoken to or by the aged Peleus.

FRAGMENTS OF KNOWN PLAYS

696

ἡ πατροκτόνος δίκη
κεκλῆτ᾽ ἂν αὐτῷ

Anonymous, *On Syntax* 128, 1 Bekker

ΦΙΛΟΚΤΗΤΗΣ ΕΝ ΤΡΟΙΑΙ

According to the Little Iliad *Philoctetes on arriving at Troy fulfilled the prediction of Heracles at* Phil. *1423 f. He was healed of his wound by Machaon, and in a duel between archers killed Paris, whose body was maltreated by Menelaus before the Trojans managed to bury it.*

697

⟨ΦΙΛΟΚΤΗΤΗΣ⟩
ὀσμῆς μόνον
ὅπως . . . μὴ βαρυνθήσεσθέ μου

Priscian, *Institutes* 18, 169 (2, 284, 5 Hertz)

μόνον ὅπως Porson: μόνον ὡς O: μου ὅπως cett.

698

ἀλλ᾽ ἔσθ᾽ ὁ θάνατος λοῖσθος ἰατρὸς νόσων

Stobaeus, *Anthology* 4, 52, 26 (5, 1080, 15 Hense)

699

μέλη βοῶν ἄναυλα καὶ ῥακτήρια

Hesychius, *Lexicon* ρ 88 Schmidt

μέλη Musurus: μέλι cod.   ἄναυλα Bergk: ἄνανδα cod.

696

He might bring an action for his father's killing.[a]

[a] In Euripides' *Andromache* and *Orestes* Neoptolemus demands that Apollo should pay him a penalty for the death of his father.

PHILOCTETES AT TROY

Quintus of Smyrna in the tenth book of his Posthomerica *gives a detailed account; the arrow only scratched Paris, but it was infected with the poison of the Hydra. But we cannot use Quintus to reconstruct the play of Sophocles, and we do not know if Sophocles mentioned Oenone, or the adventures of Philoctetes in Italy after the war.*

697

⟨PHILOCTETES⟩

Only do not be distressed by the smell of me!

698

But death is the last healer of sicknesses.

699

Uttering harsh and discordant cries . . .

701

καὶ ῥάβδος ὡς κήρυκος Ἑρμαία διπλοῦ
δράκοντος ἀμφίκρανος

Photius α 1336 Theodoridis

ΦΙΝΕΥΣ Α΄ ανδ Β΄

See on the Τυμπανισταί *(The Drummers), which
may have been identical with one of these plays. In one of
the two plays Phineus was punished for blinding his sons,
who in one version of the story were healed by Asclepius,
by being blinded himself, either by Zeus, or by the Argo-
nauts, or by Apollo, or by the Sun, and was further
afflicted by being persecuted by the Harpies, who when he
tried to eat swooped down and carried off his food.*

707

οὐδ᾿ ἂν τὸ Βοσπόρειον ἐν Σκύθαις ὕδωρ

Stephanus of Byzantium, *Ethnica* 179, 6 Meineke; Et. Sym. β
161 (p. 102, 8) Berger

707a

ἰδοὺ στυγητοῦ κρατὸς ἀγρία φόβη
τ‹ο›μαῖος

Herodian, *On Prosody in General*, cod. Vindob., ed. Hunger,
1967

701

And a staff of Hermes like that of a herald with a dragon's head at each end[a] . . .

[a] It has been conjectured that this is the staff carried by Asclepius, who Heracles at *Phil.* 1437 promises will come to Troy to heal Philoctetes' wound.

PHINEUS 1 *and* 2

But according to one story he was offered the gift of prophecy at the price of being blinded, and chose to accept the offer. In the second book of the Argonautica *of Apollonius of Rhodes, the sons of Boreas, arriving with the Argonauts, reward Phineus for guiding the expedition by driving off the Harpies. Frr. 711 and 712 have led some scholars to conjecture that one of the plays was a satyric drama. See fr. 956.*

707

Nor would the water of the Bosporus where the Scythians are . . .

707a

See, the rough hair of the hated head cut off![a]

[a] Can this describe part of the revenge of the sons of Phineus upon their stepmother?

710

(ἀντὶ γὰρ τυφλοῦ)
ἐξωμμάτωται καὶ λελάμπρυνται κόρας,
Ἀσκληπιοῦ παιῶνος εὐμενοῦς τυχών

Aristophanes, *Wealth* 634–6 and Scholia

711

βλέφαρα κέκληται δ᾽ ὡς καπηλείου θύρα

Pollux, *Vocabulary* 7, 193 (2, 105, 5 Bothe)

712

νεκρὸς τάριχος εἰσορᾶν Αἰγύπτιος

Athenaeus, *Deipnosophists* 3, 119C

ΦΟΙΝΙΞ

See on Δόλοπες, *which may well have been the same play.*

718

κύναρος ἄκανθα πάντα πληθύει γύην

Athenaeus, *Deipnosophists* 2, 70A

παντὶ . . . γύῃ?

710

(From being blind) he has been given eyes and his eye-balls have been made bright, since he has found a kindly healer in Asclepius.[a]

[a] We cannot be sure that this relates to the healing of Phineus, since Phylarchus (Jacoby, *FGrH* 81 F 18) tells us that Asclepius healed the sons of Phineus to oblige their mother Cleopatra, daughter of Erechtheus.

711

His eyes are closed as the door of a tavern is closed.[a]

[a] I.e., they are opened at very frequent intervals. This fragment has led some to infer that one of the Phineus plays must have been a satyr play, and others to suggest that a comic poet's parody of a line of Sophocles may have been mistaken for genuine Sophocles.

712

. . . looking like an Egyptian mummy . . .

PHOENIX

See on The Dolopians

718

The dog thorn abounds in every portion of the land.

ΦΡΙΞΟΣ

See on Athamas; *the* Phrixus *may have been identical with one of the two* Athamas *plays. It has been conjectured that this play used the version of the story in which*

721

ὅρια κελεύθου τῆσδε γῆς προαστίας

Stephanus of Byzantium, *Ethnica* 139, 20 Meineke

722

κυνηδὸν ἐξέπραξά νιν κνυζούμενον

Et. Gud. w (330, 39 Sturz); Et. Gen. A

ἐξέπραξά νιν Papabasileiu: ἐξέπραξαν Et. Gud.: ἐσπάραξέ νιν Blaydes

ΦΡΥΓΕΣ

Aeschylus wrote a play called Φρύγες *(The Phrygians), whose alternative title was* Ἕκτορος Λυτρά *(The Ransoming of Hector). If a scholion on* Prometheus Bound *436 is right in saying that Achilles was silent out of obstinacy* (δι᾽ αὐθάδειαν) *in the* Phrygians *of Sophocles,*

724

τοὺς εὐγενεῖς γὰρ κἀγαθούς, ὦ παῖ, φιλεῖ
Ἄρης ἐναίρειν· οἱ δὲ τῇ γλώσσῃ θρασεῖς

PHRIXUS

Phrixus' father plans to sacrifice him because of a false ac-cusation by his own wife, Phrixus' stepmother, or by Demodice the wife of Cretheus; but there is no positive ev-idence for this.

721

The boundaries of the road of this land in front of the city

722

I finished him off, while he squealed like a dog.

THE PHRYGIANS

the subject of this play was the same as that of Aeschylus' play with the same title; but in all likelihood "Sophocles" here is a mistake for "Aeschylus." We must admit, there-fore, that we do not know the subject of this play, from which we have only two quotations. See on the Priam, *which may have been the same play.*

724

My son, Ares loves to kill the noble and the valiant; and they who are brave with their tongues escape destructive

φεύγοντες ἄτας ἐκτός εἰσι τῶν κακῶν·
Ἄρης γὰρ οὐδὲν τῶν κακῶν λωτίζεται.

Stobaeus, *Anthology* 3, 8, 5 (3, 341, 10 Hense); v. 4: Schol.
BCE on *Il.* 2, 833

2 ἐναίρειν B: συναίρειν MSA   3 τῶν κακῶν] πημάτων
Wecklein   4 λωτίζεται Keil: λογίζεται Stobaeus: ληΐζεται
Schol. on Homer

725

οὐ λήξετ', οὐ παύσεσθε τούσδε τοὺς γάμους
ἀνυμεναιοῦντες;

Photius α 2154 Theodoridis

ΧΡΥΣΗΣ

Hyginus, Fables *120–1 tells us that Chryseis, the
daughter of the priest Chryses, who was carried off by Ag-
amemnon, with the results described in the first book of
the* Iliad, *had a son called Chryses, whose father, she
claimed, was Apollo. While escaping from the Taurian ty-
rant Thoas, Orestes and Iphigeneia arrived at the island
of Sminthe, where this Chryses ruled. At first he was in-
clined to hand them over, but after he had learned that
they were the children of Agamemnon, to whom he stood
in the same relation as Heracles to Amphitryon, he helped
Orestes to kill Thoas, and all of them together made their
way to Mycenae. This might be a summary of the plot of
Sophocles' play, and certain works of art have been
thought to furnish support (see* LIMC *III 1285–6); but*

forces and keep out of trouble; for Ares cuts down nothing that belongs to evil.[a]

[a] It has been conjectured that Priam spoke these words to Achilles.

725

Will you not cease to celebrate in song this wedding?[a]

[a] Cassandra may have been the speaker, perhaps with regard to the wedding that at one point was proposed between Achilles and the Trojan princess Polyxena.

CHRYSES

there can be no certainty. Dionysius of Byzantium, a geographer of the second century A.D., says that Chryses was a son of Chryseis and Agamemnon who fled from Clytemnestra and Aegisthus to seek refuge with his sister Iphigeneia among the Taurians, but died on the way and gave his name to the city of Chrysopolis. Tzetzes in his commentary on Lycophron says that Chryses and Iphigeneia were children of Agamemnon by Chryseis who after the Trojan War started for Greece, but Chryses died at Chrysopolis and Iphigeneia was captured by the Taurians and made priestess of Artemis. Either of these stories may have been used by Sophocles. Some have conjectured that it was a satyr play, but the fragments hardly provide enough evidence for this. See on the Iphigeneia.

726

ὦ πρῷρα λοιβῆς Ἑστία, κλύεις τάδε;

Schol. V(G) on Aristophanes, *Wasps* 846; Schol. BD on Pindar, *Nem.* 11, 5 (3, 186, 17 Drachmann)

727

. . . μακέλλῃ Ζηνὸς ἐξαναστραφῇ

Schol. RVEΓ on Aristophanes, *Birds* 1240

⟨ὅταν⟩, ⟨ὡς ἂν⟩, or ⟨ὃς ἂν⟩ Fritzsche

728

τοιοῦτος ὢν ἄρξειε τοῦδε τοῦ κρέως

Schol. RVE on Aristophanes, *Frogs* 191

ἄρξειε E: ἄρξει RV: ἄρξεις Aldine edition

729

ἐγὼ μίαν μὲν ἐξιονθίζω τρίχα

Apollonius Sophista, *Homeric Lexicon* 91, 33 Bekker; Hesychius, *Lexicon* ε 3907 Latte

μίαν μὲν] μέλαιναν Lehrs   τρίχα Hesych.: -ας Ap. Soph.

CHRYSES

726

O Hestia, goddess of the hearth, where the first libation is offered, do you hear this?

727

. . . it was uprooted by the mattock of Zeus.

728

. . . that being such as he is he should have power over this body.[a]

[a] The word rendered "body" properly means "meat," and its use in this sense is comic.

729

Here is one hair that my beard is sprouting![a]

[a] If the text is right, this must be a joke, and together with fr. 728 this fragment has been held to show that this was a satyr play. But if Lehrs' emendation is right, the line means "I am sprouting black hairs."

FRAGMENTS NOT ASSIGNABLE
TO ANY PLAY

730

Ed. pr. Turner, P.Oxy. 2452, Part 27, 1962, 1–20, Plates i and ii (ii = Turner, *Greek Manuscripts of the Ancient World*, 1987², no. 27); cf. Lloyd-Jones, *Gnomon* 35 (1963) 434–6; Carden, *PFS* 110–35.

P.Oxy. 2452 consists of 86 fragments of a play about the adventures of Theseus in Crete. Only seven of the fragments reach a moderate size, and since they contain no complete line and no two consecutive half-lines, they are not printed here. In fr. 730a Eriboea is addressing an

734

τὰς Ἑκαταίας μαγίδας δόρπων

Pollux, *Vocabulary* 6, 83 (2, 24, 19 Bethe)

735

τὸ πρὸς βίαν
πίνειν ἴσον πέφυκε τῷ διψῆν κακόν

Athenaeus, *Deipnosophists* 10, 428A

2 corr. Meineke, Cobet: π. ι. κ. πέφ. τῷ δ. βίᾳ codd.

FRAGMENTS NOT ASSIGNABLE
TO ANY PLAY

730

appeal in dochmiacs to Ariadne, who replies in trimeters. In fr. 730c Theseus, apparently looking forward to his struggle with the Minotaur, recalls his previous triumphs as he does at Euripides, Hippolytus *976 f and as Heracles does at Sophocles,* Trachiniae *1090f. Language and style seem a little more suggestive of Sophocles than of Euripides; Sophocles is credited with both a* Theseus *and a* Minos, *though each is quoted only once. It can hardly come from Euripides,* Theseus, *since one would expect some coincidence with frr. 381–90 Nauck.*

734

The trays that contain Hecate's suppers[a] . . .

[a] Food supposed to be for Hecate was deposited at her shrines at crossroads, and might be eaten by beggars; see S. I. Johnston, *ZPE* 88 (1991), 219–20.

735

Being forced to drink is as bad a thing as being thirsty.

FRAGMENTS NOT ASSIGNABLE

737

μισῶ μὲν ὅστις τἀφανῆ περισκοπῶν

Achilles Tatius, *Introduction to Aratus* 1 (27, 1 Maass)

738

. . . κἀνταῦθα πᾶς
προσκυνεῖ σφε τὸν στρέφοντα κύκλον ἡλίου . . .

Achilles Tatius, *Introduction to Aratus* 1 (28, 17 Maass)
Σοφοκλῆς δὲ εἰς Ἀτρέα τὴν εὕρεσιν (sc. τῆς ἀστρονομίας)
ἀναφέρει λέγων 'κἀνταῦθα . . .' κτλ

Iambic trimeters? Iambic tetrameters? I think trochaic te-
trameters are likelier, but certainty is unattainable.

2 σφε Diggle: δὲ codd.

743

Τεισὼ δ' ἄνωθεν †εστινη† αἱματορρόφος

Synagoge 362, 21 Bekker; Photius α 627 Theodoridis

Τεισὼ Pfeiffer: τίσω δ' Synag.: τίς δ' Phot. ἄνωθ'
ἔστηκεν ? Ll.-J.

745

σπουδὴ γὰρ ἡ κατ' οἶκον εὖ κεκρυμμένη
οὐ πρὸς θυραίων οὐδαμῶς ἀκουσίμη

Synagoge 373, 13 Bekker = Photius α 817 Theodoridis

1 εὖ κ. Blaydes: ἐγκ. codd.   2 πρὸς θυραίων Brunck:
προσθυραῖον Synag.: πρὸς θυραιον Phot.

737

I hate a man who, while he gazes after what cannot be
seen . . .

738

. . . here also everyone bows down before him who re-
versed the circuit of the sun.[a]

[a] For the story of how Atreus was responsible for the sun's
path being reversed, see Euripides, *Electra* 727 f and *Orestes*
1001 f. The fragment has been assigned to the *Atreus*, or to one
of the plays about Thyestes.

743

And, above, Teiso swilling blood[a] . . .

[a] Teiso is an abbreviation of Teisiphone, one of the Erinyes.

745

Activity that is well concealed at home should not by any
means be heard of by outsiders.

751

ἐτῆρας ἀμνοὺς θεοῖς ἔρεξ' ἐπακτίοις

Schol. AE on Dionysius Thrax, *Grammar* 12 (541, 5 Hilgard)

ἐτῆρας] εὔειρας v. l. ap. Schol.   ἔρεξ' L. Dindorf: ἐράξας codd.

752

Ἥλι', οἰκτίροις ἐμέ,
⟨ὃν⟩ οἱ σοφοὶ λέγουσι γεννητὴν θεῶν
πατέρα ⟨τε⟩ πάντων

Vatican Scholia 191 on Aratus i p. 42, 9 Martin

1 Ἥλι', οἰκτίροις Nauck, after Bergk: ἠελίοιο κτείρειε ἐμέ cod.   2 suppl. Petavius   3 suppl. Schneider

753

βαρὺς βαρὺς ξύνοικος, ὦ ξένοι, βαρύς

Philodemus, *On Poems*, CA iv 120, col. 12, 15 ed. Hausrath, and others who omit the author's name

754

A

καὶ πρῶτα μὲν
αἴρω ποθεινὴν μᾶζαν, ἣν φερέσβιος
Δηὼ βροτοῖσι χάρμα δωρεῖται φίλον·
ἔπειτα πνικτὰ τακερὰ μηκάδων μέλη
5 χλόην καταμπέχοντα σάρκα νεογενῆ.

B

τί λέγεις;

751

I (*or* he) sacrificed year-old lambs to the gods of the sea-shore.

752

Sun, take pity on me, you who wise men say are the begetter of the gods and father of all!

753

Hard, hard to live with, strangers, hard!

754

A

And first I lift the much-longed-for loaf, the gift to mortals of Deo,[a] bringer of our livelihood, a well-loved delight; and then the baked tender limbs of bleaters, embracing green vegetables, the meat of young ones.

B

What are you saying?

[a] A poetical name of Demeter. How much of this passage from a comedy comes from Sophocles is uncertain.

FRAGMENTS NOT ASSIGNABLE

A

τραγῳδίαν περαίνω Σοφοκλέους.

Antiphanes fr. 1 K.-A., cited by Athenaeus, *Deipnosophists* 9, 396B

2 Δηὼ Casaubon: Δημήτηρ cod.   6 περαίνω Casaubon: παραινῶ cod.

755

οὐ γάρ τι νόθος τῷδ᾽ ἀπεδείχθη,
ἀμφοῖν δὲ πατὴρ αὐτὸς ἐκλήθη·
Ζεὺς ἐμὸς ἄρχων, θνητῶν δ᾽ οὐδείς.

vv. 1–3: Aristotle, *Eudemian Ethics* 7, 10, 9, 1242 a 35 (without the author's name); v. 3: Philo, *Every Good Man is Free* 3, 19 (who names Sophocles)

1 ἀπεδείχθη] -ην Casaubon

757

ὦ γλῶσσα, σιγήσασα τὸν πολὺν χρόνον,
πῶς δῆτα τλήσῃ πρᾶγμ᾽ ὑπεξελεῖν τόδε;
ἢ τῆς ἀνάγκης οὐδὲν ἐμβριθέστερον,
ὑφ᾽ ἧς τὸ κρυφθὲν ἐκφανεῖς ἀνακτόρων.

Athenaeus, *Deipnosophists* 1, 33C

2 ὑπεξελεῖν Heimsoeth: ὑπεξελθεῖν codd.
4 ἀνακτόρων Grotius: -ον codd.

760

θάρσει· μέγας σοι τοῦδ᾽ ἐγὼ φόβου μοχλός

Athenaeus, *Deipnosophists* 3, 99C

A

I'm reciting a tragedy of Sophocles!

755

This did not prove him (*or* me?) to be a bastard, but both were said to have the same father. Zeus, and none among mortals, is my lord!

757

Tongue that has remained silent for so long, how shall you endure to bring out this matter? Indeed nothing is weightier than necessity, which shall force you to reveal the secret of the palace.

760

Be confident! You have in me a great barrier against this fear.

FRAGMENTS NOT ASSIGNABLE

761

ναῦται δ᾽ ἐμηρύσαντο ναὸς ἰσχάδα

Athenaeus, *Deipnosophists* 3, 99D

762

χορὸς δ᾽ ἀναύδων ἰχθύων ἐπερρόθει,
σαίνοντες οὐραίοισι ⟨δεσπότιν φίλην⟩

Athenaeus, *Deipnosophists* 7, 277A

2 σαίνοντες Brunck: σαίνουσιν codd.   δεσπότιν φίλην
Ll.-J.: τὴν κεκτημένην Brunck (from Athenaeus, who has οὐ τὴν
κεκτημένην, ἀλλὰ τὰς λοπάδας)

763

διψῶντι γάρ τοι πάντα προσφέρων σοφὰ
οὐκ ἂν πλέον τέρψειας ἢ πιεῖν διδούς

Athenaeus, *Deipnosophists* 10, 433E

2 ἢ Casaubon: μὴ codd.

764

⟨κακὴ⟩ κακῶς σὺ πρὸς θεῶν ὀλουμένη,
ἢ τὰς ἀρύστεις ὧδ᾽ ἔχουσ᾽ ἐκώμασας

Athenaeus, *Deipnosophists* 11, 783F

1 suppl. Meineke

767

ἴκτινος ὡς ἔκλαγξε παρασύρας κρέας

Choeroboscus on Theodosius, *Canons* 1, 267, 6 Hilgard; Et.
Gen.; Zonaras

761

And the sailors drew up the stay of the ship.

762

And a chorus of speechless fish made a din, saluting their dear mistress[a] with their tails.

[a] Amphitrite? Thetis?

763

For when a man is thirsty you cannot give him more pleasure by applying every skilful nostrum than by giving him something to drink.

764

The gods will bring you to the bad end you deserve, you who rushed drunkenly in with the ladles![a]

[a] The language shows that this must come from a satyr play.

767

He screeched like a kite that has snatched a piece of meat.

768

φυσᾷ γὰρ οὐ σμικροῖσιν αὐλίσκοις ἔτι,
ἀλλ' ἀγρίαις φύσαισι φορβειᾶς ἄτερ

Cicero, *Letters to Atticus* 2, 16, 2; [Longinus] 3, 1

769

γυναικομίμοις ἐμπρέπεις ἐσθήμασιν

Clement of Alexandria, *Paedagogus* 3, 11, 53, 4

770

πρὸς οἷον ἥξεις δαίμον' †ὡς ἔρωτα†
ὃς οὔτε τοὐπιεικὲς οὔτε τὴν χάριν
οἶδεν, μόνην δ' ἔστερξε τὴν ἁπλῶς δίκην

vv. 1–3: Clement of Alexandria, *Miscellanies* 2, 20, 123, 3; vv.
2–3: Plutarch, *Amatorius* 17, 761E

1 δ' after πρὸς deleted by Reiske   3 δ' ἔστερξε Ritschl:
δὲ στέρξαι Plutarch: δ' ἔστεργε Clement

771

καὶ τὸν θεὸν τοιοῦτον ἐξεπίσταμαι,
σοφοῖς μὲν αἰνικτῆρα θεσφάτων ἀεί,
σκαιοῖς δὲ φαῦλον κἂν βραχεῖ διδάσκαλον

vv. 1–3: Clement of Alexandria, *Miscellanies* 5, 4, 24, 2; vv. 2–
3: Plutarch, *Why are Delphic Oracles No Longer Given in Verse*
25, 406F

768

For he is blowing no longer on small pipes, but with savage blasts, without a mouthpiece.[a]

[a] It has been conjectured that this comes from an *Oreithyia*, in which according to the rhetorician Johannes Siculus Sophocles "imitated Boreas." Greek pipe-players normally used a mouthpiece.

769

You are conspicuous in clothes that imitate a woman's.

770

To what a deity shall you come . . ., who knows no fairness or gratitude, but loves only plain justice!

771

And this I know well is the god's nature: to clever men he always tells the truth in riddles, but to fools he is a poor instructor and uses few words.

FRAGMENTS NOT ASSIGNABLE

773

Θήβας λέγεις μοι καὶ πύλας ἑπταστόμους,
οὗ δὴ μόνον τίκτουσιν αἱ θνηταὶ θεούς;

Heraclides, *On the Cities of Greece* 1, 17 (80, 15 Pfister)

1 καὶ Blaydes: τὰς codd.

774

μύω τε καὶ δέδορκα κἀξανίσταμαι,
πλέον φυλάσσων αὐτὸς ἢ φυλάσσομαι

Dionysius of Halicarnassus, *On the Order of Words* 9

776

Ἄθως σκιάζει νῶτα Λημνίας βοός

Et. Gen. B; Plutarch, *The Face on the Moon* 22, 935F; Schol.
T on *Il.* 14, 229; Eustathius, *Il.* 980, 44, etc.

777

τρύχει καλυφθεὶς Θεσσαλῆς ἀπληγίδος

Et. Gen. AB = Et. Magn. 123, 14

778

ἢ σφηκιὰν βλίσσουσιν εὑρόντες τινά

Et. Gen. β 150 Berger; Et. Sym. β 131 Berger

779

ἔχω δὲ χερσὶν ἀγρ‹ί›αν βρίακχον

Et. Gen. β 254 Berger = Et. Sym. β 219 Berger

ἔχω Heinsius: ἐγὼ codd.   suppl. Brunck

773

Are you telling me of Thebes and of its seven gates, the only place where mortal women are thought to give birth to gods?[a]

  [a] I have supplied the question-mark, which was suggested to me by the ironic δή. A. F. Garvie has assigned this fragment to the *Bacchae*.

774

I see with eyes shut, and I start up, more the watcher than the watched.

776

Athos casts its shadow over the back of the cow of Lemnos.[a]

  [a] "Athos is not particularly high, 1000 m. lower than Olympus, but is particularly impresssive to seafarers because of its position and the shadow which near sunset it casts as far as Lemnos": Wilamowitz, cited by Fraenkel, *Aeschylus, Agamemnon* ii 154, n. 1. On that island there was a well-known statue of a cow.

777

Hidden by a rag from a Thessalian one-piece garment[a] . . .

  [a] A garment thrown round the shoulders like a plaid, very like the Greek chlamys.

778

. . . or they find some wasps' nest and try to rob it.

779

I hold in my arms a fierce Maenad.[a]

  [a] The line appears to be a lyric iambic trimeter.

780

οἷος γὰρ ἡμῖν δημόκοινος οἴχεται

Et. Gen. AB = Et. Magn. 265, 23

ἡμῖν Bothe: ἡμῶν codd.

783

πολὺς δὲ πηλὸς ἐκ πίθων τυρβάζεται

Et. Gen. AB = Et. Magn. 490, 3, etc.

786

ὕβρις δέ τοι
οὐπώποθ᾽ ἥβης εἰς τὸ σῶφρον ἵκετο,
ἀλλ᾽ ἐν νέοις ἀνθεῖ τε καὶ πάλιν φθίνει

Et. Gen. A = Et. Magn. 601, 56

2 ἥβης εἰς τὸ σῶφρον Pierson: ἡβήσει τῷ σώφρονι codd.

788

προσῆλθε μητρὶ καὶ φυταλμίῳ πατρί

Et. Gen. AB = Et. Sym. V = Et. Magn. 803, 4

φυταλμίῳ Sylburg: φυταλίμῳ or φυταλιμῷ Et. Magn.

793

ψακαλοῦχοι
μητέρες αἶγές τ᾽ ἐπιμαστίδιον
γόνον ὀρταλίχων ἀναφαίνοιεν

Eustathius, *Od.* 1625, 43

780

For what a public executioner have we lost!

783

And much wine-lees is stirred up from the casks.[a]

[a] R. A. Neil was probably right in guessing that this came from a satyr play.

786

But insolence never lasts until the sober stage of active life; it is in the young that it blossoms and dies away.

788

He approached his mother and the father who begot him.

793

. . . mothers with young, and may the goats display a brood of young ones at the breast!

FRAGMENTS NOT ASSIGNABLE

795

Μολοσσικαῖσι χερσὶν ἐντείνων πέδας

Choeroboscus on Hephaestion, *Handbook* 217, 13 Consbruch; Anonymus Ambrosianus, *On Metre* 2, 13

ἐντείνων Nauck: ἐκ- codd.

796

ὡς μήτε κρούσῃς μήθ' ὑπὲρ χεῖλος βάλῃς

Harpocration, *Glossary to the Ten Orators* 147, 17

799

ΟΔΥΣΣΕΥΣ

ἐγὼ δ' ἐρῶ σοι δεινὸν οὐδέν, οὔθ' ὅπως
φυγὰς πατρῴας ἐξελήλασαι χθονός,
οὔθ' ὡς ὁ Τυδεὺς ἀνδρὸς αἷμα συγγενὲς
κτείνας ἐν Ἄργει ξεῖνος ὢν οἰκίζεται,
5 οὔθ' ὡς πρὸ Θηβῶν ὠμοβρῶς ἐδαίσατο
τὸν Ἀστάκειον παῖδα διὰ κάρα τεμών

[Herodian], *On Figures* 8, 601, 10 Walz

800

Λυδία λίθος σίδηρον τηλόθεν προσηγάγου

Hesychius, *Lexicon* λ 1353 (cf. η 721) Latte

804

⟨τὰ⟩ σεμνὰ τῆς σῆς παρθένου μυστήρια

Hesychius, *Lexicon* σ 407 Schmidt

⟨τὰ⟩ (or ὡς) suppl. Wagner

795

Fitting fetters to the hands of the Molossian(s).

796

. . . so that you neither beat in the bottom of the measure nor overtop the rim.

799

ODYSSEUS

(*to Diomedes*) I shall say to you nothing dreadful, neither how you were driven out as an exile from your father's country, nor how Tydeus spilt the blood of a kinsman and settled in Argos as a guest, nor how before Thebes he made a cannibal feast off the son of Astacus, after cutting off his head.[a]

[a] As the son of Tydeus Diomedes counted as an Aetolian, although he was brought up in Argos, where his father had taken refuge after killing his uncle Alcathous. When he attacked Thebes with Adrastus and the Seven, Tydeus killed his opponent Melanippus, son of Astacus, and began to eat his brain, causing Athena, who had flown off to bring him immortality, to change her mind. Welcker seems likely to be right in referring the fragment to the *The Laconian Women*, since Odysseus and Diomedes are said to have quarrelled while they were returning to the Greek camp with the Palladium; see prefatory note to that play.

800

You were a magnet attracting iron from far off.

804

The revered mysteries of your daughter[a] . . .

[a] The person addressed must have been Demeter, and Welcker was probably right in assigning the fragment to the *Triptolemus*.

FRAGMENTS NOT ASSIGNABLE

806

λαβόντες ἄφθονον
ἄγραν πρὸς οἴκους εὐτυχοῦντες ἄξομεν

Photius α 3346 Theodoridis

807

ζημίαν λαβεῖν ἄμεινόν ἐστιν ἢ κέρδος κακόν

Lexicon Vindobonense 96, 4

808

ὅ τι γὰρ φύσις ἀνέρι δῷ,
τόδ᾽ οὔποτ᾽ ἂν ἐξέλοις

Libanius, *Orations* 64, 46

809

(ὥσπερ καὶ τὴν Τύχην Σοφοκλῆς ὕμνησε διαπορῶν
†ὑμνεῖ†)

Menander Rhetor, *The Division of Epideictic Speeches*, p. 26
Russell/Wilson

ὑμνεῖ P, om. Z: ἐν Ὕβρει? Ll.-J.

811

ὅρκους ἐγὼ γυναικὸς εἰς ὕδωρ γράφω

Helladius in Photius, *Library* 530 a 15 Bekker; Macarius,
Proverbs 6, 48

815

ἄκουε, σίγα· τίς ποτ᾽ ἐν δόμοις βοή;

Synagoge 372, 10 Bekker; Photius α 813 Theodoridis

806
We shall take measureless booty and bring it home suc-
cessfully.

807
It is better to be punished than to make a dishonest profit.

808
For what nature gives to a man you can never take away.

809
. . . as Sophocles wrote a hymn of the 'questioning' type to
Fortune.[a]

[a] Menander in his rhetorical handbook is discussing hymns
"of puzzlement and questioning," in which the poet raises ques-
tions about the subject's genealogy, or the nature of his power, or
some similar topic.

811
The oaths of a woman I write in water.[a]

[a] The comic poet Xenarchus (fr. 6 K.-A.) parodies this: "the
oath of a woman I write in wine."

815
Listen, silence! What is this cry inside the house?

FRAGMENTS NOT ASSIGNABLE

817

τὸν προβώμιον κλύω
δαίμον᾽ αἱματοσπόδητον

Photius α 626 Theodoridis

819

ἔφη⟨κ᾽⟩· ἀμούσωτος γὰρ οὐδαμῶς ἄπει

Photius α 1240 Theodoridis
ἔφη⟨κ᾽⟩ Mekler: ἔφη cod.

823

χλωροῖσι κορμοῖς ἀνδράχλης ἀναίθεται

Photius α 1739 Theodoridis

827

⟨οὐ⟩ μηκέτ᾽ ἀνθρωπιστὶ διαλέξῃ . . .
τῇδε

Photius α 1989 Theodoridis
1 suppl. Herwerden   2 τῇδε] τάδε Reitzenstein

828f

παπαῖ, χορευτὴς αὐλὸς οὐκέτι ψοφεῖ

Photius α 3180 Theodoridis

817
I hear that the god who stands before the altar was splashed with blood.[a]

[a] The reference must be to a cult statue of a god standing before an altar.

819
Come here! For by no means shall you depart without hearing the music![a]

[a] Mekler, *Berliner Philologische Wochenschrift* 27 (1907) 382, ingeniously assigned this to the *Nausicaa*, taking it to come from an account of Odysseus' encounter with the Sirens (*Od.* 12, 184 f) and supplementing accordingly.

823
It is set on fire with green logs of the andrachne.

827
You shall no longer talk in human fashion with this person![a]

[a] Mekler, in the article cited on fr. 819, thought that this was spoken by Circe to Odysseus, and that the fragment came from the *Nausicaa*.

828f
Ah, the pipe of the dance is no longer sounding!

831
ἔργου δὲ παντὸς ἤν τις ἄρχηται καλῶς,
καὶ τὰς τελευτὰς εἰκός ἐσθ᾽ οὕτως ἔχειν

Plutarch, *On Reading the Poets* 1, 15F

832
στενωπὸς Ἅιδου καὶ παλιρροία βυθοῦ

Plutarch, *On Reading the Poets* 2, 17C

833
τὸ κέρδος ἡδύ, κἂν ἀπὸ ψευδῶν ἴῃ

Plutarch, *On Reading the Poets* 4, 21A

834
οὐκ ἐξάγουσι καρπὸν οἱ ψευδεῖς λόγοι

Plutarch, *On Reading the Poets* 4, 21A
ἐξάγουσι] ἐκφέρουσι Meineke

835
γένοιτο κἂν ἄπλουτος ἐν τιμαῖς ἀνήρ

Plutarch, *On Reading the Poets* 4, 21B

836
οὐδὲν κακίων πτωχός, εἰ καλῶς φρονοῖ

Plutarch, *On Reading the Poets* 4, 21B
φρονοῖ] v.l. φρονεῖ

831

In any work, if you make a good beginning, it is likely that the finish also will be similar.

832

The gorge of Hades and the abysmal tide[a] . . .

[a] Headlam's translation.

833

Profit is sweet, even if it comes from lies.

834

False words bear no fruit.

835

Even without wealth a man may acquire honours.

836

A poor man is no worse than another, if his mind should be good.

FRAGMENTS NOT ASSIGNABLE

837

ὡς τρισόλβιοι
κεῖνοι βροτῶν, οἳ ταῦτα δερχθέντες τέλη
μόλωσ᾽ ἐς Ἅιδου· τοῖσδε γὰρ μόνοις ἐκεῖ
ζῆν ἔστι, τοῖς δ᾽ ἄλλοισι πάντ᾽ ἔχειν κακά

Plutarch, *On Reading the Poets* 4, 21E; Arsenius, *Violarium*, p. 203 Walz

4 ἔχειν Paton: ἐκεῖ, ἐκεῖνα Plutarch: ἐκτόπως Arsenius

838

τυφλὸς γάρ, ὦ γυναῖκες, οὐδ᾽ ὁρῶν Ἄρης
συὸς προσώπῳ πάντα τυρβάζει κακά

Plutarch, *On Reading the Poets* 6, 23B; *Amatorius* 13, 757A

839

οὐκ ἔστ᾽ ἀπ᾽ ἔργων μὴ καλῶν ἔπη καλά

Plutarch, *On Reading the Poets* 8, 27F; Stobaeus, *Anthology* 3, 3, 32 (3, 205, 1 Hense)

840

μολυβδὶς ὥστε δίκτυον κατέσπασεν

Plutarch, *Progress in Virtue* 1, 75B; Et. Gen. AB

841

ὅτῳ δ᾽ ἔρωτος δῆγμα παιδικὸν προσῇ

Plutarch, *Progress in Virtue* 4, 77B; *Table Talk* 1, 2, 6, 619A

παιδικὸν] -οῦ Valckenaer

837

Since thrice fortunate are those among mortals who have seen these rites before going to Hades; for they alone have life there, while others have every kind of misery.[a]

[a] Apparently a reference to the Eleusinian Mysteries.

838

Ares is blind, women, and cannot see, he who with his pig's face stirs up every kind of evil.

839

No noble words come from ignoble deeds.

840

. . . just as the leaden sink carries down the net.

841

But for him who has been stung by love for a boy . . .

FRAGMENTS NOT ASSIGNABLE

842

πρὸς ἅσπερ οἱ μαργῶντες ἐντονώτατοι

Plutarch, *Progress in Virtue* 13, 84A

843

τὰ μὲν διδακτὰ μανθάνω, τὰ δ' εὑρετὰ
ζητῶ, τὰ δ' εὐκτὰ παρὰ θεῶν ᾐτησάμην

Plutarch, *Fortune* 2, 97F

844

βᾶτ' εἰς ὁδὸν δὴ πᾶς ὁ χειρῶναξ λεώς,
οἳ τὴν Διὸς γοργῶπιν Ἐργάνην στατοῖς
λίκνοισι προστρέπεσθε ‹καὶ› παρ' ἄκμονι
τυπάδι βαρείᾳ

Plutarch, *Fortune* 4, 99A; vv. 1–3 βᾶτ' . . . προστρέπεσθε:
Clement of Alexandria, *Protrepticus* 10, 97, 2; cf. Plutarch, *Rules for Politicians* 5, 802A

3 suppl. Gataker

845

σὺ δ' ἄνδρα θνητὸν εἰ κατέφθιτο στένεις,
εἰδὼς τὸ μέλλον οὐδὲν εἰ κέρδος φέρει;

Plutarch, *Consolation to Apollonius* 11, 107A

846

οὐ κόσμος, οὔκ, ὦ τλῆμον, ἀλλ' ἀκοσμία
φαίνοιτ' ἂν εἶναι σῶν τε μαργότης φρενῶν

Plutarch, *Advice on Marriage* 26, 141D

842

Men who are mad about these women are most intense.[a]

[a] But Pearson translated "wherein the frenzied are most vehement," which may be right; it would depend on the context.

843

What can be taught, I learn; what can be found, I look for; what can be prayed for I beg of the gods.

844

Be on your way, all people who work with your hands, you who entreat Zeus' daughter, Ergane of the terrible eyes, with baskets placed before her, and by the anvil with heavy hammer[a] . . .

[a] Ergane was the cult title borne by Athena as the patroness of manual workers, who in Athens celebrated in her honour the feast of the Chalkeia on the last day of the month Pyanopsion.

845

And do you lament the death of a mortal, when you have no idea whether the future will bring him any gain or not?

846

This is not an adornment, no, unhappy one, it would seem to be disorder and the madness of your thinking! [a]

[a] Hartung conjectured that these words were spoken to Eriphyle in the *Epigoni*. Jewellery, such as the necklace for which Eriphyle betrayed her husband, could be called κόσμος, an adornment; but the word also means order as opposed to disorder.

FRAGMENTS NOT ASSIGNABLE

847

εὔκαρπον Κυθέρειαν

Plutarch, *Advice on Marriage* 42, 144B

848

σὺ δὲ σφαδάζεις πῶλος ὡς εὐφορβίᾳ·
γαστήρ τε γάρ σου καὶ γνάθος πλήρης ⟨βορᾶς⟩

Plutarch, *Roman Questions* 71, 280F
2 suppl. E. A. J. Ahrens

849

ἔναυλα κωκυτοῖσιν, οὐ λύρα, φίλα

Plutarch, *The Delphic 'E'* 21, 394B

851

ΑΔΜΗΤΟΣ

οὑμὸς δ᾽ ἀλέκτωρ αὐτὸν ἦγε πρὸς μύλην

Plutarch, *Oracles in Decline* 15, 417E

852

ἀεὶ δ᾽ ἀοιδῶν μοῦνος ἐν στέγαις ἐμαῖς
κωκυτὸς ἐμπέπτωκεν

* * *

μοῦσα καὶ σειρὴν μία

Plutarch, *Curiosity* 6, 518B; *The Control of Anger* 15, 463B

847

. . . fruitful Cytherea[a] . . .

[a] Greek cults of Aphrodite had not much to do with agricultural fertility, but she had a festival at Amathus in Cyprus called κάρπωσις, the feast of fruits.

848

You toss yourself about like an overfed colt, because your stomach and your mouth are crammed with food.

849

Pipe music, not the lyre, is suited to laments.

851

ADMETUS

My cock used to summon him to the mill.[a]

[a] As a punishment for killing the Cyclopes Apollo was condemned to be slave for a year to the Thessalian king Admetus. Presumably Admetus is saying that the crowing of his cock summoned Apollo to work at the mill, one of the most disagreeable tasks imposed on slaves. The tone suggests a satyr play. There is no evidence that Sophocles wrote a play with Admetus as a character; but he wrote an *Eumelus* (q.v.), and note fr. 911.

852

Always the only song that has descended on my house is one of lamentation . . . Muse and one Siren.[a]

[a] Plutarch quotes this fragment twice without mentioning the author's name; but Wilamowitz assigned it to Sophocles on the somewhat tenuous ground that he alone of the tragedians uses the Ionic form μοῦνος. Sirens, often depicted in funerary art, are associated with lamentation.

FRAGMENTS NOT ASSIGNABLE

853

τὰ πλεῖστα φωρῶν αἴσχρ' ἐφευρήσεις βροτῶν

Plutarch, *The Control of Anger* 16, 463C; *Brotherly Love* 8, 481E

αἴσχρ' ἐφευρήσεις F. W. Schmidt: αἰσχρὰ φωράσεις codd.

854

πικρὰν πικροῖς κλύζουσι φαρμάκοις χολήν

Plutarch, I *Quiet of Mind* 7, 468B; II *The Face in the Moon* 7, 923F; III *The Control of Anger* 16, 463E

πικρὰν πικροῖς . . . II: πικρῷ πικρὰν . . . φαρμάκῳ III: πικρὰν χ. κλ. φαρμάκῳ πικρῷ I

855

ΝΕΣΤΩΡ

οὐ μέμφομαί σε· δρῶν γὰρ εὖ κακῶς λέγεις

Plutarch, *Talkativeness* 4, 504B; *Rules for Politicians* 14, 810B

856

οὐ γάρ τι βουλῆς ταὐτὸ καὶ δρόμου τέλος

Plutarch, *Talkativeness* 19, 511E

858

βραδεῖα μὲν γὰρ ἐν λόγοισι προσβολὴ
μόλις δι' ὠτὸς ἔρχεται ῥυπωμένου·
πρόσω δὲ λεύσσων ἐγγύθεν γε πᾶς τυφλός

Plutarch, *Table Talk* 1, 8, 1, 625C

2 ῥυπωμένου Meineke: τρυπωμένου codd.   3 πρόσω Dindorf: πόρρω codd.   γε Ll.-J.: δὲ codd.

853

If you investigate, you will find that most of what men do is low.

854

They wash away bitter bile with bitter medicines.

855

NESTOR

I do not blame you; for though your words are bad, your actions are good.[a]

[a] Nestor says this to Ajax. Welcker assigned the fragment to the *Palamedes*, but it might have come in any one of the many plays about the matter of Troy.

856

For the end of deliberation is not the same as the end of a race.

858

The impact of the words comes slowly, and has difficulty in getting through an ear that is blocked; a man who can see from far off is altogether blind close up.

FRAGMENTS NOT ASSIGNABLE

859

φίλιπποι καὶ κερουλκοί,
σὺν σάκει δὲ κωδωνοκρότῳ παλαισταί

Plutarch, *Table Talk* 2, 5, 2, 639F (of the Trojans)

860

οὐ πάντα τἀγένητα πρῶτον ἦλθ᾽ ἅπαξ;

Plutarch, *Table Talk* 8, 9, 3, 732D; Artemidorus 4, 59

οὐ πάντα Ll.-J.: ἅπαντα codd. τἀγένητα Porson: τὰ γένη
τοῦ Plutarch: τἀδόκητα Artemidorus

861

ΟΔΤΣΣΕΤΣ
Σειρῆνας εἰσαφικόμην,
Φόρκου κόρας, θροοῦντε τοὺς ῎Αιδου νόμους

Plutarch, *Table Talk* 9, 14, 6, 745F

1 εἰσαφικόμην Brunck (ὁ Σοφοκλέους ᾽Ο. φησι Σειρῆνας
εἰσαφικέσθαι codd.)   2 θροοῦντε Lobeck: αἰθροῦντος
codd.

863

φίλων τοιούτων οἱ μὲν ἐστερημένοι
χαίρουσιν, οἱ δ᾽ ἔχοντες εὔχονται φυγεῖν

Plutarch, *Amatorius* 23, 768E; *On Having Many Friends* 3,
94C

859

Lovers of horses and drawers of bows, and wrestlers with shield with jingling bells.[a]

[a] Hartung assigned this to the *Shepherds*.

860

Did not all things that did not yet exist come once as new things?

861

ODYSSEUS

I came to the Sirens, daughters of Phorcus, singing the songs of Hades.[a]

[a] Brunck assigned this to the *Phaeacians* (perhaps identical with the *Nausicaa*), Welcker to the *Odysseus Wounded by the Spine*.

863

Such friends as these people are glad to be deprived of, and if they are not they pray that they may escape them.

864

λάμπει γὰρ ἐν χρείαισιν ὥσπερ εὐγενὴς
χαλκός· χρόνῳ δ᾽ ἀργῆσαν ἤμυσε στέγυς

Plutarch, *Old Men in Politics* 15, 791E; ib. 8, 788B; *Live Unknown* 4, 1129C

865

δεινὸν τὸ τᾶς Πειθοῦς πρόσωπον

Plutarch, *Herodotus' Malice* 1, 854F

867

εὖ γὰρ καὶ διχοστατῶν λόγος
σύγκολλα τἀμφοῖν ἐς μέσον τεκταίνεται

Plutarch, *The Intelligence of Animals* 37, 985C

868

ἤρθη χαρᾷ
γραίας ἀκάνθης πάππος ὣς φυσώμενος

Plutarch, *Not Even a Pleasant Life is Possible on Epicurean Principles* 19, 1100C

1 ἤρθη χαρᾷ Hartung: ... ὅπως ὑπὸ χαρᾶς ἤρθη κατὰ τὸν Σοφοκλέα 'γραίας ... φυσώμενος' codd.

869

πολλῶν χαλινῶν ἔργον οἰάκων θ᾽ ἅμα

Plutarch, *Life of Alexander* 7, 2; *Amatorius* 21, 767E

870

ταχεῖα πειθὼ τῶν κακῶν ὁδοιπορεῖ

Plutarch, *Life of Artaxerxes* 28, 4; John Scylitzes, *Synopsis of the Histories* 321, 70 Thurn

864
For . . . shines out in time of need like fine bronze; but if the house is neglected, it collapses.

865
Awesome is the face of Persuasion.

867
Discussion, even when men disagree, welds the arguments of both sides compactly together.

868
He was lifted up by his delight like the down of gray thistle when it is blown.

869
A task requiring many bridles and many rudders all at once.

870
Persuasion moves fast when it is moving men to evil.

FRAGMENTS NOT ASSIGNABLE

871

ΜΕΝΕΛΑΟΣ

ἀλλ' οὑμὸς ἀεὶ πότμος ἐν πυκνῷ θεοῦ
τροχῷ κυκλεῖται καὶ μεταλλάσσει φύσιν,
ὥσπερ σελήνης ὄψις εὐφρόνας δύο
στῆναι δύναιτ' ἂν οὔποτ' ἐν μορφῇ μιᾷ,
5 ἀλλ' ἐξ ἀδήλου πρῶτον ἔρχεται νέα,
πρόσωπα καλλύνουσα καὶ πληρουμένη,
χὤτανπερ αὐτῆς εὐπρεπεστάτη φανῇ,
πάλιν διαρρεῖ κἀπὶ μηδὲν ἔρχεται.

Plutarch, I *Life of Demetrius* 45, 3; II *Roman Questions* 76, 282A (vv. 5–8); III *Curiosity* 5, 517D (vv. 5–8)

3 σελήνης Gomperz: σελήνης δ' codd.   εὐφρόνας Grotius: -αις codd.   7 εὐπρεπεστάτη III DZa: εὐγενεστάτη III cett., I, II   8 κεὶς τὸ I

872

καὶ τὰν νέορτον, ἇς ἔτ' ἄστολος χιτὼν
θυραῖον ἀμφὶ μηρὸν
πτύσσεται, Ἑρμιόναν

Plutarch, *Comparison of Lycurgus and Numa* 3, 5

1 νέορτον Valckenaer: νεοργὸν codd.

873

ὅστις γὰρ ὡς τύραννον ἐμπορεύεται
κείνου 'στι δοῦλος, κἂν ἐλεύθερος μόλῃ

Plutarch, *Life of Pompey* 78, 7; *Sayings of Kings and Commanders* 204D; Appian, *Civil Wars* 2, 85; Dio Cassius 42, 4, 3; Plutarch, *On Reading the Poets* 12, 33C; Diogenes Laertius, *Lives of Eminent Philosophers* 2, 82; Macarius, *Proverbs* 6, 50

871

MENELAUS

But my fate is always revolving on the fast-moving wheel
of the goddess[a] and changing its nature, just as the ap-
pearance of the moon cannot remain for two nights in the
same shape, but first emerges from obscurity as new,
making its face more beautiful and coming to fullness,
and when it is at its loveliest, it dissolves once more and
comes to nothing.

[a] Tyche (Fortune).

872

. . . and the young one, whose still ungirt tunic falls around
the thigh which it reveals, Hermione[a] . . .

[a] Brunck assigned this fragment to the Ἑλένης Ἀπαίτησις.

873

For whoever journeys to a tyrant is his slave, even if he is
free when he sets out.[a]

[a] Pompey is said to have quoted these lines to his wife and son
just before entering the boat in which he was murdered by the
emissaries of the King of Egypt.

873.1 γὰρ ὡς App., Dio, D. L.: δὲ πρὸς Plut.

874

ὦ θεοί, τίς ἆρα Κύπρις ἢ τίς Ἵμερος
τοῦδε ξυνήψατ';

Plutarch, *Life of Timoleon* 36, 2

879

βομβεῖ δὲ νεκρῶν σμῆνος ἔρχεταί τ' ἄνω

Porphyry, *Cave of the Nymphs* 18

879a

οὐ χρή ποτ' ἄνθρωπον μέγαν ὄλβον ἀπο-
βλέψαι· τανυφλοίου γάρ ἰσαμέριος
ὅστις αἰγείρου βιοτὰν ἀποβάλλει . . .

Porphyry, *On the Styx*, in Stobaeus, *Anthology* 4, 41, 57

1 ἄνθρωπον Gleditsch: -ων codd.

880

Ἀλφεσίβοιαν, ἣν ὁ γεννήσας πατήρ

Priscian, *On the Metres of Terence* 23

881

ἐδοξάτην μοι τὼ δύ' ἠπείρω μολεῖν

Schol. M on Aeschylus, *Persians* 181

874

O gods, what Aphrodite or what Desire had a finger in this?

879

And the dead in a swarm hum and rise up.[a]

[a] Porphyry in the passage in which he quotes this fragment says that "the ancients" called the souls awaiting birth "bees"; cf. Virgil, *Aeneid* 6, 706–9.

879a

A man must never fasten his gaze on great prosperity; for one whose lifespan is equal to that of the poplar with its long-furrowed bark and who sheds his livelihood[a] . . .

[a] Bergk, Nauck and Pearson thought this came from the same context as fr. 593; but Radt rightly points out that passages in dactylo-epitrite metre may well show the same metrical pattern without belonging to the same context.

880

Alphesiboea, whom the father who begot her[a] . . .

[a] This is quoted as an example of the rare iambic trimeter with a choriamb as its first metron. Alphesiboea, daughter of Phegeus, was Alcmeon's first wife; see the prefatory note on the *Alcmeon*, to which Welcker assigned this fragment.

881

I thought the two continents came[a] . . .

[a] This must come from a description of a dream like that in the passage of Aeschylus which the scholiast quoted this to illustrate.

FRAGMENTS NOT ASSIGNABLE

884

ὁ σκηπτροβάμων αἰετός, κύων Διός

Schol. ΓV on Aristophanes, *Birds* 515

885

σαίνεις δάκνουσα καὶ κύων λαίθαργος εἶ

Suetonius, *On Abusive Terms* (93 Taillardat); Eustathius, *Od.* 1493, 32; Schol. on Aristophanes, *Knights* 1068 b, e; Suda λ 178

σαίνεις δάκνουσα Schol. Ar., Suda: σαίνουσα δάκνειν Suetonius: σαίνουσα δάκνεις Eustathius

885a

οἴμοι, πέπρακται τοῦ θεοῦ τὸ θέσφατον

Aristophanes, *Knights* 1248 (where Schol. Γ2 attribute the line to Sophocles)

887

Ζεὺς νόστον ἄγοι τὸν νικόμαχον
καὶ παυσανίαν καὶ ἀτρείδαν

Schol. E on Aristophanes, *Clouds* 1163; Tzetzes on *Clouds* 1160a; Suda λ 853

1 νικόμαχον Heath: νικομάχαν codd.   2 κατ᾽ Ἀτρειδᾶν Bentley

890

†ἐπειγομένων οὐ† κερκίδος ὕμνους,
ἢ τοὺς εὕδοντας ἐγείρει

Schol. VE on Aristophanes, *Wealth* 541

1 ἐπειγομένων οὐ omitted by E. ἐξ Ἐπιγόνων? Ll.-J.

884

The eagle on the sceptre, the faithful bird of Zeus[a] . . .

[a] For the eagle on the sceptre of Zeus, compare Pindar, *First Pythian Ode* line 6.

885

You fawn on men as you bite them and are a treacherous dog.

885a

Alas, the god's oracle has been accomplished!

887

May Zeus bring about a return with victory in battle and an end of pain and of fear![a]

[a] The three adjectives are also proper names.

890

. . . the songs of the distaff, which awakens sleepers.[a]

[a] Nauck assigned this to the *Tereus*, comparing fr. 595, κερκίδος φωνή.

FRAGMENTS NOT ASSIGNABLE

892

παῖδας γὰρ οὓς ἔφυσ᾽ ἀναλώσας ἔχει

Schol. B on Euripides, *Medea* 33 Schwartz

893

εὐφημίαν μὲν πρῶτα κηρύξας ἔχω

Schol. B on Euripides, *Medea* 33; Schol. on *Orestes* 451

894

ὀργὴ γέροντος ὥστε μαλθακὴ κοπὶς
βραδεῖα θήγειν, ἐν τάχει δ᾽ ἀμβλύνεται

Schol. MTAB on Euripides, *Orestes* 490

2 βραδεῖα θήγειν Ll.-J.: ἐν χειρὶ θήγει codd.: ἐν χειρὶ
θήγειν Diels: ταχεῖα θήγειν Wecklein

895

ἀεὶ γὰρ εὖ πίπτουσιν οἱ Διὸς κύβοι

Schol. MTAB on Euripides, *Orestes* 603; Berlin Photius 37,
13; Suda α 607; Stobaeus 1, 3, 32 (1, 58, 7 Wachsmuth);
Paroemiographers

896

εἴθ᾽ ἦσθα σώφρων ἔργα τοῖς λόγοις ἴσα

Schol. A on [Euripides], *Rhesus* 105

897

δάφνην φαγὼν ὀδόντι πρῖε τὸ στόμα

Schol. on Hesiod, *Theogony* 30

892

For he has destroyed the children I begot.[a]

[a] Perhaps said by Priam of Achilles; but there are many other possibilities.

893

First, I have made a solemn call for silence.

894

An old man's anger, like a blunt cleaver, takes a long time to sharpen and soon grows blunt.

895

For in dice-play Zeus's throw is always lucky.

896

I wish you were as sensible in your actions as in your words.

897

When you eat bay, bite your lips with your teeth.[a]

[a] The bay was sacred to Apollo, and was particularly associated with his oracle.

FRAGMENTS NOT ASSIGNABLE

898

ἐγὼ κατ' αὐτόν, ὡς ὁρᾷς, ἐξέρχομαι

Aristarchus ap. Schol. A on Homer *Il.* 1, 423–4

900

ὃς μὴ πέπονθε τἀμά, μὴ βουλευέτω

Schol. bT on Homer, *Il.* 9, 453a

βουλευέτω Bekker: -ηται b: -εται T

902

ὡς ἂν Διὸς μέτωπον ἐκταθῇ χαρᾷ

Schol. T on Homer, *Il.* 15, 103; Schol. RΓ on Aristophanes, *Lysistrata* 8 = Suda τ 772

903

οὐ πώποθ' ὑμᾶς συμβαλεῖν ἐπίσταμαι

Schol. bT on Homer, *Il.* 16, 142

904

σὺν τοῖσιν ἵπποις τοῖσιν ἐκλελεγμένοις
ἥδιον ἂν χωροῖμεν ἢ παντὶ σθένει

Schol. T on Homer, *Il.* 18, 274

1 σὺν Schneidewin: ἐν cod.   ἐκλελεγμένοις Schneidewin: ἐκλελειμμένος cod.   2 ἥδιον Hecker: ἴδιον cod.

898

I am going out after him, as you see.

900

Let no one give counsel who has not suffered what I have suffered!

902

So that the brow of Zeus may be unknitted with delight.

903

I have never been able to understand you.

904

We should rather go with the chosen horses than in full strength.

905

ὃς παρακτίαν
στείχων ἀνημέρωσα κνωδάλων ὁδόν

Schol. on Pindar, Hypothesis to *Isthmian Odes*

1 ὥς? Snell

907

ἤδη γὰρ ἕδρᾳ Ζεὺς ἐν ἐσχάτῃ θεῶν

Schol. BD on Pindar, *Nemeans* 10, 57c

908

λύσω γάρ, εἰ καὶ τῶν τριῶν ἓν οἴσομαι

Schol. ACEHQ on Pindar, *Olympians* 1, 97 f.

909

ὠνὴν ἔθου καὶ πρᾶσιν, ὡς Φοῖνιξ ἀνήρ,
Σιδώνιος κάπηλος

Schol. BDEFGQ on Pindar, *Pythians* 2, 125a

910

χῶρος γὰρ αὐτός ἐστιν ἀνθρώπου φρενῶν
ὅπου τὸ τερπνὸν καὶ τὸ πημαῖνον φέρει·
δακρυρροεῖ γοῦν καὶ τὰ χαρτὰ τυγχάνων

Schol. BDEGQ on Pindar, *Pythians* 4, 217

1 αὐτός Bamberger: οὗτός codd.   2 τερπνὸν] τέρπον
Cobet   φέρει Ll.-J.: φύει codd.   3 χαρτὰ Conington:
καὶ τὰ codd.

905
I who on my way purged the coastal road of monsters[a] . . .

  [a] The speaker must be Theseus; see on fr. 730.

907
For has Zeus in the highest seat among the gods ever . . .?[a]

  [a] "Has Zeus ever . . .?" or "Zeus has already . . ."; we cannot be sure, since the sentence is incomplete.

908
For I shall open it, even if I shall get one of the three things![a]

  [a] This is thought to allude to the story that a consulter of the Delphic oracle might be given his response in an envelope, and if he opened it before an appointed day might lose an eye, an arm, or his tongue.

909
You bought and sold, like a Phoenician, a Sidonian merchant.

910
Delightful things and painful things occupy the same place in a man's mind, for he weeps even when something pleasant happens to him.

FRAGMENTS NOT ASSIGNABLE

911

ὦ γῆ Φεραία, χαῖρε, σύγγονόν θ' ὕδωρ
Ὑπέρεια κρήνη, νᾶμα θεοφιλέστατον

Schol. DEGQ on Pindar, *Pythians* 4, 221b

913

⟨τὸ⟩ πάνσοφον κρότημα, Λαέρτου γόνος

Schol. UEAP on Theocritus 15, 48–50

suppl. Valckenaer

915

ἔστιν τις αἶα, Θεσσαλῶν παγκληρία

Stephanus of Byzantium, *Ethnica* 36, 16 Meineke

916

Ἀνακτόρειον τῆσδ' ἐπώνυμον χθονός

Stephanus of Byzantium, *Ethnica* 92, 15 Meineke

917

τί μέλλετ', Ἀρτακῆς τε καὶ Περκώσιοι;

Stephanus of Byzantium, *Ethnica* 127, 13 Meineke

Ἀρτακῆς Dindorf: -εῖς codd.

918

πάντ' ἐκκαλύπτων ὁ χρόνος εἰς ⟨τὸ⟩ φῶς ἄγει

Stobaeus, *Anthology* 1, 8, 1 (1, 93, 17 Wachsmuth); cf. [Menander], *Monosticha* 639 and 839

suppl. Grotius

911

Land of Pherae, hail, and you, water of my kindred, spring
of Hypereia, stream most dear to the gods![a]

[a] Pherae is in Thessaly, and Admetus ruled there; see fr. 851.
Hypereia was a fountain, located at Pherae by Pindar, *Pyth*. 4,
125.

913

The all-cunning piece of mischief, the son of Laertes[a] . . .

[a] This may come from any of the plays in which Odysseus was
a character.

915

There is a land which the Thessalians all together possess.

916

Anactorium, which gave its name to this land[a] . . .

[a] Anactorium is in Acarnania, on the Gulf of Ambracia.

917

Why do you hesitate, men of Artace and Percote?[a]

[a] These places are on the Hellespont, near Abydos; the frag-
ment may come from the *Shepherds*.

918

Time uncovers all things and brings them to the light.

919

ἀλλ᾽ οὐ γὰρ ἂν τὰ θεῖα κρυπτόντων θεῶν
μάθοις ἄν, οὐδ᾽ εἰ πάντ᾽ ἐπεξέλθοις σκοπῶν

Stobaeus, *Anthology* 2, 1, 4 (2, 4, 4 Wachsmuth)

920

ἀμνήμονος γὰρ ἀνδρὸς ὄλλυται χάρις

Stobaeus, *Anthology* 2, 46, 6 (2, 260, 17 Wachsmuth):
Σοφοκλέους Gaisford: Θεοκρίτου codd.

921

σκαιοῖσι πολλοῖς εἷς σοφὸς διόλλυται

Stobaeus, *Anthology* 3, 2, 16 (3, 181, 15 Hense)

922

A

ἐσθλοῦ γὰρ ἀνδρὸς τοὺς πονοῦντας ὠφελεῖν.

B

ἀλλ᾽ ἡ φρόνησις ἀγαθὴ θεὸς μέγας.

Stobaeus, *Anthology* 3, 3, 4 (3, 192, 12 Hense)

923

ἀλλ᾽ οἱ κακῶς πράσσοντες οὐ κωφοὶ μόνον,
ἀλλ᾽ οὐδ᾽ ὁρῶντες εἰσορῶσι τἀμφανῆ

Stobaeus, *Anthology* 3, 4, 1 (3, 219, 14 Hense)

919

But since you could not learn about matters that concern the gods if the gods concealed them, not even if you were to go over all things in your scrutiny . . .

920

For if a man is forgetful, gratitude is done away with.

921

One wise man is ruined by many blunderers.

922

A

For it is the way of a good man to help those in trouble.

B

But sound thinking is a great god.

923

But the unfortunate are not only dumb, but even when they have sight they do not see things that are clearly visible.

FRAGMENTS NOT ASSIGNABLE

924

ὡς δυσπάλαιστόν ‹ἐστιν› ἀμαθία κακόν

Stobaeus, *Anthology* 3, 4, 5 (3, 220, 9 Hense)

δυσπάλαιστόν Nauck: δυσπέλαστον codd. suppl. Grotius

925

ἡ δὲ μωρία
μάλιστ᾽ ἀδελφὴ τῆς πονηρίας ἔφυ

Stobaeus, *Anthology* 3, 4, 19 (3, 223, 6 Hense)

926

χαίρειν ἐπ᾽ αἰσχραῖς ἡδοναῖς οὐ χρή ποτε

Stobaeus, *Anthology* 3, 5, 3 (3, 256, 9 Hense)

927

οὐ τοῖς ἀθύμοις ἡ τύχη ξυλλαμβάνει

Stobaeus, *Anthology* 3, 8, 11 (3, 342, 9 Hense); Arsenius, *Proverbs* 41, 75 (who gives it to Menander)

927a

ἐλευθέρα γὰρ γλῶσσα τῶν ἐλευθέρων

Stobaeus, *Anthology* 3, 13, 16 (3, 456, 10 Hense)

927b

Ἐλευθερία Διὸς ὄλβιον τέκος

Stobaeus, *Anthology* 3, 13, 17 (3, 456, 12 Hense)

924

What a difficult plague to wrestle with is stupidity!

925

Foolishness is indeed the sister of wickedness.

926

One should never delight in pleasures that are disgraceful.

927

Fortune does not help the spiritless.

927a

Free men have free tongues!

927b

Freedom, happy child of Zeus!

928

αἰδὼς γὰρ ἐν κακοῖσιν οὐδὲν ὠφελεῖ·
ἡ γὰρ σιωπὴ τῶγκαλοῦντι σύμμαχος

Stobaeus, *Anthology* 3, 13, 27 (3, 458, 7 Hense); Arsenius,
Proverbs 22, 28

τῶγκαλοῦντι Cobet: τῷ λαλοῦντι codd.

929

τί ταῦτ' ἐπαινεῖς; πᾶς γὰρ οἰνωθεὶς ἀνὴρ
ἥσσων μὲν ὀργῆς ἐστι, τοῦ δὲ νοῦ κενός.
φιλεῖ δὲ πολλὴν γλῶσσαν ἐκχέας μάτην
ἄκων ἀκούειν οὓς ἑκὼν εἶπεν λόγους.

Stobaeus, *Anthology* 3, 18, 1 (3, 512, 14 Hense); Clement of
Alexandria, *Paedagogus* 2, 2, 4; vv. 3–4: Plutarch, *How to Profit
from your Enemies* 5, 89A

930

κλέπτων δ' ὅταν τις ἐμφανῶς ἐφευρεθῇ,
σιγᾶν ἀνάγκη, κἂν λάλον φορῇ στόμα

Stobaeus, *Anthology* 3, 24, 4 (3, 602, 4 Hense)

2 λάλον Blaydes: καλὸν codd.   φορῇ Cobet: φέρῃ codd.

931

ἦ δεινὸν ἆρ' ἦν, ἡνίκ' ἄν τις ἐσθλὸς ὢν
αὑτῷ συνειδῇ

Stobaeus, *Anthology* 3, 24, 6 (3, 602, 4 Hense)

928

Shamefastness is of no use when one is in trouble; for silence is on the side of the accuser.

929

Why do you praise this? Every man who gets drunk is at the mercy of his anger, and is empty of good sense. And when he has poured out many a foolish word he is sorry to hear the things he was so glad to utter.

930

But when one has been caught red-handed in a theft, one must keep silent, even if one carries about a chattering tongue.

931

So it turns out to be a bad thing when a man is conscious of his own goodness.

932

ὅρκοισι γάρ τοι καὶ γυνὴ φεύγει πικρὰν
ὠδῖνα παίδων· ἀλλ' ἐπεὶ λήξῃ κακοῦ,
ἐν τοῖσιν αὐτοῖς δικτύοις ἁλίσκεται
πρὸς τοῦ παρόντος ἱμέρου νικωμένη

Stobaeus, *Anthology* 3, 28, 4 (3, 617, 7 Hense)

2 ἐπεὶ Ellendt: ἐπὰν codd.

933

ὅρκος γὰρ οὐδεὶς ἀνδρὶ φιλήτῃ βαρύς

Stobaeus, *Anthology* 3, 28, 6 (3, 618, 1 Hense)

934

οἴκοι μένειν δεῖ τὸν καλῶς εὐδαίμονα

Stobaeus, *Anthology* 3, 39, 14 (3, 724, 10 Hense); Diogenes
Laertius, *Lives of Eminent Philosophers* 7, 35; Clement of Alex-
andria, *Miscellanies* 6, 2, 7, 6

935

μήποτε κρυφαῖον μηδὲν ἐξείπῃς ἔπος·
κλῇθρον γὰρ οὐδὲν ὧδ' ἂν εὐπαγὲς λάβοις
γλώσσης, κρυφαῖον οὐδὲν οὗ διέρχεται

Stobaeus, *Anthology* 3, 41, 3 (3, 758, 1 Hense)

1 μήποτε Ll.-J.: μή μοι codd.: alii alia   2 εὐπαγὲς Cobet:
εὐπετὲς codd.   3 οὗ Gomperz: οὐ codd.

932

For a woman swears that she will avoid the bitter pangs of childbirth; but once she has respite from the pain, she is caught in the same nets, overcome by the desire of the moment.

933

For no oath weighs heavy on a man who is a thief.

934

The man who is truly fortunate should stay at home.[a]

[a] Clement attributes this line to Aeschylus, and it is fr. 317 in Radt's edition.

935

Never betray a secret; for you will find no lock for the tongue so secure that no secret passes through it.

936

ὅπου γὰρ οἱ φύσαντες ἡσσῶνται τέκνων,
οὐκ ἔστιν αὕτη σωφρόνων ἀνδρῶν πόλις

Stobaeus, *Anthology* 4, 1, 11 (4, 4, 2 Hense)

1 φύσαντες Pierson: φυλάσσοντες codd.

937

νόμοις ἕπεσθαι τοῖσιν ἐγχώροις καλόν

Stobaeus, *Anthology* 4, 1, 25 (4, 7, 9 Hense); Arsenius, *Proverbs* 37, 31; [Menander], *Monosticha* 518

938

πολλῶν πόνων δεῖ τῷ καλόν τι μωμένῳ,
σμικροῦ δ' ἀγῶνος οὐ μέγ' ἔρχεται κλέος

Stobaeus, *Anthology* 4, 4, 11 (4, 186, 15 Hense)

1 πόνων Nauck: καλῶν codd.   καλόν τι μωμένῳ Nauck: καλῶς τιμωμένῳ codd.   2 σμικροῦ Cobet: μικροῦ codd.

939

γνῶμαι πλέον κρατοῦσιν ἢ σθένος χερῶν

Stobaeus, *Anthology* 4, 13, 7 (4, 348, 12 Hense); Arsenius, *Proverbs* 15, 17

κρατοῦσιν ἢ σθένος] σθένουσιν ἢ κράτος Nauck

940

εἰ σῶμα δοῦλον, ἀλλ' ὁ νοῦς ἐλεύθερος

Stobaeus, *Anthology* 4, 19, 33 (4, 428, 2 Hense); Arsenius, *Proverbs* 22, 2

936

For a city where the fathers are defeated by the children,
that is not a city of reasonable men.

937

It is proper to obey the laws of the country.

938

The man who aims at something noble must endure many
toils, and no great fame comes from a petty contest.

939

Right judgments have more power than strength of arm.

940

If the body is a slave's, the mind is that of a free man.

FRAGMENTS NOT ASSIGNABLE

941

ὦ παῖδες, ἥ τοι Κύπρις οὐ Κύπρις μόνον,
ἀλλ᾽ ἐστὶ πολλῶν ὀνομάτων ἐπώνυμος.
ἔστιν μὲν Ἅιδης, ἔστι δ᾽ ἄφθιτος βίος,
ἔστιν δὲ λύσσα μανιάς, ἔστι δ᾽ ἵμερος
5 ἄκρατος, ἔστ᾽ οἰμωγμός. ἐν κείνῃ τὸ πᾶν
σπουδαῖον, ἡσυχαῖον, ἐς βίαν ἄγον.
ἐντήκεται γάρ †πλευμόνων† ὅσοις ἔνι
ψυχή· τίς οὐχὶ τῆσδε τῆς θεοῦ βορός;
εἰσέρχεται μὲν ἰχθύων πλωτῷ γένει,
10 χέρσου δ᾽ ἔνεστιν ἐν τετρασκελεῖ γονῇ,
νωμᾷ δ᾽ ἐν οἰωνοῖσι τοὐκείνης πτερόν.

* * *

ἐν θηρσίν, ἐν βροτοῖσιν, ἐν θεοῖς ἄνω.
τίν᾽ οὐ παλαίουσ᾽ ἐς τρὶς ἐκβάλλει θεῶν;
εἴ μοι θέμις—θέμις δὲ—τἀληθῆ λέγειν,
15 Διὸς τυραννεῖ πλευμόνων ἄνευ δορός,
ἄνευ σιδήρου· πάντα τοι συντέμνεται
Κύπρις τὰ θνητῶν καὶ θεῶν βουλεύματα.

Stobaeus, *Anthology* 4, 20, 6 (4, 435, 12 Hense); Plutarch,
Amatorius 13, 757A (lines 1–4)

3 βίος Bothe: βία codd.   4 μανιάς Porson: μανίας
Plutarch: μαινάς Stobaeus   7 ἐντήκεται] ἀνθάπτεται
Meineke: ἐξάπτεται? cf. Plutarch fr. 137 (7, 84 Sandbach)
        8 οὐχὶ Grotius: οὔτι codd.   10 χέρσου δ᾽ ἔνεστιν ἐν
Nauck: ἔνεστι δ᾽ ἐν χέρσου codd.   11 lacuna after this
line (Radt)

404

941

Children, the Cyprian is not the Cyprian alone, but she is called by many names. She is Hades, she is immortal life, she is raving madness, she is unmixed desire, she is lamentation; in her is all activity, all tranquillity, all that leads to violence. For she sinks into the vitals of all that have life; who is not greedy for that goddess? She enters into the swimming race of fishes, she is within the four-legged brood upon dry land, and her wing ranges among birds . . . among beasts, among mortals, among the race of gods above. Which among the gods does she not wrestle and throw three times? If I may speak out—and I may speak out—to tell the truth, she rules over the heart of Zeus, without spear, without iron. All the plans of mortals and of gods are cut short by the Cyprian.

942

τίς δ' οἶκος ἐν βροτοῖσιν ὠλβίσθη ποτὲ
γυναικὸς ἐσθλῆς χωρὶς ὀγκωθεὶς χλιδῇ;

Stobaeus, *Anthology* 4, 22, 6 (4, 495, 9 Hense)

943

κατ' ὀρφανὸν γὰρ οἶκον ἀνδρόφρων γυνή

Stobaeus, *Anthology* 4, 22, 178 (4, 558, 8 Hense)

944

πενία δὲ συγκραθεῖσα δυσσεβεῖ τρόπῳ
ἄρδην ἀνεῖλε καὶ κατέστρεψεν βίον

Stobaeus, *Anthology* 4, 32, 27 (5, 790, 6 Hense)

945

ὦ θνητὸν ἀνδρῶν καὶ ταλαίπωρον γένος,
ὡς οὐδέν ἐσμεν πλὴν σκιαῖς ἐοικότες,
βάρος περισσὸν γῆς ἀναστρωφώμενοι

Stobaeus, *Anthology* 4, 34, 1 (5, 824, 4 Hense)

1 θνητὸν Gesner: θνητῶν codd.   3 ἀναστρωφώμενοι
Gesner: ἀναστρεφόμενοι codd.

946

οὐ γὰρ θέμις ζῆν πλὴν θεοῖς ἄνευ κακῶν

Stobaeus, *Anthology* 4, 34, 49 (5, 840, 7 Hense)

942
But what house among mortals was ever thought happy without a good wife, though it was loaded with luxury?

943
For in a house that is bereft a woman thinking like a man . . .

944
But poverty combined with an impious character has utterly ruined and upset (his?) life.

945
O mortal and miserable race of men, since we are nothing but creatures like shadows, walking about as a superfluous burden upon the earth!

946
For it is ordained that none except the gods shall live without misfortunes.

FRAGMENTS NOT ASSIGNABLE

947

στέργειν δὲ τἀκπεσόντα καὶ θέσθαι πρέπει
σοφὸν κυβευτήν, ἀλλὰ μὴ στένειν τύχην

Stobaeus, *Anthology* 4, 44, 43 (5, 969, 8 Hense); Hesychius, *Lexicon* κ 4369 Latte

948

ἐλπὶς γὰρ ἡ βόσκουσα τοὺς πολλοὺς βροτῶν

Stobaeus, *Anthology* 4, 46, 14 (5, 999, 20 Hense); Arsenius, *Proverbs* 23, 13; [Menander], *Monosticha*, cod. Σ (App. 1)

949

πάντ᾽ ἐμπέφυκε τῷ μακρῷ γήρᾳ κακά,
νοῦς φροῦδος, ἔργ᾽ ἀχρεῖα, φροντίδες κεναί

Stobaeus 4, 50, 64 (5, 1044, 1 Hense); v. 2: Clement of Alexandria, *Protrepticus* 10, 89, 3

950

οὐκ ἔστι γῆρας τῶν σοφῶν, ἐν οἷς ὁ νοῦς
θείᾳ ξύνεστιν ἡμέρᾳ τεθραμμένος.
[προμηθία γὰρ κέρδος ἀνθρώποις μέγα]

Stobaeus, *Anthology* 4, 50 III (5, 1055, 6 Hense)

1 ἐν οἷς] ὅσοις Blaydes   3 Bothe saw that this line was placed here by mistake.

947

The clever dice-player must put up with the throw of the dice and make the best of it, but not lament his fortune.

948

For it is hope that is the sustenance of most mortals.

949

All evils are part of great age; mind gone, actions feeble, futile worries.

950

Old age does not come to the wise, who live with an intelligence nurtured by the daylight of the gods. [For foresight is a great boon to men.]

951

ὅστις δὲ θνητῶν θάνατον ὀρρωδεῖ λίαν,
μῶρος πέφυκε. τῇ τύχῃ μέλει τάδε.
ὅταν δ᾽ ὁ καιρὸς τοῦ θανεῖν ἐλθὼν τύχῃ,
οὐδ᾽ ἂν πρὸς αὐλὰς Ζηνὸς ἐκφύγοις μολών.

Stobaeus, *Anthology* 4, 51, 10 (5, 1068, 5 Hense)

3 δ᾽ Grotius: γὰρ cod.   4 ἐκφύγοις Dindorf: -ῃ cod.: -οι
Halm

952

ὅστις γὰρ ἐν κακοῖσιν ἱμείρει βίου
ἢ δειλός ἐστιν ἢ δυσάλγητος φρένας

Stobaeus, *Anthology* 4, 53, 21 (5, 1103, 16 Hense)

953

A

θανόντι κείνῳ συνθανεῖν ἔρως μ᾽ ἔχει.

B

ἥξεις—ἐπείγου μηδέν—εἰς τὸ μόρσιμον.

Stobaeus, *Anthology* 4, 54, 12 (5, 1115, 7 Hense)

954

χρόνος δ᾽ ἀμαυροῖ πάντα κεἰς λήθην ἄγει

Stobaeus, *Anthology* 4, 58, 8 (5, 1143, 9 Hense); [Menander],
Monosticha 831

1 ἀμαυροῖ] ἀναιρεῖ Mon.

951

Any mortal who is excessively afraid of death is a fool.
This depends on fortune; but when the moment of death
comes, you could not escape even if you came to the
courts of Zeus.

952

For whoever though miserable longs for life is either a
coward or insensible.

953

A

He being dead, I long to die with him.

B

You will come—do not make haste!—to your fated end.

954

Time makes all things dark and brings them to oblivion.

FRAGMENTS NOT ASSIGNABLE

955

τἀληθὲς ἀεὶ πλεῖστον ἰσχύει λόγου

Stobaeus, *Anthology* 3, 11, 5 (3, 430, 8 Hense)

ἰσχύει λόγου] ἰσχύειν λέγω Nauck

956

. . . εἴ τινα Σοφοκλῆς τραγῳδεῖ περὶ τῆς Ὠρειθυίας
λέγων ὡς ἀναρπαγεῖσα ὑπὸ Βορέου κομισθείη
   ὑπέρ τε πόντον πάντ᾽ ἐπ᾽ ἔσχατα χθονὸς
   νυκτός τε πηγὰς οὐρανοῦ τ᾽ ἀναπτυχάς,
   Φοίβου τε παλαιὸν κῆπον

Strabo, *Geography* 7, 3, 1 p. 295C

3 τε deleted by Hermann

957

νὴ τὼ Λαπέρσα, νὴ τὸν Εὐρώταν τρίτον
νὴ τοὺς ἐν Ἄργει καὶ κατὰ Σπάρτην θεούς,

Strabo, *Geography* 8, 5, 3 p. 364C

2 comes before 1 in the mss.; Nauck transposed them. Radt in
Strabone in Grecia (ed. A.M. Biraschi, 1999, 68–9), defends the
order in the manuscript.

958

ἐδέξατο ῥαγεῖσα Θηβαία κόνις
αὐτοῖσιν ὅπλοις καὶ τετρωρίστῳ δίφρῳ

Strabo, *Geography* 9, 1, 22 p. 399C

955

In any question the truth has always greatest strength.

956

. . . if Sophocles in a tragedy says of Oreithyia that she was snatched up by Boreas and carried 'far beyond the sea to the confines of earth, and the sources of Night, and the expanse of Heaven, and the ancient garden of Phoebus'[a]

[a] Ruhnken assigned this to the *Oreithyia*, others to the *Phineus* or the *Drummers*.

957

By the gods of Argos and of Sparta, by the sackers of Las, and thirdly by the Eurotas![a]

[a] The sackers of Las, a stronghold on a spur of Taygetus, are the Dioscuri.

958

The dusty ground of Thebes burst open and received him, arms and four-horse chariot and all.[a]

[a] The person referred to is Amphiaraus; the play might be the *Amphiaraus*, the *Alcmeon*, the *Eriphyle* or the *Epigoni*.

959

ὅθεν κατεῖδον τὴν βεβακχιωμένην
βροτοῖσι κλεινὴν Νῦσαν, ἣν ὁ βούκερως
Ἴακχος αὑτῷ μαῖαν ἡδίστην νέμει,
ὅπου τίς ὄρνις οὐχὶ κλαγγάνει;

Strabo, *Geography* 15, 1, 7 p. 687 C

2 Νῦσαν Kramer: νύσσαν codd.

960

θαυμαστὰ γὰρ τὸ τόξον ὡς ὀλισθάνει

Suda ω 213 Adler

961

θεοῦ δὲ πληγὴν οὐχ ὑπερπηδᾷ βροτός

Theophilus, *Letter to Autolycus* 2, 8; Stobaeus, *Anthology* 1, 3, 7 (1, 53, 15 Wachsmuth); [Menander], *Monosticha* 345

πληγήν] παγίδας Heimsoeth   ὑπερπηδᾷ] ὑπεκπηδᾷ Herwerden

962

εἰ δείν᾽ ἔδρασας, δεινὰ καὶ παθεῖν σε δεῖ

Theophilus, *Letter to Autolycus* 2, 37; Stobaeus, *Anthology* 1, 3, 48a (1, 61, 3 Wachsmuth); Schol. on Dionysius Thrax, *Grammar* 20 Hilgard

959

From here I caught sight of Nysa, haunt of Bacchus, famed among mortals, which Iacchus of the bull's horns counts as his beloved nurse; here what bird does not cry[a] . . .?

[a] For the identification of Dionysus with the Eleusinian deity Iacchus, compare *Antigone* 1146–52. Nysa is a mythological and not a real place.

960

For it is amazing how the bow slips.[a]

[a] Perhaps from the Νίπτρα (*The Foot-Washing*); one thinks of the attempts to string the bow in the twenty-first book of the *Odyssey*.

961

A mortal cannot leap clear of a blow from a god.

962

If you have acted dreadfully, you must suffer dreadfully.

963

οἱ γὰρ γύνανδροι καὶ λέγειν ἠσκηκότες

Trypho, *On Tropes* 8; Polybius of Sardis, *On Figures* p. 612 Walz

964

θεοῦ τὸ δῶρον τοῦτο· χρὴ δ᾽ ὅσ᾽ ἂν θεοὶ
διδῶσι, φεύγειν μηδέν, ὦ τέκνον, ποτέ

[Plutarch], *Life of Homer* 158

965

ΟΔΥΣΣΕΥΣ

ὀρθῶς δ᾽ Ὀδυσσεύς εἰμ᾽ ἐπώνυμος κακῶν·
πολλοὶ γὰρ ὠδύσαντο δυσμενεῖς ἐμοί

Life of Sophocles 20

1 κακῶν Blaydes: κακοῖς, -ός, -ῶς codd.   2 δυσμενεῖς Nauck: δυσσεβεῖς codd.

966

ὅταν τις ᾄδῃ τὸν Βοιώτιον νόμον,
τὰ πρῶτα μὲν σχολαῖον, εἶτα δ᾽ ἔντονον

Codex Parisinus suppl. gr. 676 (Corpus Paroemiographorum) 70 = Zenobius, *Proverbs* 2, 65

2 εἶτα δ᾽ ἔντονον Blaydes: εὔτονος ἀεί cod.: ἐντείνων δ᾽ ἀεί Radt

966a

ἰσχυρὸν ὀργῆι καὶ λελειμμένον φρενόσ.

In σχέδη in four thirteenth-century MSS deriving from Herodian; see J. J. Keaney, *AJP* 122 (2001), 173.

963

Woman-men and those who have studied oratory . . .

964

This is the god's gift; and we ought never to avoid any of the things the gods give us, my son.

965

ODYSSEUS

I am rightly called Odysseus, after something bad; for many enemies have been angry with me.[a]

[a] Odysseus is punning on his name; see Homer, *Od*. 19, 407 f.

966

When someone sings the Boeotian nome, leisurely at first, but later vehement[a] . . .

[a] On nomes, see West, *Ancient Greek Music* (1992) 215 f.; "it is said that it [the Boeotian nome] began quietly and ended in a wild fashion" (W.J.M. Starkie on Aristophanes, *Acharnians* 14).

966a

Strong in anger and bereft of sense.

DOUBTFUL FRAGMENT

ΟΙΝΕΥΣ ?

Ed. pr. of P.Oxy. 1083 Hunt, *P.Oxy.* viii (1911), 60 f, with Plate iii. See Page, *GLP* no. 31; Maas, *BPW* 32 (1912) 1426 f = *Kleine Schriften* 50 f; Wilamowitz, *NJKA* 29 (1912) 449 = *Kl. Schr.* 347; Pfeiffer, *WS* 79 (1966) 65 f; Carden, 135 f (with bibliography); Radt, 636 f. See on Μάντεις (*The Prophets*).

The publication in 1962 of new fragments of this papyrus as P.Oxy. 2453 showed that not all of its contents came from the same play; see on the Μάντεις *and the* Ἀνδρομέδα. *The presence of a rare word quoted as from the latter play (see fr. 133) has strengthened the case for thinking that fr. 1130 is by Sophocles. There is a gap before the name of Oeneus opposite line 19, and* Σχ]οινεύς *(Schoeneus) has been suggested. Both he and Oeneus had daughters who were the objects of competition; but*

1130

⟨ΧΟΡΟΣ⟩

. . . .
κυρεῖν δρῶντα· δηλοῦν τί· χρη[
    ἐργάτην τοιοῦδ᾽ ἀγῶνος αἰχμαλ[ωτ

418

DOUBTFUL FRAGMENT

OENEUS?

Schoeneus' daughter Atalanta used to challenge her suitors to race her, which does not fit the situation described in this fragment. Does Oeneus fit it any better? It has been objected that his daughter Deianeira was fought over by Heracles and Achelous (see The Women of Trachis), *but was not the prize in an open competition. However, supposing Oeneus was simply trying to find someone to fight Achelous for his daughter, the satyrs might well have volunteered. Apart from this fragment, "the evidence for this title is meagre and inconclusive," as Pearson (I p. 121) put it. But though Radt has placed it among the "Dubia et Spuria," it seems to me highly probable that this fragment is from an* Oeneus *by Sophocles.*

1130
⟨CHORUS OF SATYRS⟩

. . . to explain what . . . was doing. He who is the cause of such a struggle should (be made a) prisoner!

⟨ΟΙΝΕΥΣ⟩

ἀλλ᾽ ἐξεροῦμεν. ἀλλὰ πρῶτα βούλομ[αι
γνῶναι τίνες πάρεστε καὶ γένους ὅ[του
5 βλαστόντες· οὐ γ[ὰρ] νῦν γέ πω μαθ[ὼν ἔχω.

ΧΟ(ΡΟΣ) ΣΑΤΤ(ΡΩΝ)

ἅπαντα πεύσῃ. νυμφίοι μὲν ἥ[κομε]ν,
παῖδες δὲ νυμφῶν, Βακχίου δ᾽ ὑπηρέται,
θεῶν δ᾽ ὅμαυλοι· πᾶσα δ᾽ ἥρμοσται τέχνη
πρέπουσ᾽ ἐν ἡμῖν· ἔστι μὲν τὰ πρὸς μάχην
10 δορός, πάλης ἀγῶνες, ἱππικῆς, δρόμου,
πυγμῆς, ὀδόντων, ὄρχεων ἀποστροφαί,
ἔνεισι δ᾽ ᾠδαὶ μουσικῆς, ἔνεστι δὲ
μαντεῖα παντάγνωτα κοὐκ ἐψευσμένα,
ἰαμάτων τ᾽ ἔλεγχος, ἔστιν οὐρανοῦ
15 μέτρησις, ἔστ᾽ ὄρχησις, ἔστι τῶν κάτω
λάλησις· ἆρ᾽ ἄκαρπος ἡ θεωρία;
ὧν σοι λαβεῖν ἔξεστι τοῦθ᾽ ὁποῖον ἂν
χρῄζῃς, ἐὰν τὴν παῖδα προστιθῇς ἐμοί.

]ΟΙΝΕΥΣ

ἀλλ᾽ οὐχὶ μεμπτὸν τὸ γένος. ἀλλὰ βούλομαι
20 καὶ τόνδ᾽ ἀθρῆσαι πρῶτον ὅστις ἔρχεται

13 παντάγνωτα (rather than πάντ᾽ ἄγνωτα) Maas: πάντα
γνωτὰ Hunt

420

DOUBTFUL FRAGMENT

⟨OENEUS⟩

Why, I will tell you! But first I wish to know who you are
that come, and of what family. I have not yet learned this!

CHORUS OF SATYRS

You shall learn all! We come as suitors, we are sons of
nymphs and ministers of Bacchus and neighbours of the
gods. Every proper trade is part of our equipment—fight-
ing with the spear, contests of wrestling, riding, running,
boxing, biting, twisting people's balls; we have songs of
music, we have oracles quite unknown and not forged,
and tests for ways of healing; we can measure the skies,
we can dance, our lower parts can speak.[a] Is our study
fruitless? You can avail yourself of whatever thing you
like, if you assign your daughter to me.

OENEUS

Why, I cannot fault your family. But first I wish to look
also at this man who is coming.[b]

[a] They are boasting of their farting power.

[b] I suspect that the person whom Oeneus had seen coming
turned out to be Heracles, who often figured in satyric dramas.

INDEX

All page references are to Volume III of the edition, which contains the fragments. *Aj[ax]*, *El[ectra]*, and *O[edipus] T[yrannus]* are in Volume I; the other four plays are in Volume II. Parentheses mark references when a person or place is alluded to but not named.

Abae *O.T.* 900

Acamas (*Ph.* 562)

Acarnania fr. 271, 3

Acastus pp. 252–257

Acestes fr. 672

Achaeans *Aj.* 560, 573, 638, 999, 1053, 1098; *El.* 571, 701; *Ph.* 59, 595, 609, 616, 623, 916, 1243, 1250, 1306, 1404; pp. 56–57; fr. 210, 53

Achelous *Tr.* 9, 510; fr. 271, 4; (pp. 418–421)

Acheron *El.* 183; *Ant.* 812, 816; fr. 523, 3

Achilles *Aj.* 41, 442, 1337, 1341; *Ph.* 4, 50, 57, 62, 241, 331, 358, 364, 542, 582, 940, 1066, 1220, 1237, 1312, 1433; pp. 58–63; fr. 210, 2; pp. 256–267, 280–285, (330–333?)

Acrisius pp. 28–33, 200–203

Admetus fr. 386, 1; fr. 851

Adrastus *O.C.* 1302; pp. 72–79

Aeacidae *Aj.* 645; fr. 487, 1

Aeetes pp. 186–189, 268–271 (?), 274–277

Aegean Sea *Aj.* 461; fr. 371, 1

Aegeus *O.C.* 69, 549, 607, 940, 1154, 1518, 1538, 1754; pp. 18–23

Aegisthus *El.* 97–98, 267, 310, 386, 517, 627, 661, 667, 957, 965, 1101, 1107, 1290, 1308, 1403, 1409, 1415, 1428, 1442–end; pp. 106–112

Aeneas fr. 373, 1

Aenians *El.* 706, 724

Aerope (*Aj.* 1295)

Aetolia *El.* 704; *Tr.* 8; *O.C.* 1315

Agamemnon *Aj.* 1223–1373; *El.* 2, 95, 124–125, 182, 695; (*Ph.* 1376–1377); pp. 263–267, 280–285. *See* Atreidae

Agenor *O.T.* 268

Aidoneus *O.C.* 1558–1559. *See* Hades

Aidos *O.C.* 1268; fr. 928

423

INDEX

Ajax (son of Oileus) pp. 12–17

Ajax (son of Telamon) *Aj. passim*; *O.C.* 1–847, 1096–end

Alcmene *Aj.* 1303; *Tr.* 19, 97, 181, 644, 1148

Alcmeon pp. 72–79

Aleus pp. 32–41

Alexander pp. 40–43. *See* Paris

Alphesiboea fr. 880

Alpheus fr. 652d, 3

Althaea pp. 212–213 (?)

Amphiaraus *El.* 837; *O.C.* 1313; pp. 46–47, 72–79; (fr. 958)

Amphilochia fr. 271, 3

Amphion *Ant.* 1155; pp. 226–235

Amphitrite *O.T.* 195; (fr. 762, 2 ?)

Amphitryon pp. 48–49

Amycus pp. 44–45

Anactorium fr. 916

Anchises (fr. 373, 2)

Andromache p. 48

Andromeda pp. 50–53

Antenor pp. 54–55

Antigone *Ant. passim*; *O.C.* 1–848, 1096–1555, 1670–end

Antilochus *Ph.* 425

Aphrodite *Ant.* 800; *O.C.* 693; fr. 277; pp. 194–195. *See* Cypris, Cythereia

Apia *O.C.* 1303. *See* Peloponnese

Apollo *Aj.* 703; *El.* 655, 1376, 1379, 1425; *O.T.* 80, 377, 470, 498, 720, 909, 919, 1329; *Tr.* 209; *Ph.* 102; *O.C.* 1091; pp. 141–177, 226–235;

(fr. 771); (fr. 851). *See* Loxias, Lycean, Paian, Phoebus

Apsyrtus pp. 274–277

Ara *El.* 111; *O.T.* 418; *Tr.* 1239

Arcadia *O.C.* 1320; fr. 272; (pp. 141–177)

Areopagus *O.C.* 947

Ares *Aj.* 254, 614, 1196; *El.* 96, 1243, 1385, 1423; *O.T.* 190; *Ant.* 125, 139, 952, 970; *Tr.* 653; *O.C.* 947, 1046, 1065, 1391, 1659; fr. 256; fr. 724, 2, 4; fr. 838

Argives *Aj.* 44, 67, 95, 186, 420, 440, 498, 663, 774, 1331, 1340, 1383; *El.* 535, 693, 1459; *Ant.* 15; *Ph.* 67, 554, 560, 630, 944, 1064; *O.C.* 1316; fr. 10c, 2; fr. 432, 1; fr. 462, 2

Argos (country) *El.* 4; *Ant.* 104(?); *O.C.* 378, 1167, 1301, 1325, 1387, 1401, 1416; fr. 270, 3; fr. 271, 5; fr. 799, 4; fr. 957, 1

Argos (guard of Io) pp. 112–135

Ariadne fr. 730

Artace fr. 917

Artemis *Aj.* 172; *El.* 563, 570, 626; *O.T.* 161, 207; *Tr.* 214; (fr. 401, 2); pp.226–235

Asclepius *Ph.* 1437; fr. 710, 3

Asia *O.C.* 695; fr. 411, 1

Astacus fr. 799, 6

Astyoche pp. 82–95

Atalanta *O.C.* 1321–1322; pp. 212–213

Ate *Ant.* 185, 614, 625; *Tr.* 851, 1104; *Ph.* 705; *O.C.* 1244

INDEX

Athamas pp. 10–12
Athena *Aj.* 1–133, 402, 450,
  757, 771; *O.T.* 159, 188; *Ph.*
  134; *O.C.* 706, 1071, 1090;
  fr. 10c; pp. 194–195; (fr. 844).
  See Pallas, Ergane
Athens *Aj.* 861, 1222; *El.* 707,
  731; *O.C.* 24, 58, 108, 260,
  283, (1066), (1125–1127),
  1759
Athos fr. 237; fr. 776
Atlas fr. 314, 267
Atreidae *Aj.* 57, 97, 302,
  389–390, 445, 461, 469, 620,
  667, 718, 838, 931, 948, 960,
  1319, 1349 (*sing.*); *El.* 651,
  1068; *Ph.* (6), 314, 321, 323,
  361, 389, 396, 455, 510, 566,
  586, 598, (723), 872, 916,
  (1023–1024), 1285, (1355),
  1384, 1390; fr. 887(?)
Atreus *El.* 1508; *Ph.* 1023, 1355,
  1376; pp. 54–55, 106–112
Auge pp. 32–41
Aulis *El.* 564
Autolycus fr. 242

Bacchae *Ant.* 1122, 1129. *See*
  Briacchos, Maenads,
  Thyiades
Bacchus *O.T.* 211, 1105; *Ant.*
  154, 1121, 1129; *Tr.* 219, 510,
  704; fr. 1130, 7. *See* Dionysus
Barce *El.* 727. *See* Libya
Bellerophon (pp. 134–135?)
Boeotia *El.* 708; fr. 966
Boreas *Ant.* 985; (fr. 768?);
  fr. 956

Bosporus *Aj.* 882; *Ant.* 969; fr.
  503, 3; fr. 707
Briacchos fr. 770. *See* Bacchae,
  Maenads, Thyiades
Briseis (pp. 24–25?)

Cadmeans *O.T.* 1, 29, 35, 144,
  223, 268, 273, 1288; *Ant.* 508,
  1115, 1162; *Tr.* 116; *O.C.* 354,
  380, 399, 409, 451, 736, 741,
  1394. *See* Cadmus
Cadmus *O.T.* 1; *Ant.* 1155
Calchas *Aj.* 746, 750, 783
Camicus pp. 178–181
Capaneus *Ant.* (131–137), 1319
Carthage fr. 602
Cassandra (pp. 40–43?),
  182–183
Castalia *Ant.* 113
Cedalion pp. 182–185
Celmis pp. 194–195
Cenaeum *Tr.* 238, 753, 996
Centaur *Tr.* 680, 831, (1095–
  1096), 1141, 1162
Cephallenia *Ph.* 254, 791
Cephalus pp. 268–269
Cephisus *O.C.* 687
Cerberus (*Tr.* 1098);
  pp. 182–183
Chalcodon *Ph.* 489; pp. 276–281
Chaldea fr. 637
Charnabon fr. 604
Chiron *Tr.* 715; (pp. 68–69?)
Chronos *Aj.* 646, 713; *O.T.* 614,
  1213; *O.C.* 7, 609, 618, 1454;
  El. 179; fr. 301; fr. 918, fr. 954
Chryse *Ph.* 194, 270, 1327;
  pp. 24–25; fr. 384;
  pp. 340–343

425

Chryseis pp. 24–25, 340–343
Chryses pp. 340–343
Chrysothemis *El.* 157, 324–471, 871–1057
Cilla fr. 40
Cithaeron *O.T.* 421, 1026, 1089, 1127, 1134, 1391, 1452
Cleopatra (*Ant.* 980–987); pp. 308–309(?)
Clytemnestra *El.* 97, 273, 516–803, 1400–1415, 1473–1475; pp. 138–141, pp. 184–185
Cnossos *Aj.* 699
Cocalus pp. 178–181
Coeranus fr. 391
Colchis pp. 186–189; fr. 638
Colonus *O.C.* 59, 670
Corinth *O.T.* 774, 794, 936, (939), 955, 997, 1119, 1394
Coronus fr. 384, 2
Corycus *Ant.* 1128
Creon *O.T.* 70, 78–150, 288, 378–379, 385, 400, 411, 426, 513–678, 701, 1416–1523; *Ant.* 21, 31, 47, 156, 162–326, 386–1114, 1257–end; *O.C.* 367, 396, 455, 723, 728–1043
Crete *Aj.* 1295; *Tr.* 119; (pp. 206–212); (fr. 730)
Cretheus (pp. 312–321?)
Creusa pp. 188–193. *See* Ion
Crisa *El.* 180, 730
Cycnus pp. 256–263
Cyllene *Aj.* 605; *O.T.* 1104; pp. 141–177
Cypris *Tr.* 497, 515, 860; pp. 194–195; fr. 874, 1;

fr. 941, 1–17. *See* Aphrodite, Cythereia
Cythereia fr. 847

Daedalus pp. 64–65, 178–181
Dais fr. 605
Danaans *Aj.* 138, 144, 225
Danae *Ant.* 944; pp. 28–33, 64, 200–203
Daphnae (*O.C.* 1048–1049)
Dardanus *Ph.* 69
Daulis *O.T.* 734
Deianeira *Tr.* 1–496, 531–632, 663–812; (pp. 418–421?)
Deidameia pp. 276–281
Delos *Aj.* 704; *O.T.* 154
Delphi *O.T.* 463, 734; *O.C.* 413. *See* Pytho
Demeter *O.C.* 1600; pp. 300–305; (fr. 804). *See* Deo
Demophon (*Ph.* 562)
Deo *Ant.* 1121; fr. 754, 3. *See* Demeter
Dike *Aj.* 1390; *El.* 476, 528; *O.T.* 274, 885; *Ant.* 451, 854; *O.C.* 1382; fr. 12, 1
Diomedes (*Ph.* 570, 592); pp. 196–197; (fr. 799)
Dionysus *Ant.* 957, (1115); *O.C.* 679; pp. 66–67; (fr. 314, 224); pp. 182–185; fr. 668; (fr. 773)
Dioscuri pp. 44–45, (pp. 310–311?); (fr. 957, 2)
Dirce *Ant.* 104, 844
Doctor *Tr.* 974–1020
Dodona (Dodo) *Tr.* 172, (1167); fr. 455; fr. 456; fr. 460; fr. 461

INDEX

Dolopians pp. 68–69. *See* Phoenix

Dorians *O.T.* 775; *O.C.* 696, 1301; fr. 314, 34

Dotium fr. 380; fr. 384; fr. 492

Dryas *Ant.* 955; fr. 10c, 1

Echidna *Tr.* 1099

Echo *Ph.* 189

Edonians *Ant.* 956

Egypt *O.C.* 337; fr. 712

Eidothea (*Ant.* 973); pp. 308–309; (fr. 707a?)

Elatus fr. 380

Electra *El. from* 86 *passim*

Eleusis *Ant.* 1120; pp. 300–305; (fr. 837)

Eleutheria fr. 927

Elpis *Ant.* 615; fr. 948

Enyalios *Aj.* 179. *See* Ares

Eos pp. 268–269

Epigonoi pp. 72–77

Epistrophus pp. 24–25

Erechtheus *Aj.* 202; *Ant.* 982

Ergane fr. 844. *See* Athena

Eriboea *Aj.* 569; fr. 730

Erichthonius fr. 242, 1. *See* Hermes

Erigone (daughter of Aegisthus) pp. 100–101

Erigone (daughter of Icarius) pp. 100–101

Erinys *Aj.* 837, 843, 1034, 1390; *El.* 112, 276, 491, 1080; *Ant.* 603, 1075; *Tr.* 809, 895, 1051; *O.C.* 1299, 1434. *See* Eumenides

Eriphyle (*El.* 844); pp. 72–79

Eris pp. 76–77

Eros *Ant.* 781–782; *Tr.* 354, 441; fr. 684; fr. 770

Erymanthus *Tr.* 1097

Eteocles *Ant.* 23, (55), (169), 194; *O.C.* (421 f.), 1295

Eteoclus *O.C.* 1316

Ethiopians pp. 22–23. *See* Memnon

Etna *O.C.* 312; fr. 162

Etruria *Aj.* 17; fr. 270, 4; fr. 598, 2

Euboea *Tr.* 74, 237, 401, 752, 788; *Ph.* 489; fr. 24, 3; fr. 255, 2

Eumelus pp. 82–83

Eumenides *O.C.* (39–40), 42, (84), (106), (466), 486, (864). *See* Erinyes

Eumolpidae *O.C.* 1053

Europia fr. 39

Eurotas fr. 957, 2

Euryalus pp. 82–83

Eurydice *Ant.* 1180–1243

Eurypylus pp. 82–95

Eurysaces *Aj.* 340, 545–595, (983), (1409); pp. 96–97

Eurystheus *Tr.* 1049

Eurytus *Tr.* 74, 244, 260, 316, 353, 363, 380, 420, 750, 1220

Evenus *Tr.* 559

Ganymedes fr. 345

Ge (Gaia) *Ph.* 391; *O.C.* 40, 1574

Geras fr. 949; fr. 950

Getae fr. 604

Glaucus (son of Minos) pp. 206–213

Great Bear *Tr.* 130

INDEX

Guard (Theban) *Ant.* 223–331, 384–445

Hades *Aj.* 517, 608, 635, 660, 865, (1035?), 1192; *El.* 110, 137, (184), 463, 542, 835, 949, 1342; *O.T.* 30, 972; *Ant.* 519, 542, 575, 581, 654, 777, 780, 811, 822, 911, 1075, 1205, 1241, 1284; *Tr.* 4, 120, 282, 501, 1040, 1098, 1161; *Ph.* 449, 624, 861, 1211, 1349; *O.C.* 1221, 1440, 1461, 1552, 1572, (1606?), 1690; fr. 832; fr. 861, 2; fr. 941, 3. *See* Aidoneus
Haemon *Ant.* (568), 572, 626–765, 1175, 1217
Hecate fr. 535, 2; fr. 734
Hector *Aj.* 662, 817, 1027, 1029; pp. 256–263; fr. 566, 4
Hecuba (fr. 620)
Helen pp. 68–73, 196–197, (310–311?)
Helenus *Ph.* 606, 1338
Helicaon pp. 12–17, 82–95
Helios *Aj.* 846, 857; *El.* 424, 824; *O.T.* 661, 1426; *Ant.* 1065; *Tr.* 96, (145), 869; fr. 535, 1; fr. 582; fr. 752
Hellespont fr. 503, 2
Hephaestus *Ant.* 123, 1007; *Ph.* 987; fr. 156; pp. 250–253(?)
Hera *El.* 8; pp. 112–135; fr. 270, 3; fr. 314, 266; pp. 194–195
Heracles *Aj.* 1303; *Tr.* (19), 27, 51, (97), 156, 170, (181), 233, 391, 406, 428, 460, 476, 540, 550, 563, 576, 585, 668, 872,

913, 916, (956), 971–end; *Ph.* 262, (727), 802, 943, 1131, 1406, 1409–end; pp. 96–99; (fr. 1130, 20?)
Hermaion (mountain) *Ph.* 1459
Hermes *Aj.* 832; *El.* 111, 1395–1396; (*O.T.* 1104); *Tr.* 620; *Ph.* 133; *O.C.* 1548; pp. 112–135, 141–177; fr. 701. *See* Erichthonius
Hermione pp. 80–81; fr. 872
Hestia fr. 726
Himeros fr. 874, 1
Hippodameia pp. 242–249
Hippolytus pp. 322–331
Hippomedon *O.C.* 1317
Hipponous pp. 136–137
Horkos *O.C.* 1765; fr. 933
Hybris pp. 320–321; (fr. 809)
Hydra *Tr.* 574, 1094
Hyllus *Tr.* 56, 61–93, 734–820, 971–end
Hypereia fr. 911
Hypnos *Aj.* 675; *Ph.* 828
Hypsipyle pp. 204–205

Iacchus *Ant.* 1152; fr. 959, 3
Icarian Sea *Aj.* 702
Ida *Aj.* 434, 601; fr. 522, 1. *See* Olympus 3
Idaean Dactyls pp. 194–195
Ilium *Ph.* 61, 245, 247, 454, 548, 1200, 1438. *See* Troy
Inachus *El.* 5; pp. 112–135
India *Ant.* 1038
Io *El.* 5; pp. 112–135
Iobates pp. 134–137
Iocaste *O.T.* (573), 631–862, 911–1072; (*Ant.* 53);

(*O.C.* 525–528, 978–987)
Iole *Tr.* (307), 381, 420, 1220
Ion pp. 178–179. *See* Creusa
Ionian Sea fr. 337
Iphianassa *El.* 157
Iphigeneia pp. 138–141, 340–343
Iphitus *Tr.* 28, 270
Iris (fr. 272)
Ismene *Ant.* 1–99, 526–581; *O.C.* 310–509, (818), 1096–1555, 1668–end
Ismenos *O.T.* 21; *Ant.* 1124
Istros fr. 210, 67
Italy *Ant.* 1119; fr. 600
Itys *El.* 14; pp. 290–301
Ixion (*Ph.* 676–679); pp. 134–135

Jason pp. 186–189, 204–205, 268–289, 274–277
Jocaste *see* Iocaste

Keres *O.T.* 472
Kronos *Tr.* 128, 500; *Ph.* 679; *O.C.* 712; fr. 126, 2

Labdacus *O.T.* 224, 267, 489, 496; *Ant.* 594, 862; *O.C.* 221
Lacmus fr. 271, 2
Laconia *Aj.* 8; fr. 176; pp. 196–197. *See* Sparta
Laertes *Aj.* 1393; *Ph.* 87, 366, 628, 1357; fr. 913. *See* Lartius
Laius *O.T.* 103, 126, 224, 308, 451, 558, 573, 703, 711, 721, 740, 753, 759, 814, 852, 906, 1042, 1117, 1122, 1139, 1167,

1216; *O.C.* 220, 553, (991–999)
Laocoon pp. 198–201
Laomedon *Aj.* 130
Lapiths fr. 384, 2
Larissa pp. 200–203
Lartius *Aj.* 1, 380; *Ph.* 1386. *See* Laertes
Las fr. 957, 2
Leda (pp. 310–311?)
Lemnos *Ph.* 2, 800, 986, (989), 1060, 1464; pp. 204–205; fr. 776
Lerna *Tr.* 574, 1094
Lethe fr. 670
Leto *El.* 570; fr. 401, 2; pp. 226–235
Libya *El.* 702; fr. 11, 2; fr. 133. *See* Barce
Lichas *Tr.* 189, 229–334, 392–496, 757, 773
Liguria fr. 599, 3
Locri *Tr.* 788
Loxias *O.T.* 853, 994, 1102. *See* Apollo
Lycean Agora *El.* 7
Lycean (as title of Apollo) *El.* 645, 1379; *O.T.* 203, 919
Lycia *O.T.* 208
Lycomedes *Ph.* 243; pp. 276–281
Lycurgus (*Ant.* 955), (fr. 10c, 1). *See* Dryas
Lycus fr. 24, 2
Lydia *Tr.* 70, 248, 356, 432; fr. 91a; fr. 412, 2; fr. 800
Lyrcus fr. 271, 6

Maenads *O.T.* 212; (*Ant.* 963);

(fr. 779). *See* Bacchae, Briacchos, Thyiades
Magnesia *El.* 705
Maia *El.* 1395; fr. 314, 267–268
Medea pp. 186–189, 268–271
Megareus *Ant.* 1303
Melanippus (fr. 799)
Meleager pp. 212–213
Melis *Tr.* 194, 636; *Ph.* 4, 725
Memnon fr. 210, 80; pp. 215–216. *See* Ethiopians
Menelaus *Aj.* 1045–1160; *El.* 537, 545, 576; fr. 177, 2; pp. 80–81, 263–267; fr. 871. *See* Atreidae
Menoeceus *O.T.* 69, 85, 1453; *Ant.* 156 (?), 211, 1098
Merchant (pretended) *Ph.* 543–627
Merope *O.T.* 775, 990
Messengers (1) Corinthian *O.T.* 924–1185; (2) Second Messenger *O.T.* 1223–1296; (3) *Ant.* 1155–1346; (4) *Tr.* 180–496; (5) Messenger in *Laocoon* fr. 373
Minos (pp. 64–5); pp. 178–181, 206–213, 214–215; fr. 730
Minotaur fr. 730
Moirai *Ant.* 987; *Ph.* 1466
Molossia fr. 795
Momus pp. 218–219
Morios *O.C.* 705
Muses *O.C.* 691; pp. 214–215; (fr. 568, 1); fr. 852, 3
Mycenae *El.* 9, 161, 423, 1459; *Ph.* 325; pp. 54–55
Mynes pp. 24–25
Myrtilus *El.* 509; pp. 242–249

Mysia *Aj.* 699; fr. 210, 74; pp. 216–217. *See* Aleus, Eurypylus, Telephus

Nauplius pp. 218–225
Nausicaa pp. 224–227, 322–323
Neleus pp. 312–321
Nemea *Tr.* 1092
Nemesis *El.* 792, 1467
Neoptolemus *Ph.* 1–1080, 1222–end; pp. 80–81, 82–95, 252–257, 276–281, 330–333
Nereids *O.C.* 719; fr. 562, 2
Nessus *Tr.* 558, 1141
Nestor *Ph.* 422; fr. 144a; fr. 855
Nike *Ant.* 148; *Ph.* 134
Niobe (*Ant.* 824); pp. 226–235
Nisus fr. 24, 4
Nurse *Tr.* 49–93, 871–946
Nymphs *O.T.* 1108; *Ant.* 1129; *Tr.* 215; *Ph.* 1454, 1470
Nysa *Ant.* 1130; fr. 959, 2
Nyx fr. 433. *See* Skotos

Oceanus fr. 270, 2
Odysseus *Aj.* 1–133, 303, 371–384, 954–958, 971, 1318–1401; *Ph.* 1–134, 314, 321, 344, 429, 441, 568, 572, 592, 596, 608, (628), 636, (852), 974–1080, 1218–1262, 1293–1302; fr. 305; pp. 196–197, 224–227, 236–242, 276–281, 280–285, 286–289; fr. 799; (fr. 913); fr. 965
Oea *O.C.* 1061
Oeax fr. 434a
Oechalia *Tr.* 354, 478, 859

Oedipus *O.T.* and *O.C. passim*; *Ant.* 2, (49), 167, 193, (471), 600, 1018; fr. 401

Oeneus *Tr.* 6, 405, 569, 598, 665, 792, 1050; *O.C.*, 1315; pp. 135–137, 242–243, 418–421

Oeniadae *Tr.* 510

Oenomaus pp. 242–249

Oenopion pp. 182–185

Oenotria fr. 599, 2

Oeta *Tr.* 200, 436, 635, 1191; *Ph.* 453, 479, 490, 664, 728, 1430

Oileus pp. 286–289

Olenus fr. 300

Olympia *O.T.* 901

Olympus 1 (home of the gods) *El.* 209; *O.T.* 867, 1088; *Ant.* 609, 758; *Tr.* 275; *Ph.* 315; *O.C.* 1655; fr. 535, 3

Olympus 2 (in Mysia) *Aj.* 881

Olympus 3 (one of the four peaks of Ida so called) fr. 522

Omphale *Tr.* (70), 252, 356

Oreithyia fr. 956. *See* Cleopatra, Phineus

Orestes *El.* 1–85, 163, 182, 294–297, 303, 317, 455, 602, 673, 676, 681 f., 789, 795, 808 f., 877, 904, 915, 933, 1098–1375; pp. 80–81, 340–343

Orion pp. 182–185

Ortygia *Tr.* 21

Pactolus *Ph.* 394

Paian *O.T.* 154; *Tr.* 221; *Ph.* 822. *See* Apollo

Paidagogos of Orestes *El.* 1–85, 660–803, 1326–1375

Paidagogos of Troilus pp. 306–307

Palamedes pp. 218–225, 248–251. *See* Nauplius

Palladium pp. 196–197(?)

Pallas (Athena) *Aj.* 954; *O.T.* 20; *Ant.* 1184; *Tr.* 1031; *O.C.* 107, 1009

Pallas (brother of Aegeus) fr. 24, 7

Pan *Aj.* 694–695; *O.T.* 1100; (pp. 320–321)

Pandora pp. 250–253

Paris *Ph.* 1425; pp. 194–195, (332–335?). *See* Alexander

Parnassus *O.T.* 475; *Ant.* 114

Parthenopaeus *O.C.* 1320

Peasant (of Colonus) *O.C.* 28–80

Peitho *Tr.* 66; fr. 865; fr. 870

Pelasgia fr. 270, 4; fr. 379

Peleus *Ph.* 333; fr. 150; fr. 151; pp. 68–69, 252–257; (fr. 618); pp. 330–333

Pelias pp. 268–269 (?), 312–321

Pelion (Mount) fr. 154

Pelopia pp. 106–107

Pelopidae *El.* 10

Peloponnese *O.C.* 696. *See* Apia

Pelops *El.* 502; *O.C.* 69; pp. 242–249

Peparethus *Ph.* 549

Percote fr. 917

Perithus (=Peirithous) *O.C.* 1594

Perrhaebia fr. 271, 2

Persephone *El.* 110; *O.C.* 1548; (fr. 804). *See* Phersephassa

INDEX

Perseus pp. 28–33, 200–203

Phaedra pp. 322–331

Phamenus fr. 392

Phanoteus *El.* 45, 670

Pherae fr. 911

Pheres fr. 386, 1

Phersephassa *Ant.* 894. *See* Persephone

Philammon (fr. 242)

Philoctetes *Ph.* (4–11), (40–47), 54, 101–107, 219–end; pp. 332–335

Philomela pp. 290–301

Philonis (fr. 242)

Phineus *Ant.* 971; pp. 308–309 (?), 334–337

Phocis *El.* 45, 670, 759, 1107, 1442; *O.T.* 733

Phoebus *Aj.* 186; *El.* 35, 637, 645; *O.T.* 71, 96, 133, 149, 162, 279, 285, 305, 712, 788, 1011, 1096; *Ph.* 335; *O.C.* 414, 454, 623, 665, 793; fr. 314, 48, 82, 85, 163; fr. 442, 3. *See* Apollo, Loxias, Paian

Phoenix *Ph.* 562, 565; fr. 153; pp. 68–69, 276–281, 336–337; fr. 861, 2. *See* Dolopians

Phorcus fr. 861, 2

Phrixus pp. 338–339. *See* Athamas

Phrygians *Aj.* 210, 488, 1054, 1292; *Ant.* 824; fr. 210, 77; fr. 412, 1; pp. 338–341

Phthia pp. 330–333

Pieria fr. 568, 1

Pindus fr. 271, 2

Pleuron *Tr.* 7

Pluto *Ant.* 1200; fr. 273; fr. 283. *See* Hades

Poeas *Ph.* 5, 263, 318, 329, (492), 1230, 1261, 1410, 1439

Polybus *O.T.* 489, 774, 827, 941, 956, 972, 990, 1016–1017, 1394

Polydeuces pp. 44–45. *See* Dioscuri

Polydorus *O.T.* 267

Polyidus pp. 206–213

Polynices *Ant.* 26, (55), 110, (169), 198, 902, (1018), 1198; *O.C.* 375, (421 f.), 1249–1446

Polyxena pp. 262–267, 306–307

Pontus *Tr.* 100

Poseidon *Tr.* 502; *O.C.* 55, 713, 1158, 1494; fr. 371, 1; fr. 506

Priam *Ph.* 605; pp. 82–95, 266–267

Priest of Zeus *O.T.* 14–150

Procne pp. 290–301

Procris pp. 268–269

Prometheus *O.C.* 56; pp. 194–195, 250–253

Protesilaus pp. 256–263

Pylades *El.* 1–85, 1098–1375

Pylos *Ph.* 422

Pytho *El.* 32–33, 49; *O.T.* 70, 152, 242, 603, 788, 965; fr. 460, 1; fr. 490. *See* Delphi

Rhea *O.C.* 1073; pp. 194–195

Rhipaean Mountains *O.C.* 1248

Salamis *Aj.* 135, 596, 860; pp. 286–289

Salmoneus fr. 10c, 6; pp. 270–273, 312–321

Salmydessus *Ant.* 970

Sardis *Ant.* 1037; fr. 210, 67

Sarpedon fr. 210, 80

Sarpedonian Rock fr. 637

Satyr *see list of satyr-plays*, p. 8

Scamander *Aj.* 418

Scythia fr. 427; fr. 473;
    pp. 274–277; fr. 707

Selli *Tr.* 1167

Semele (*Ant.* 1115–1116); (fr.
    773)

Shepherd (Theban) *O.T.* (756),
    (837), (1048), 1110–1185

Sidero pp. 312–321

Sigeum *Ph.* 355

Silenus pp. 141–177

Sinon pp. 274–275

Sipylus *Ant.* 825

Siren fr. 852, 3; fr. 861

Sisyphus *Aj.* 189, 1311; *Ph.* 417,
    1311; pp. 274–275; fr. 567

Skotos *O.C.* 40, 106. *See* Nyx

Skyros *Ph.* 240, 326, 381, 459,
    970, 1368; pp. 276–281

Sparta *Aj.* 1102; *El.* 701; *Ph.* 325;
    fr. 957. *See* Laconia

Spercheius *Ph.* 492, 726

Sphinx *O.T.* (36), 130, (1199)

Strophius *El.* 111

Styx *O.C.* 1564

Sunium *Aj.* 1220

Syagrus (dog) fr. 15

Syria fr. 637

Taenarum pp. 76–77

Talaus *O.C.* 1318

Talos (pp. 64–65)

Tantalus *Ant.* 825; pp. 226–235,
    286–287

Tartarus *O.C.* 1389, 1574; fr.
    442, 8

Tecmessa *Aj.* 201–595, 784–814,
    891–989

Teiso (=Tisiphone) fr. 743

Telamon *Aj.* 134, 183, 204, 463,
    569, 763, 767, 1008, 1299;
    pp. 286–289

Telephus pp. 32–41, 82–95,
    290–291. *See* Aleus,
    Eurypylus, Mysia

Teleutas *Aj.* 210, 331

Tereus pp. 290–301

Teucer *Aj.* 342, 562, 688, 741,
    751, 782, 795, 797, 804, 827,
    921, 975–1184; *Ph.* 1057;
    pp. 286–289

Thamyras pp. 102–105

Thanatos (*Aj.* 854); *Tr.* 834; *Ph.*
    797

Thebes *O.T.* 153, 1524; *Ant.* 102,
    149, 733, 834, 937, 940, 988,
    1122, 1135; *Tr.* 511, 1154;
    O.C. (399), 406, 415, 616,
    791, 919, 1305, 1312, 1319,
    1355, 1372, 1769; fr. 773, 1;
    fr. 799, 5; fr. 958, 1

Themis *El.* 1064

Thermopylae *Tr.* 639

Thersites *Ph.* 442

Theseus *Ph.* 562; *O.C.* 69,
    (296 f.), 549–667, 887–1041,
    1066, 1096–1210, 1350,
    1500–1555, 1593, 1657,
    1751–end; pp. 106–107,
    322–331; fr. 730; fr. 905

Thessaly *El.* 703; *O.C.* 314;
    fr. 777; fr. 915. *See*
    Pherae

INDEX

Thestor *Aj.* 801

Thetis fr. 151; pp. 252–257, 280–285; fr. 618

Thoas (pp. 340–343?)

Thoricus *O.C.* 159

Thrace *O.T.* 197; *Ant.* 589; fr. 237; pp. 290–301. *See* Edonians

Thyestes pp. 54–55, 106–112

Thyiades *Ant.* 1151. *See* Bacchae

Tiresias *O.T.* 285, 297–462, (747); *Ant.* 988–1090; fr. 392

Tiryns *Tr.* 270, 1152

Tisiphone *see* Teiso

Trachis *Tr.* 39, 371, 423, 1140; *Ph.* 491

Triptolemus pp. 300–305

Troilus pp. 306–307

Trojans *Aj.* 467; *Ph.* 113, 1253

Troy *Aj.* 415, 424, 438, 459, 819, 862, 984, 1021, 1190, 1210; *El.* 1; *Ph.* (69), 112, 197, 353, 611, 915, 920, 941, 998, 1175, 1332, 1337, 1341, 1347, 1363, 1376, 1392, 1401, 1423, 1428, 1435; fr. 10c, 2; fr. 566, 1. *See* Ilium

Tyche *O.T.* 1080; fr. 314, 79; fr. 809

Tydeus *Ph.* 570, 592; *O.C.* 1316; pp. 136–137; fr. 799, 3

Tyndareus pp. 310–311

Tyro pp. 312–321

Tyrrhenia *see* Etruria

Xantha (?) fr. 392

Zeus *Aj.* 91, 172, 186, 387, 401, 450, 708, 824, 831, 953; *El.* 149, 162, 175, 209, 659, 756, 823, 1063, 1097, 1466; *O.T.* 18, 151, 188, 202, 470, 498, 738, 904, 1198; *Ant.* 127, 143, 184, 450, 487, 604, 658, 950, 1040, 1041, 1117, 1149; *Tr.* 19, 26, (128), 140, 200, 251, 270, 279, 288, 303, 399, 437, (500), 513, 566, 644, 753, 826, 956, 983, 995, 1002, 1022, 1048, 1106, 1148, 1188, 1191, 1278; *Ph.* 140, 393, 484, (679), 802, 943, 989–990, 1233, 1289, 1324, 1415, 1443; *O.C.* 95, 143, 310, 532, 623, 705, (712), 793, 882, (1073), 1079, 1086, 1267, 1382, 1435, 1456, 1460, 1471, 1485, 1502, 1606, 1748, 1767; fr. 10c, 6; fr. 237; pp. 112–135; fr. 314, 257, 340, 401; fr. 425; fr. 455; fr. 524, 3, 7; fr. 590, 3; fr. 682, 2; fr. 684, 5; fr. 727; fr. 755, 3; fr. 844, 2; fr. 887; fr. 895; fr. 907; fr. 927b; fr. 941, 15; fr. 951, 4

434